image® comics presents:

PvP™
PLAYER vs. PLAYER

the **dork** ages

collecting issues 1-6 of PvP, volume 1,
originally published by Dork Storm Press

For Image Comics:
Publisher: Jim Valentino
Director of Marketing: Eric Stephenson
Director of Production: Brent Braun
Controller/Foreign Licensing: Traci Hale
Art Director: Brett Evans
Web Developer: Allen Hui
Accounting assistant: Cindie Espinoza
Book Trade Coordinator: Tim Hegarty
Production Assistant: Jon Malin

image
IMAGECOMICS.COM

PvP: The Dork Ages, February 2004. First Printing. Published by Image Comics. Office of publication: 1071 N. Batavia street, Suite A, Orange, CA. PvP is TM and © 2004 Scott R. Kurtz. All rights reserved. Any similarities between characters and persons living or dead are purely coincidental. No portion of this book may be reproduced without the written permission of the author. Image and its logo are ® and ©2004 Image Comics, Inc. All rights reserved. Printed in Canada. Face it, you're a neomaxizoomdweebie.

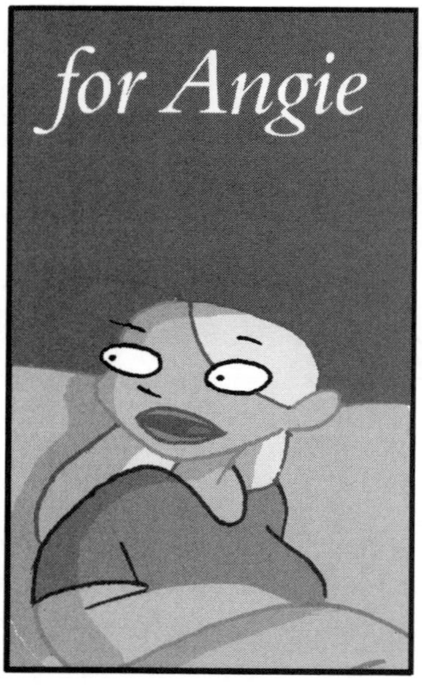
for Angie

INTRODUCTION

by Aaron Williams

Scott Kurtz has a guest room in his house where he stores visiting artists. You'd think it would have comic posters, statues of Hellboy, console video games, and the smell of wood pulp pages doused in ink. Instead, it's the "Woodland Sprite" suite, complete with translucent green drapes over the bed, prints of flowers and fruit, and a dragonfly night light. All I need to complete the ensemble is some slippers with bells on the toes. This is the setting I find myself in. Locked in Oberon and Titania's spare bedroom, not being allowed to emerge until I present an introduction for this book. I wanted to write it from Scott's commode, but the holy of holies must remain unsullied. So onward we go...

I met Scott for the first time while in St. Louis, during what might be called the dawn of the season of our discontent. Neither one of us knew the rocky road we had ahead of us as we chowed down on Blueberry Hill's signature cheeseburgers and talked about PvP becoming its own self-published comic book. We were filled with promise and new hope, as those of

us who had been publishing a while could give Scott some wisdom on how to get a comic produced in exchange for promotion from Scott's enormous presence on the web. In the end, I think I've learned more about publishing from him than he ever learned from me, but that's a story for another time. Flash forward a few years. We're older, wiser, and for Scott, the birthing pains are over. PvP had spread its wings, slapped on a JATO unit and took off for the upper ozone layer. And Scott has brought me along for the ride, thanks to the internet. Not only do I get to read his on-line material like every other rabid fan, I get to watch the sausage as it's made, thanks to Microsoft Instant Messenger.

Instant Messaging is an oft-scorned means of communication. Full of LOL'ers and OMFG'ers, IM'ing is seen as juvenile and a means for hackers to gain control of your system. In the hands of the artistically insane, however, it's the next best thing to a Vulcan mind-meld. Scott and I have spent countless hours bleeping and blooping ideas back-and-forth. PDF's of our comics have been sent in seconds, allowing one part of our virtual mega-brain to tell the other side that it misspelled "the" on page four. Twice. In two different ways.

I've seen him craft jokes that would ache the ribs of the gods themselves, and I've seen him bang his head on his desk in frustration, crying to the universe to deliver unto him a punchline. I've seen his characters grow and change, as well as remain so faithfully true to themselves, that I practically consider them real people. I think he's crossed that threshold where he can't help but tell the stories of this motley crew, because the characters themselves wouldn't let him stop.

This volume is the record of a beginning. It's not the beginning of PvP as a comic strip. It's another kind of beginning, as a full-fledged graphic publication. As the cover implies, this could be thought of as PvP's adolescence, where it practiced kissing in the mirror and tried to comb its hair before it went to the prom with Image. And even that is only a beginning.

So where will it all end? I learned how PvP will conclude from Scott himself. He has the final strip planned in his head, and I'm sure you'd agree it finishes everything satisfactorily, even without knowing everything that will come before it. But that's another story we'll all have to wait for.

Well, except for me. But don't worry; it'll be worth it.

Aaron

Aaron Williams is the author/illustrator for the comic books "Nodwick" and "ps238." When not drawing, he finds time to pester Scott Kurtz and make his daily cartoon late.

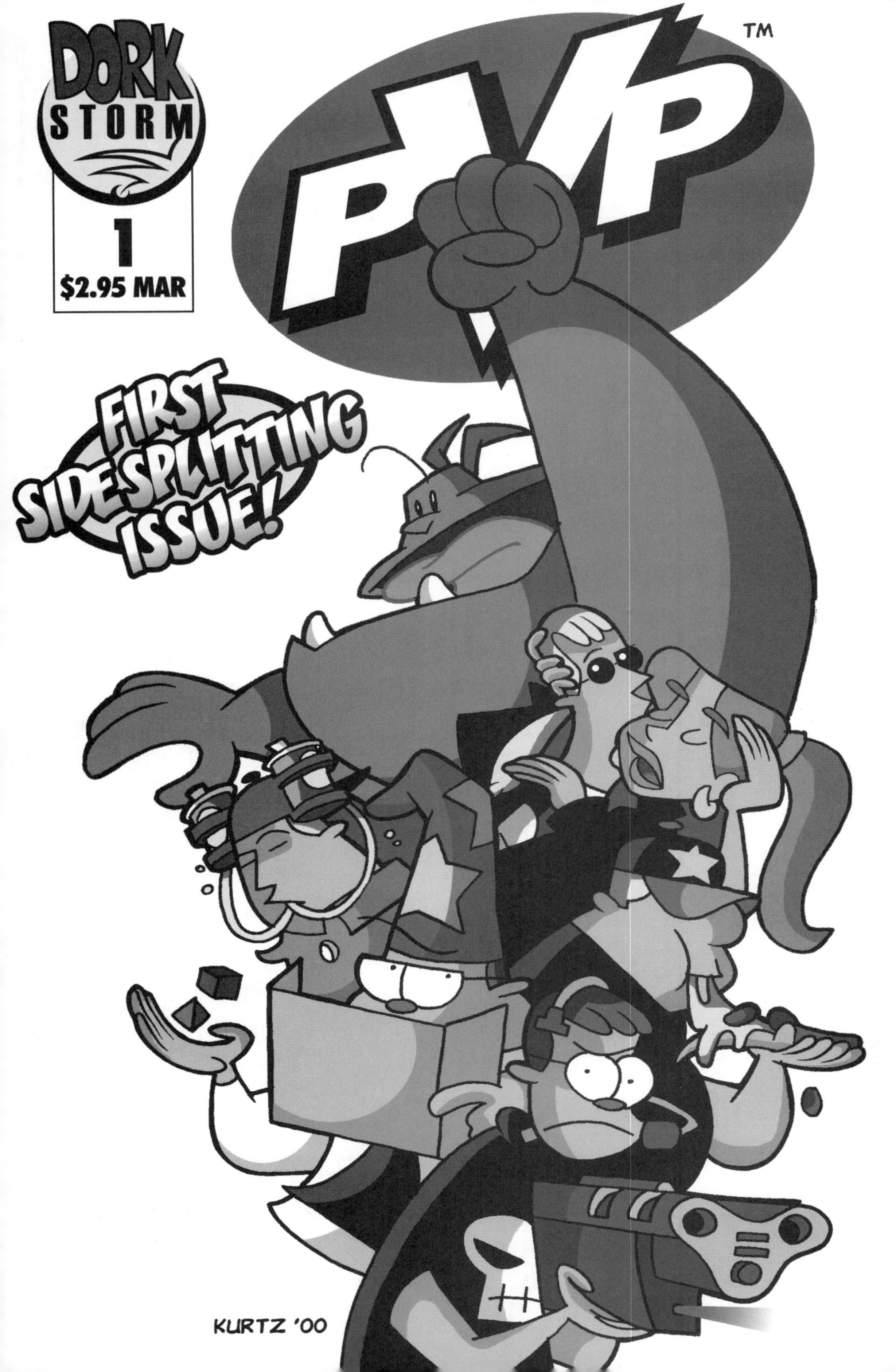
DORK STORM
1
$2.95 MAR
PVP™
FIRST SIDESPLITTING ISSUE!
KURTZ '00

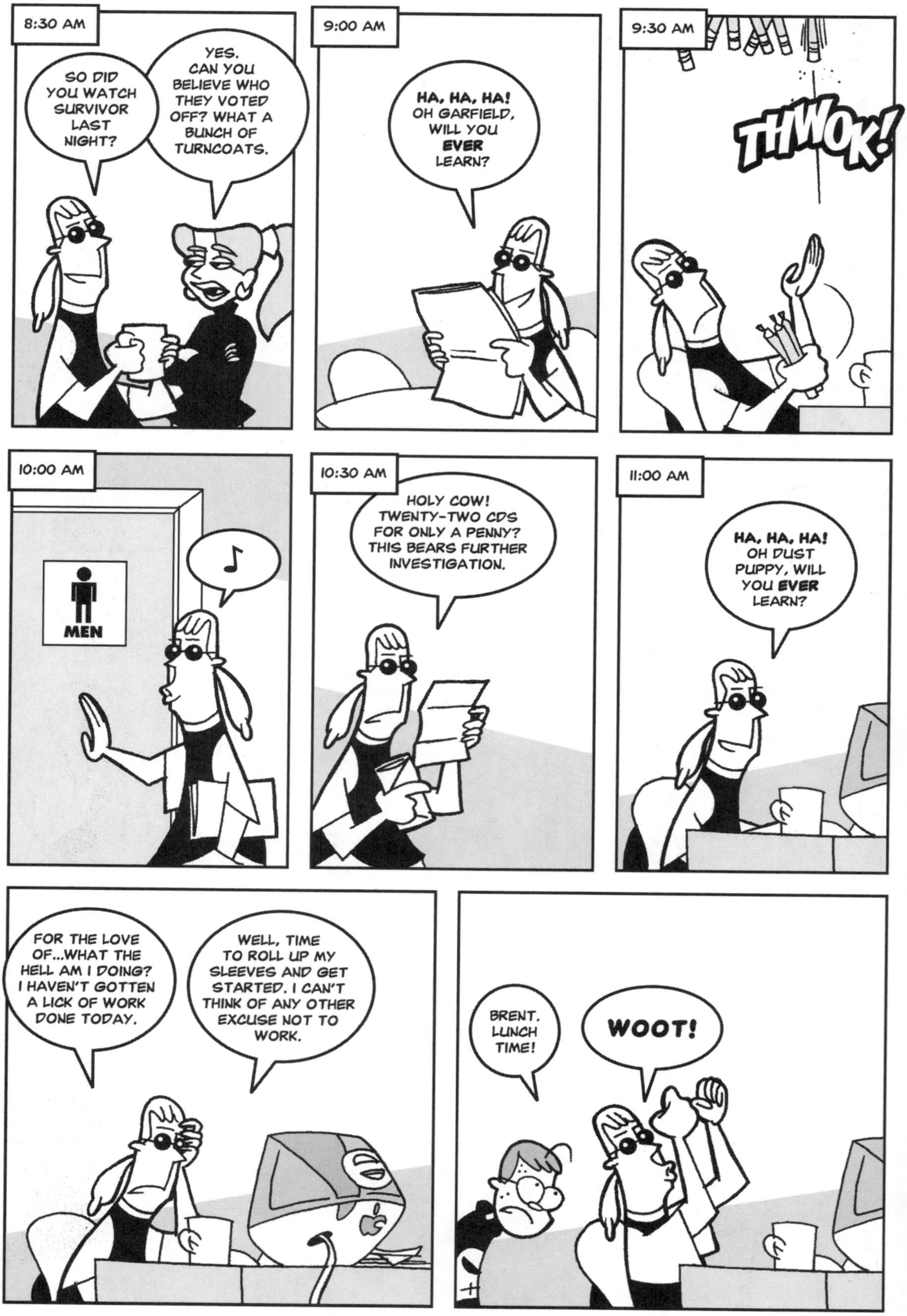
8:30 AM
SO DID YOU WATCH SURVIVOR LAST NIGHT?
YES. CAN YOU BELIEVE WHO THEY VOTED OFF? WHAT A BUNCH OF TURNCOATS.
9:00 AM
HA, HA, HA! OH GARFIELD, WILL YOU EVER LEARN?
9:30 AM
THWOK!
10:00 AM
MEN
♪
10:30 AM
HOLY COW! TWENTY-TWO CDS FOR ONLY A PENNY? THIS BEARS FURTHER INVESTIGATION.
11:00 AM
HA, HA, HA! OH DUST PUPPY, WILL YOU EVER LEARN?
FOR THE LOVE OF...WHAT THE HELL AM I DOING? I HAVEN'T GOTTEN A LICK OF WORK DONE TODAY.
WELL, TIME TO ROLL UP MY SLEEVES AND GET STARTED. I CAN'T THINK OF ANY OTHER EXCUSE NOT TO WORK.
BRENT. LUNCH TIME!
WOOT!

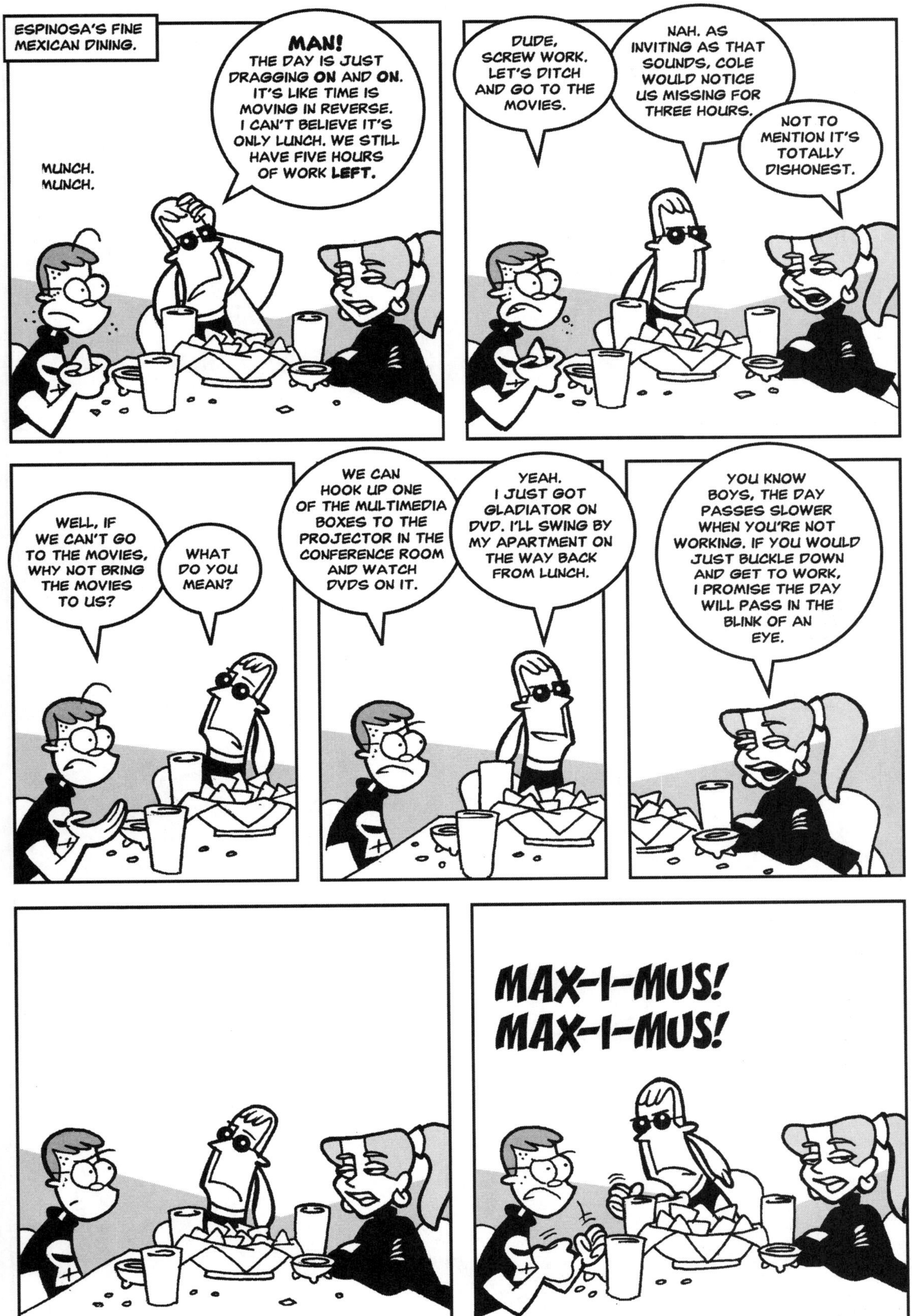
ESPINOSA'S FINE MEXICAN DINING.
MUNCH. MUNCH.
MAN! THE DAY IS JUST DRAGGING ON AND ON. IT'S LIKE TIME IS MOVING IN REVERSE. I CAN'T BELIEVE IT'S ONLY LUNCH. WE STILL HAVE FIVE HOURS OF WORK LEFT.
DUDE, SCREW WORK. LET'S DITCH AND GO TO THE MOVIES.
NAH. AS INVITING AS THAT SOUNDS, COLE WOULD NOTICE US MISSING FOR THREE HOURS.
NOT TO MENTION IT'S TOTALLY DISHONEST.
WELL, IF WE CAN'T GO TO THE MOVIES, WHY NOT BRING THE MOVIES TO US?
WHAT DO YOU MEAN?
WE CAN HOOK UP ONE OF THE MULTIMEDIA BOXES TO THE PROJECTOR IN THE CONFERENCE ROOM AND WATCH DVDS ON IT.
YEAH. I JUST GOT GLADIATOR ON DVD. I'LL SWING BY MY APARTMENT ON THE WAY BACK FROM LUNCH.
YOU KNOW BOYS, THE DAY PASSES SLOWER WHEN YOU'RE NOT WORKING. IF YOU WOULD JUST BUCKLE DOWN AND GET TO WORK, I PROMISE THE DAY WILL PASS IN THE BLINK OF AN EYE.
MAX-I-MUS! MAX-I-MUS!

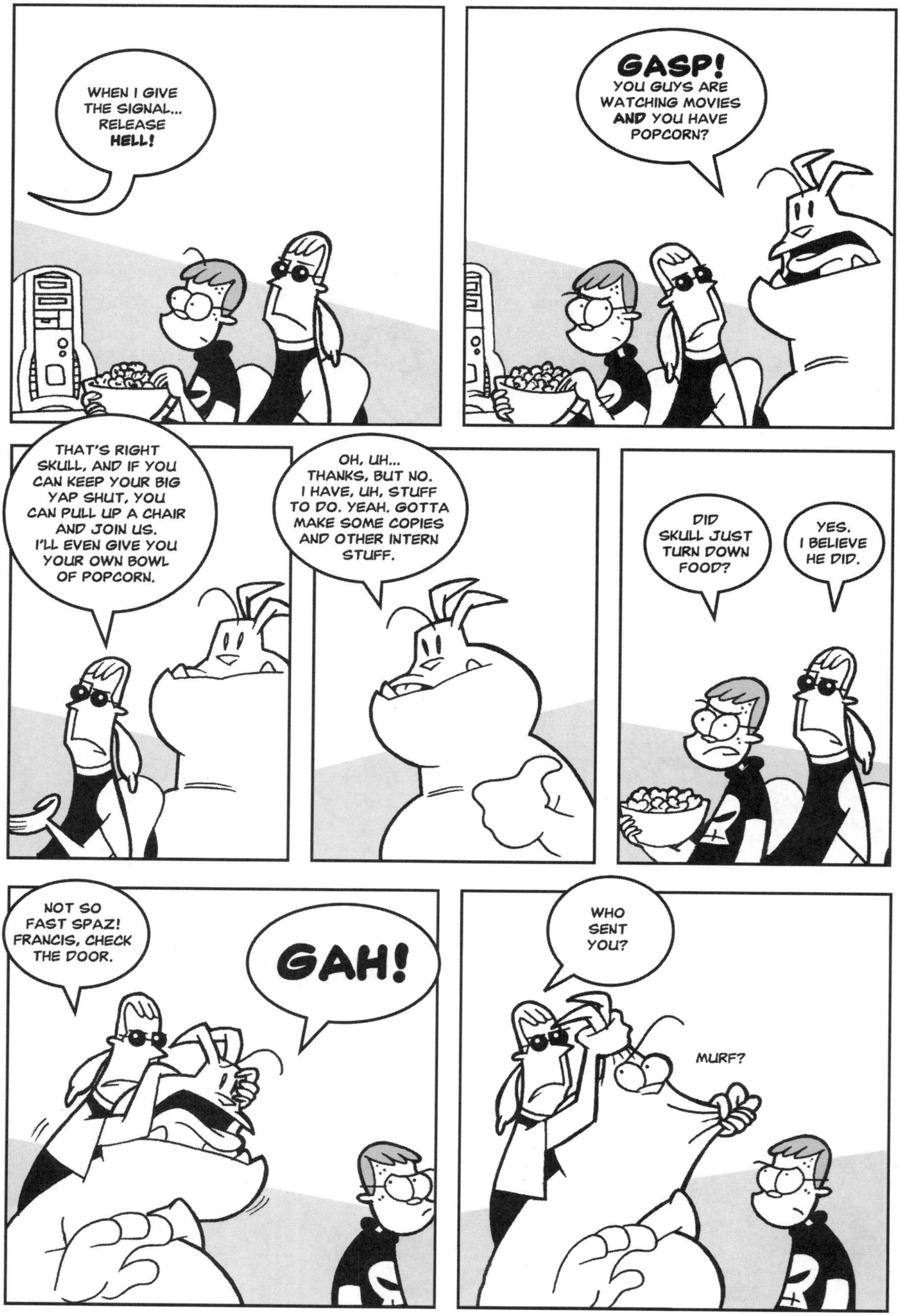
WHEN I GIVE THE SIGNAL... RELEASE **HELL!**
GASP! YOU GUYS ARE WATCHING MOVIES **AND** YOU HAVE POPCORN?
THAT'S RIGHT SKULL, AND IF YOU CAN KEEP YOUR BIG YAP SHUT, YOU CAN PULL UP A CHAIR AND JOIN US. I'LL EVEN GIVE YOU YOUR OWN BOWL OF POPCORN.
OH, UH... THANKS, BUT NO. I HAVE, UH, STUFF TO DO. YEAH. GOTTA MAKE SOME COPIES AND OTHER INTERN STUFF.
DID SKULL JUST TURN DOWN FOOD?
YES. I BELIEVE HE DID.
NOT SO FAST SPAZ! FRANCIS, CHECK THE DOOR.
GAH!
WHO SENT YOU?
MURF?

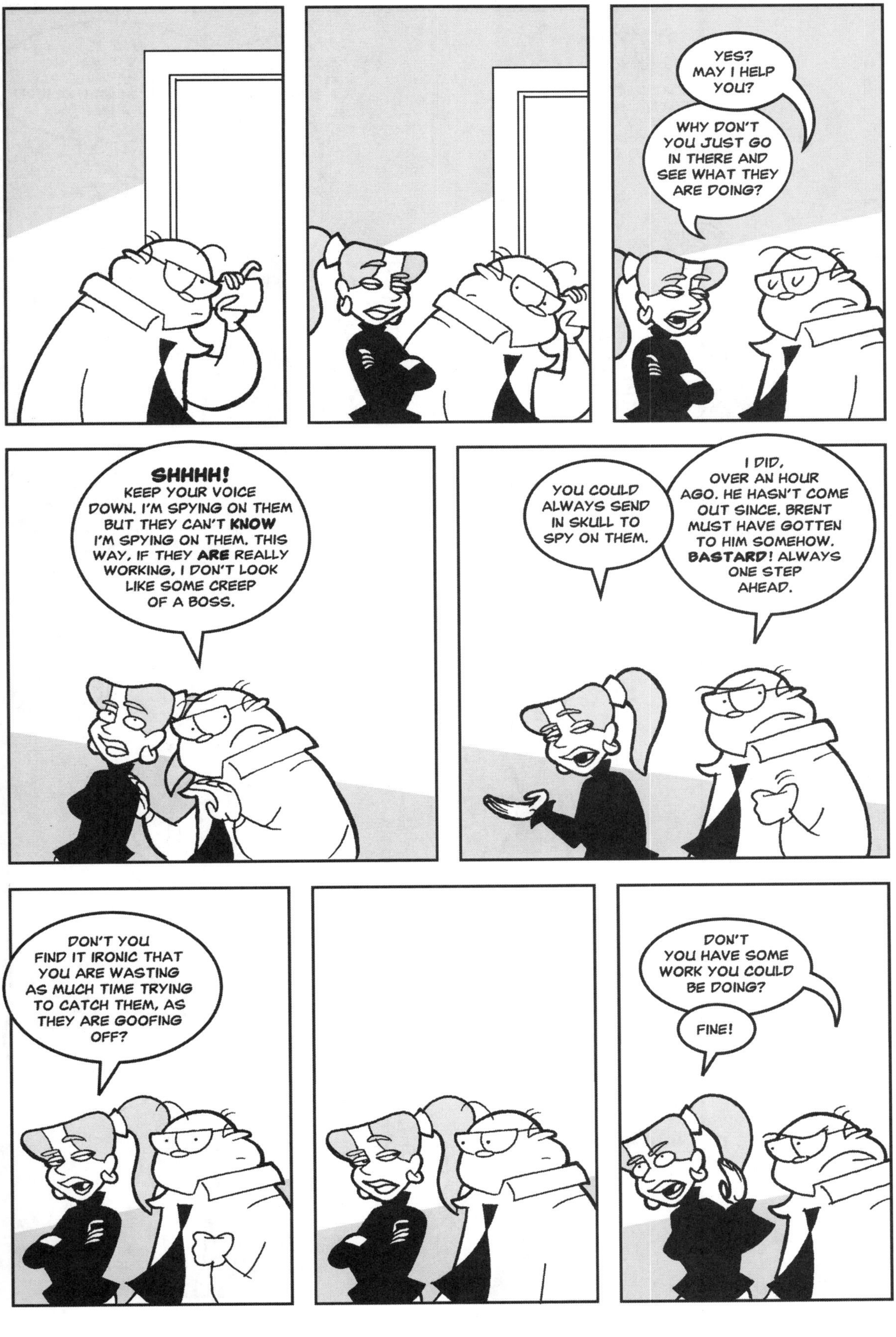
YES? MAY I HELP YOU?
WHY DON'T YOU JUST GO IN THERE AND SEE WHAT THEY ARE DOING?
SHHHH! KEEP YOUR VOICE DOWN. I'M SPYING ON THEM BUT THEY CAN'T KNOW I'M SPYING ON THEM. THIS WAY, IF THEY ARE REALLY WORKING, I DON'T LOOK LIKE SOME CREEP OF A BOSS.
YOU COULD ALWAYS SEND IN SKULL TO SPY ON THEM.
I DID, OVER AN HOUR AGO. HE HASN'T COME OUT SINCE. BRENT MUST HAVE GOTTEN TO HIM SOMEHOW. BASTARD! ALWAYS ONE STEP AHEAD.
DON'T YOU FIND IT IRONIC THAT YOU ARE WASTING AS MUCH TIME TRYING TO CATCH THEM, AS THEY ARE GOOFING OFF?
DON'T YOU HAVE SOME WORK YOU COULD BE DOING?
FINE!

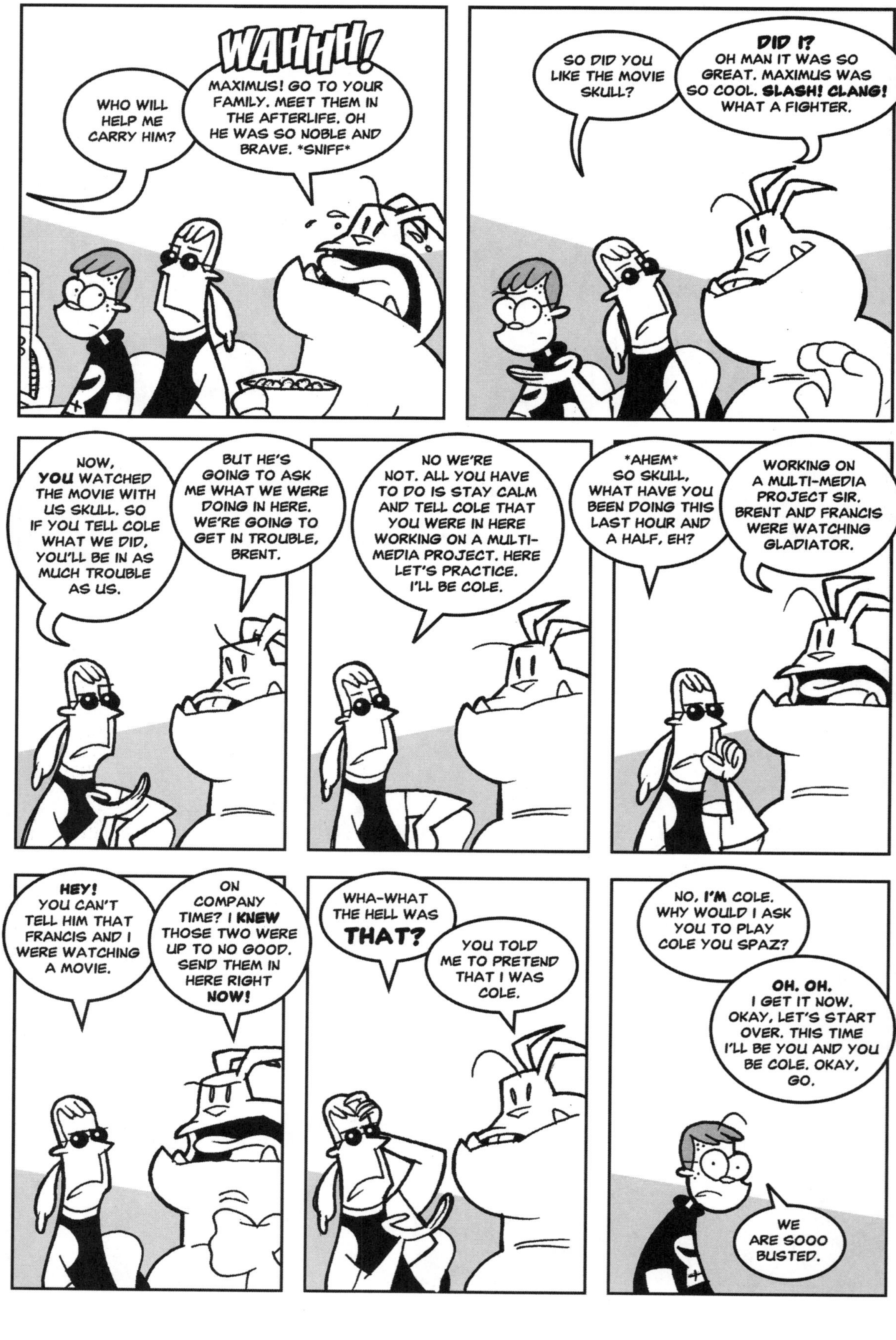
WHO WILL HELP ME CARRY HIM?
WAHHH!
MAXIMUS! GO TO YOUR FAMILY. MEET THEM IN THE AFTERLIFE. OH HE WAS SO NOBLE AND BRAVE. *SNIFF*
SO DID YOU LIKE THE MOVIE SKULL?
DID I? OH MAN IT WAS SO GREAT. MAXIMUS WAS SO COOL. SLASH! CLANG! WHAT A FIGHTER.
NOW, YOU WATCHED THE MOVIE WITH US SKULL. SO IF YOU TELL COLE WHAT WE DID, YOU'LL BE IN AS MUCH TROUBLE AS US.
BUT HE'S GOING TO ASK ME WHAT WE WERE DOING IN HERE. WE'RE GOING TO GET IN TROUBLE, BRENT.
NO WE'RE NOT. ALL YOU HAVE TO DO IS STAY CALM AND TELL COLE THAT YOU WERE IN HERE WORKING ON A MULTI-MEDIA PROJECT. HERE LET'S PRACTICE. I'LL BE COLE.
AHEM SO SKULL, WHAT HAVE YOU BEEN DOING THIS LAST HOUR AND A HALF, EH?
WORKING ON A MULTI-MEDIA PROJECT SIR. BRENT AND FRANCIS WERE WATCHING GLADIATOR.
HEY! YOU CAN'T TELL HIM THAT FRANCIS AND I WERE WATCHING A MOVIE.
ON COMPANY TIME? I KNEW THOSE TWO WERE UP TO NO GOOD. SEND THEM IN HERE RIGHT NOW!
WHA-WHAT THE HELL WAS THAT?
YOU TOLD ME TO PRETEND THAT I WAS COLE.
NO, I'M COLE. WHY WOULD I ASK YOU TO PLAY COLE YOU SPAZ?
OH. OH. I GET IT NOW. OKAY, LET'S START OVER. THIS TIME I'LL BE YOU AND YOU BE COLE. OKAY, GO.
WE ARE SOOO BUSTED.

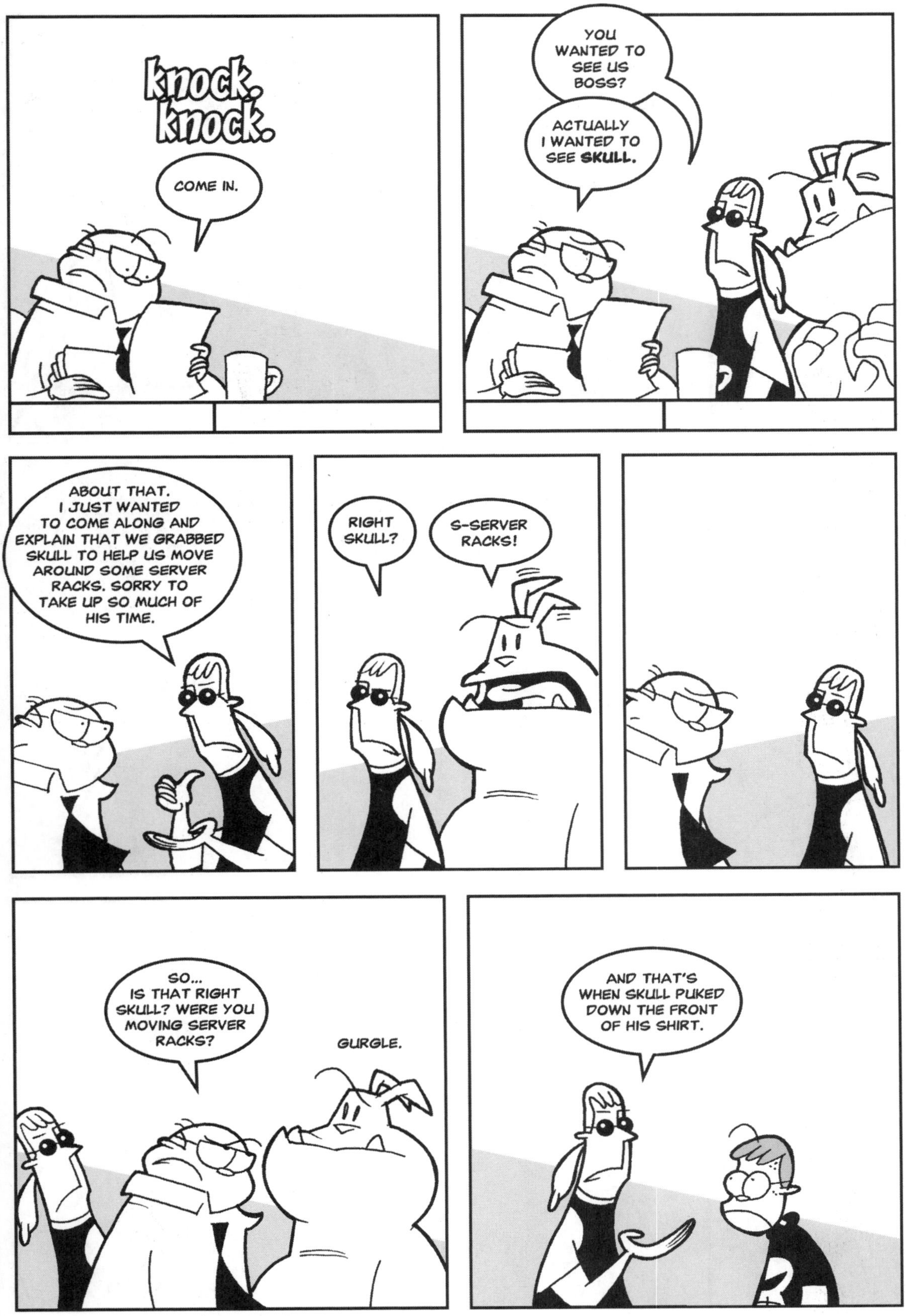
knock. knock.
COME IN.
YOU WANTED TO SEE US BOSS?
ACTUALLY I WANTED TO SEE **SKULL.**
ABOUT THAT. I JUST WANTED TO COME ALONG AND EXPLAIN THAT WE GRABBED SKULL TO HELP US MOVE AROUND SOME SERVER RACKS. SORRY TO TAKE UP SO MUCH OF HIS TIME.
RIGHT SKULL?
S-SERVER RACKS!
SO... IS THAT RIGHT SKULL? WERE YOU MOVING SERVER RACKS?
GURGLE.
AND THAT'S WHEN SKULL PUKED DOWN THE FRONT OF HIS SHIRT.

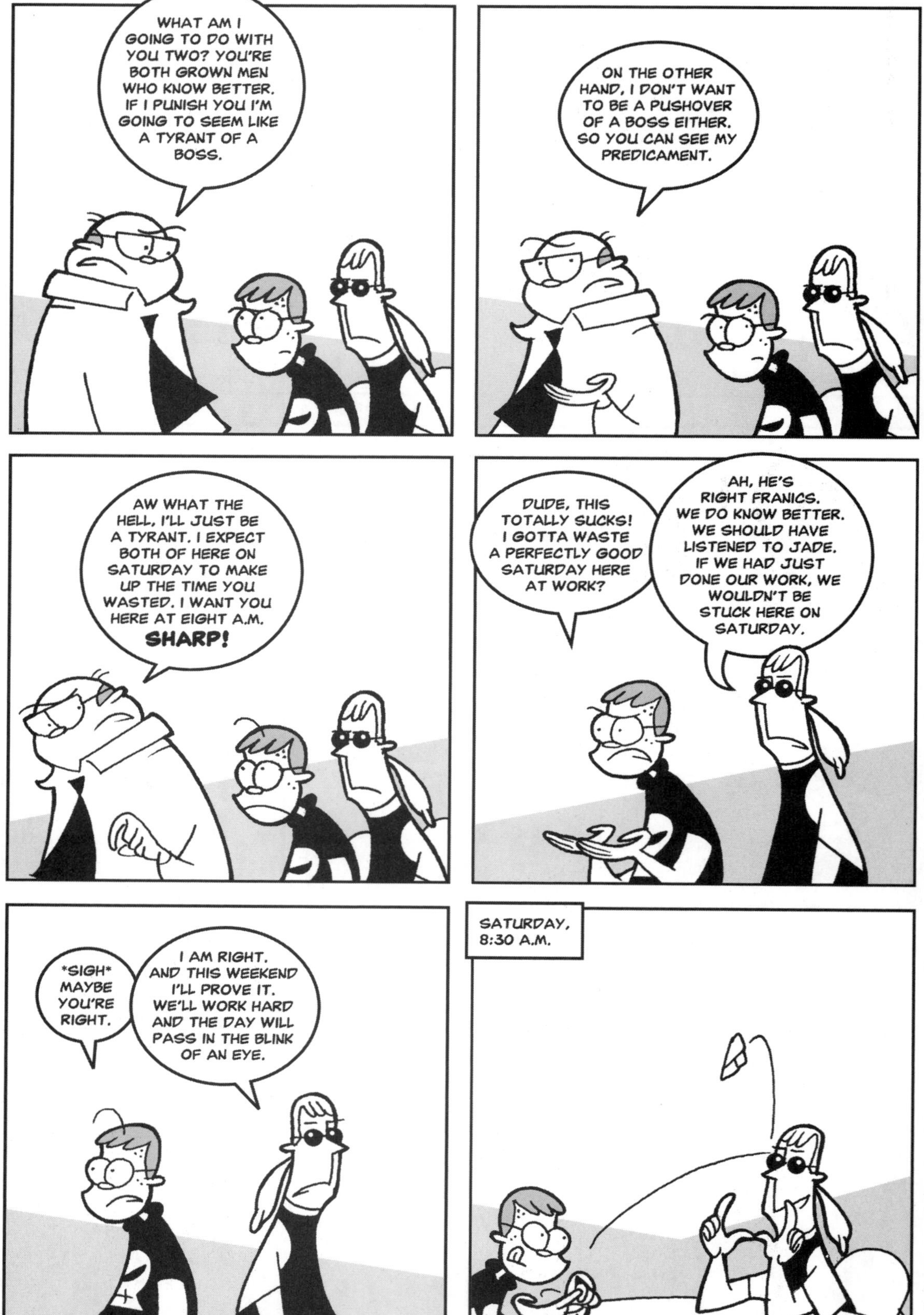
WHAT AM I GOING TO DO WITH YOU TWO? YOU'RE BOTH GROWN MEN WHO KNOW BETTER. IF I PUNISH YOU I'M GOING TO SEEM LIKE A TYRANT OF A BOSS.
ON THE OTHER HAND, I DON'T WANT TO BE A PUSHOVER OF A BOSS EITHER. SO YOU CAN SEE MY PREDICAMENT.
AW WHAT THE HELL, I'LL JUST BE A TYRANT. I EXPECT BOTH OF HERE ON SATURDAY TO MAKE UP THE TIME YOU WASTED. I WANT YOU HERE AT EIGHT A.M. SHARP!
DUDE, THIS TOTALLY SUCKS! I GOTTA WASTE A PERFECTLY GOOD SATURDAY HERE AT WORK?
AH, HE'S RIGHT FRANICS. WE DO KNOW BETTER. WE SHOULD HAVE LISTENED TO JADE. IF WE HAD JUST DONE OUR WORK, WE WOULDN'T BE STUCK HERE ON SATURDAY.
SIGH MAYBE YOU'RE RIGHT.
I AM RIGHT. AND THIS WEEKEND I'LL PROVE IT. WE'LL WORK HARD AND THE DAY WILL PASS IN THE BLINK OF AN EYE.
SATURDAY, 8:30 A.M.

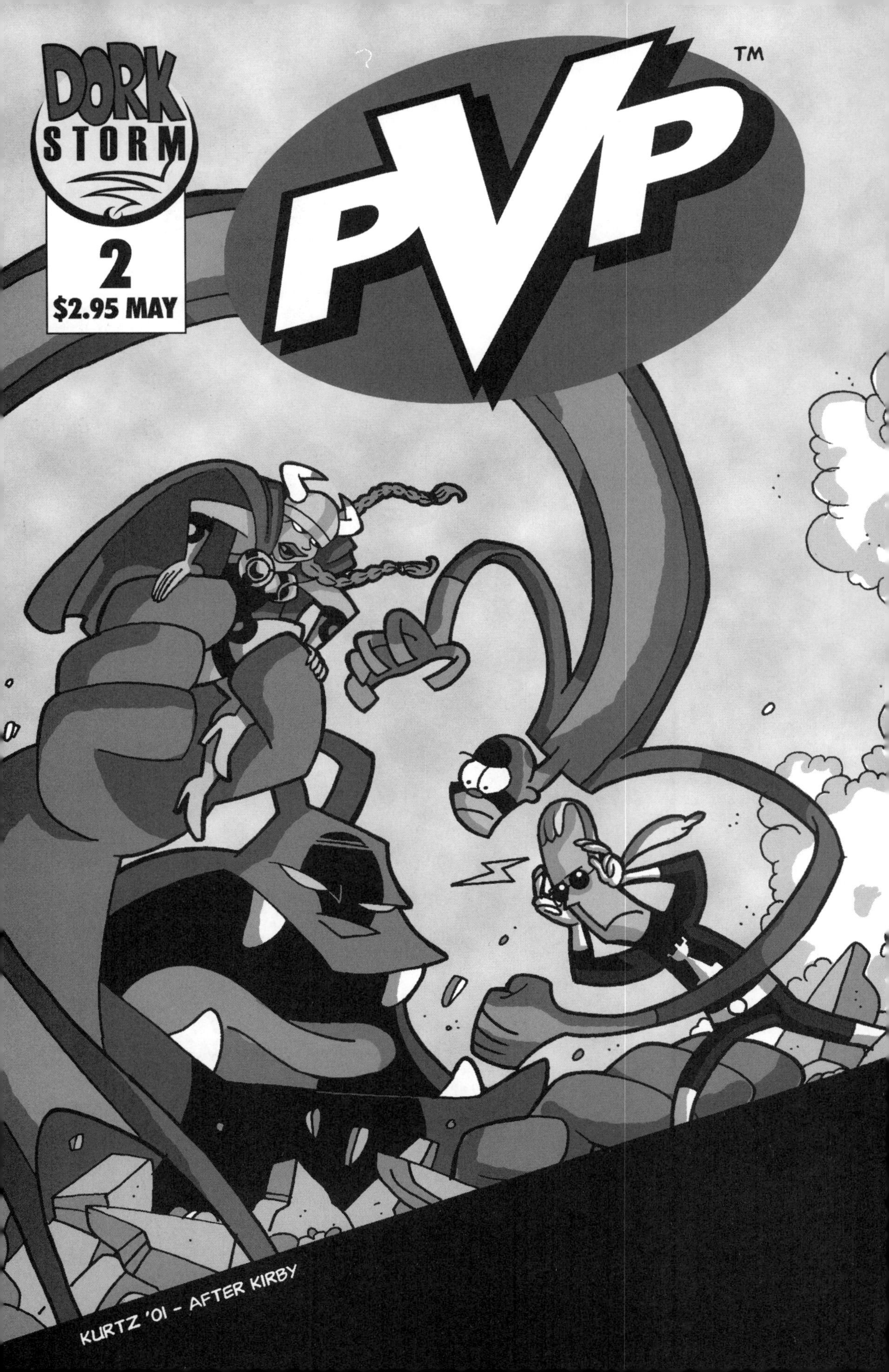
DORK STORM
2
$2.95 MAY
PVP™
KURTZ '01 - AFTER KIRBY

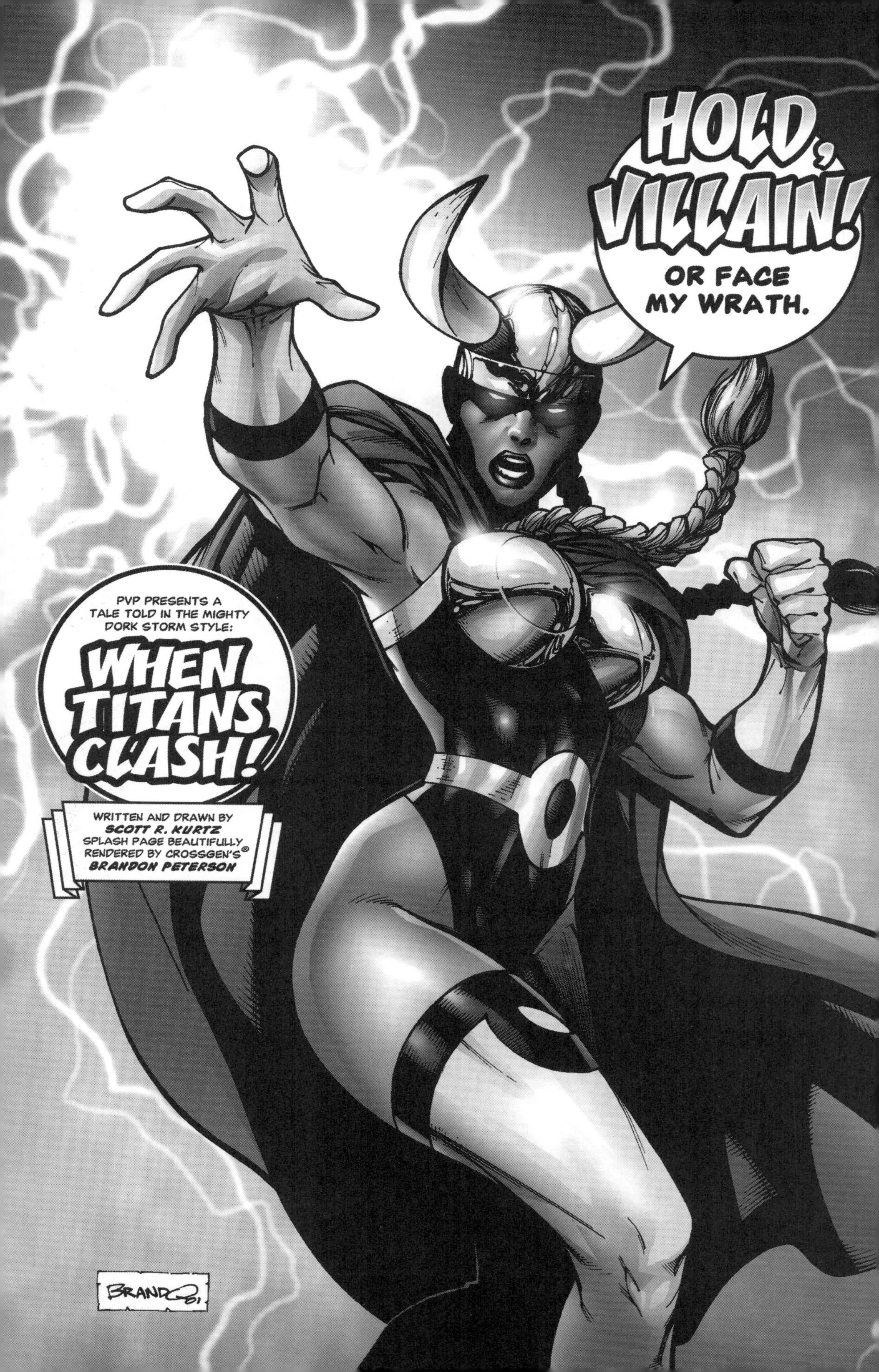
HOLD, VILLAIN! OR FACE MY WRATH.
PVP PRESENTS A TALE TOLD IN THE MIGHTY DORK STORM STYLE:
WHEN TITANS CLASH!
WRITTEN AND DRAWN BY SCOTT R. KURTZ SPLASH PAGE BEAUTIFULLY RENDERED BY CROSSGEN'S® BRANDON PETERSON
BRAND '01

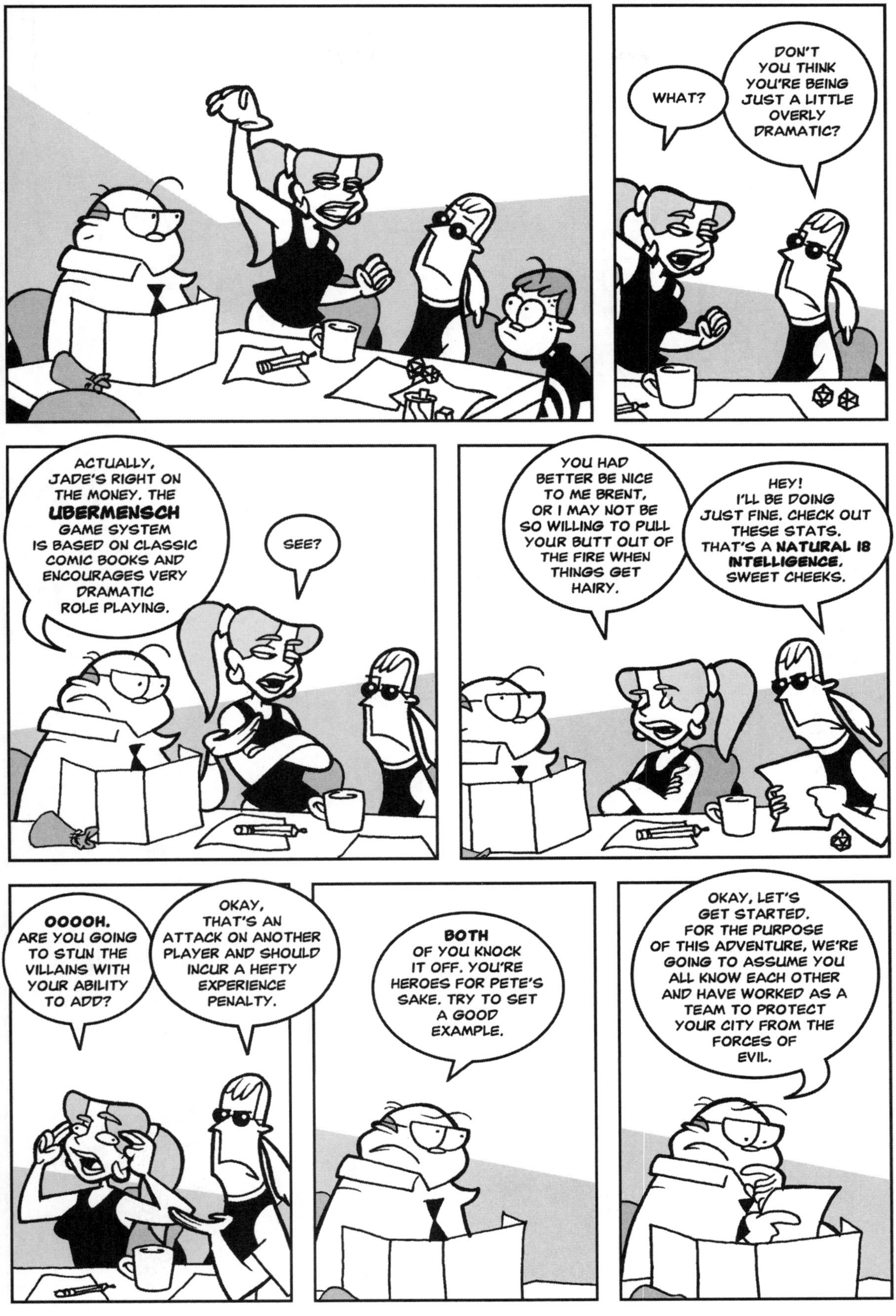
WHAT?
DON'T YOU THINK YOU'RE BEING JUST A LITTLE OVERLY DRAMATIC?
ACTUALLY, JADE'S RIGHT ON THE MONEY. THE **UBERMENSCH** GAME SYSTEM IS BASED ON CLASSIC COMIC BOOKS AND ENCOURAGES VERY DRAMATIC ROLE PLAYING.
SEE?
YOU HAD BETTER BE NICE TO ME BRENT, OR I MAY NOT BE SO WILLING TO PULL YOUR BUTT OUT OF THE FIRE WHEN THINGS GET HAIRY.
HEY! I'LL BE DOING JUST FINE. CHECK OUT THESE STATS. THAT'S A **NATURAL 18 INTELLIGENCE,** SWEET CHEEKS.
OOOOH. ARE YOU GOING TO STUN THE VILLAINS WITH YOUR ABILITY TO ADD?
OKAY, THAT'S AN ATTACK ON ANOTHER PLAYER AND SHOULD INCUR A HEFTY EXPERIENCE PENALTY.
BOTH OF YOU KNOCK IT OFF. YOU'RE HEROES FOR PETE'S SAKE. TRY TO SET A GOOD EXAMPLE.
OKAY, LET'S GET STARTED. FOR THE PURPOSE OF THIS ADVENTURE, WE'RE GOING TO ASSUME YOU ALL KNOW EACH OTHER AND HAVE WORKED AS A TEAM TO PROTECT YOUR CITY FROM THE FORCES OF EVIL.

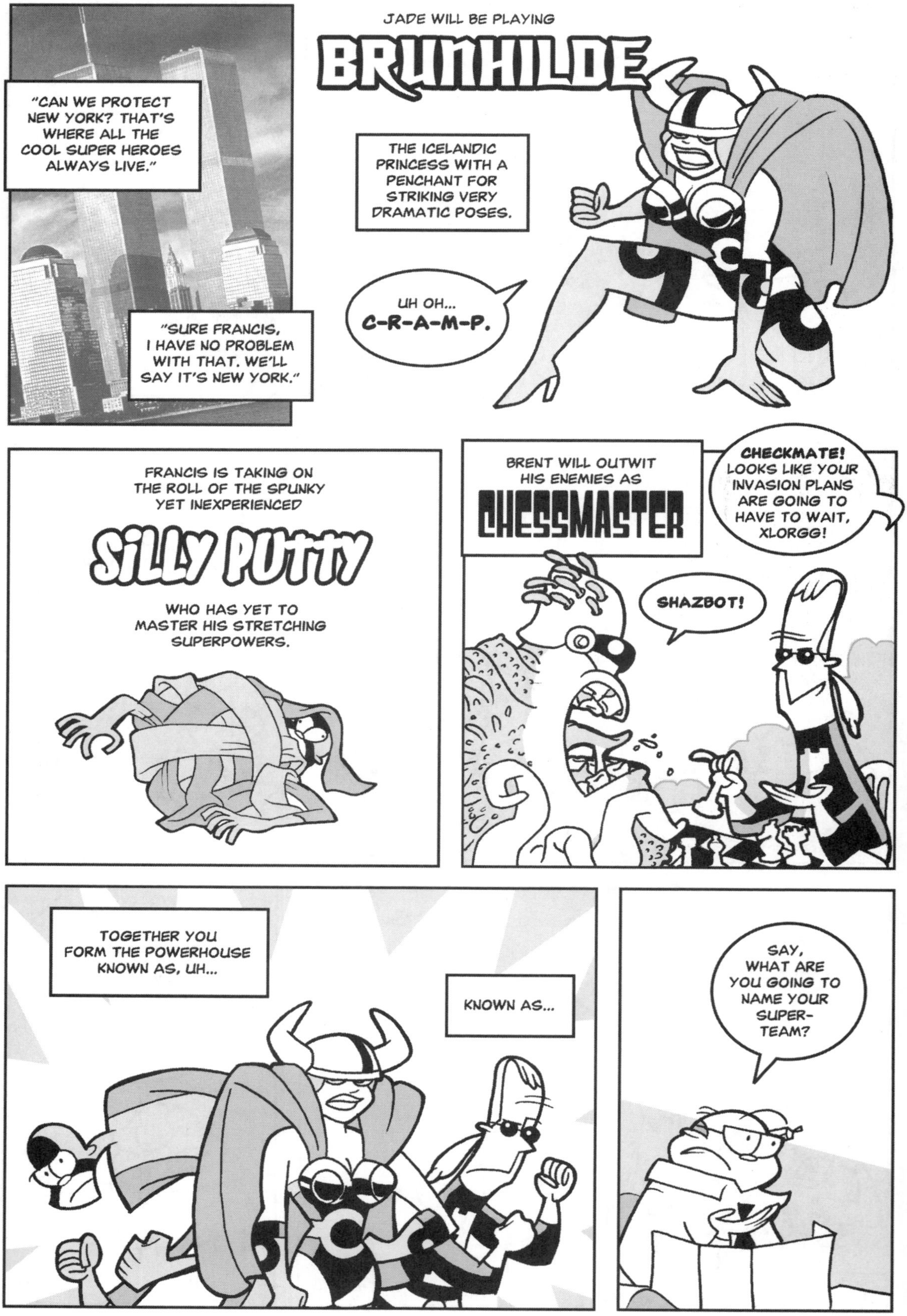
"CAN WE PROTECT NEW YORK? THAT'S WHERE ALL THE COOL SUPER HEROES ALWAYS LIVE."
"SURE FRANCIS, I HAVE NO PROBLEM WITH THAT. WE'LL SAY IT'S NEW YORK."
JADE WILL BE PLAYING
BRUNHILDE
THE ICELANDIC PRINCESS WITH A PENCHANT FOR STRIKING VERY DRAMATIC POSES.
UH OH... C-R-A-M-P.
FRANCIS IS TAKING ON THE ROLL OF THE SPUNKY YET INEXPERIENCED
SILLY PUTTY
WHO HAS YET TO MASTER HIS STRETCHING SUPERPOWERS.
BRENT WILL OUTWIT HIS ENEMIES AS
CHESSMASTER
CHECKMATE! LOOKS LIKE YOUR INVASION PLANS ARE GOING TO HAVE TO WAIT, XLORGG!
SHAZBOT!
TOGETHER YOU FORM THE POWERHOUSE KNOWN AS, UH...
KNOWN AS...
SAY, WHAT ARE YOU GOING TO NAME YOUR SUPER-TEAM?

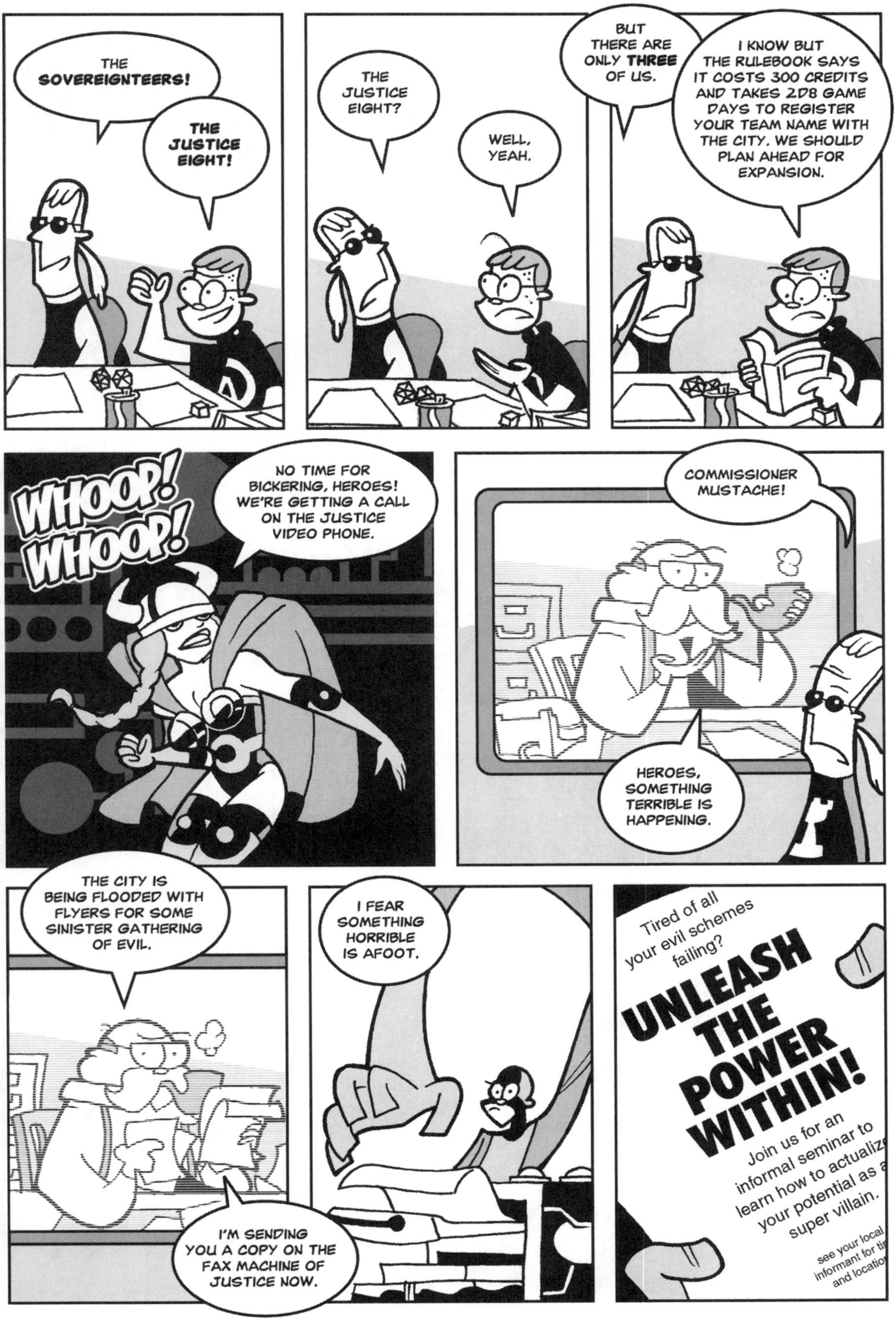

THE SOVEREIGNTEERS!
THE JUSTICE EIGHT!
THE JUSTICE EIGHT?
WELL, YEAH.
BUT THERE ARE ONLY THREE OF US.
I KNOW BUT THE RULEBOOK SAYS IT COSTS 300 CREDITS AND TAKES 2D8 GAME DAYS TO REGISTER YOUR TEAM NAME WITH THE CITY. WE SHOULD PLAN AHEAD FOR EXPANSION.
WHOOP! WHOOP!
NO TIME FOR BICKERING, HEROES! WE'RE GETTING A CALL ON THE JUSTICE VIDEO PHONE.
COMMISSIONER MUSTACHE!
HEROES, SOMETHING TERRIBLE IS HAPPENING.
THE CITY IS BEING FLOODED WITH FLYERS FOR SOME SINISTER GATHERING OF EVIL.
I'M SENDING YOU A COPY ON THE FAX MACHINE OF JUSTICE NOW.
I FEAR SOMETHING HORRIBLE IS AFOOT.
Tired of all your evil schemes failing?
UNLEASH THE POWER WITHIN!
Join us for an informal seminar to learn how to actualiz your potential as a super villain.
see your local informant for ti and locatio

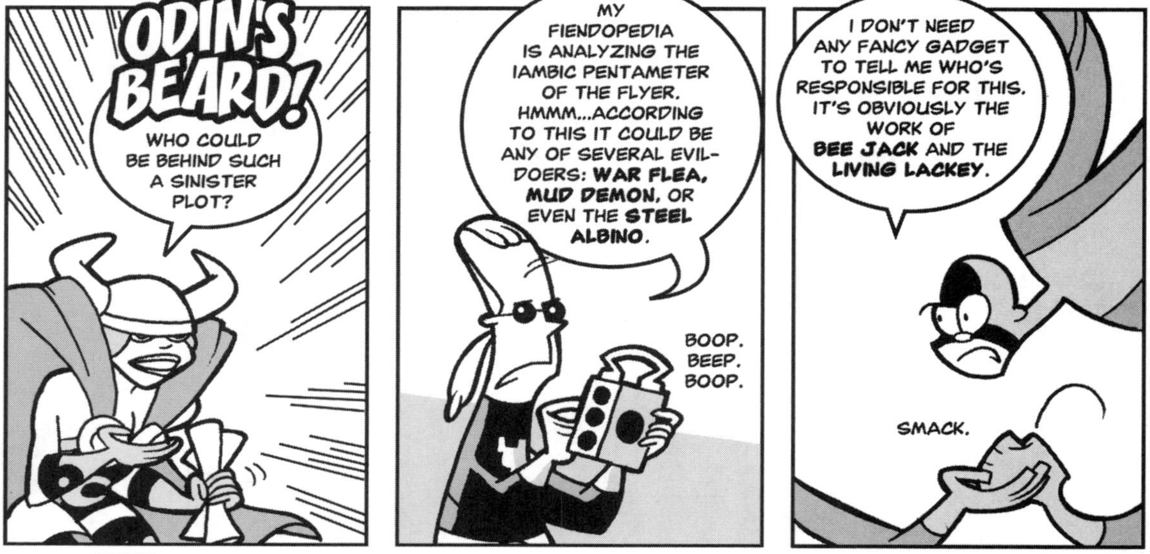
ODIN'S BEARD!
WHO COULD BE BEHIND SUCH A SINISTER PLOT?
MY FIENDOPEDIA IS ANALYZING THE IAMBIC PENTAMETER OF THE FLYER. HMMM...ACCORDING TO THIS IT COULD BE ANY OF SEVERAL EVIL-DOERS: WAR FLEA, MUD DEMON, OR EVEN THE STEEL ALBINO.
BOOP. BEEP. BOOP.
I DON'T NEED ANY FANCY GADGET TO TELL ME WHO'S RESPONSIBLE FOR THIS. IT'S OBVIOUSLY THE WORK OF BEE JACK AND THE LIVING LACKEY.
SMACK.

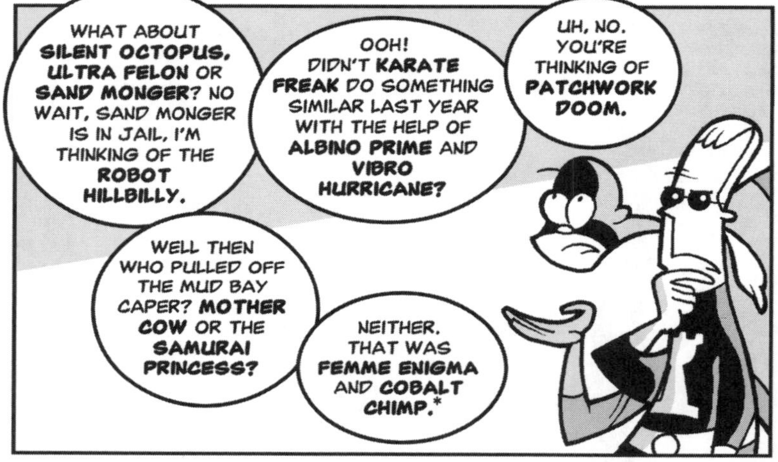
WHAT ABOUT SILENT OCTOPUS, ULTRA FELON OR SAND MONGER? NO WAIT, SAND MONGER IS IN JAIL, I'M THINKING OF THE ROBOT HILLBILLY.
OOH! DIDN'T KARATE FREAK DO SOMETHING SIMILAR LAST YEAR WITH THE HELP OF ALBINO PRIME AND VIBRO HURRICANE?
UH, NO. YOU'RE THINKING OF PATCHWORK DOOM.
WELL THEN WHO PULLED OFF THE MUD BAY CAPER? MOTHER COW OR THE SAMURAI PRINCESS?
NEITHER. THAT WAS FEMME ENIGMA AND COBALT CHIMP.*

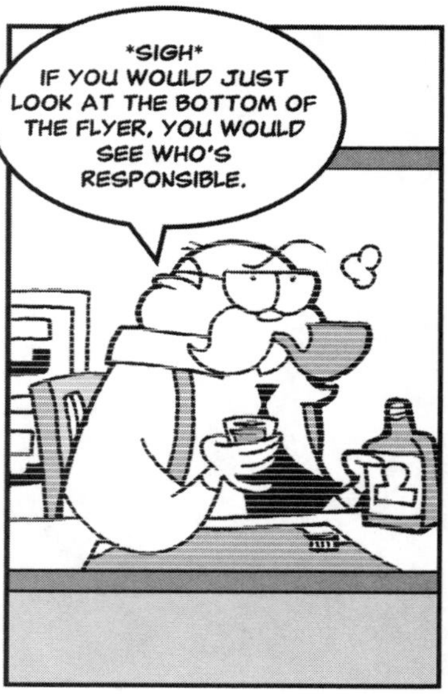
SIGH IF YOU WOULD JUST LOOK AT THE BOTTOM OF THE FLYER, YOU WOULD SEE WHO'S RESPONSIBLE.

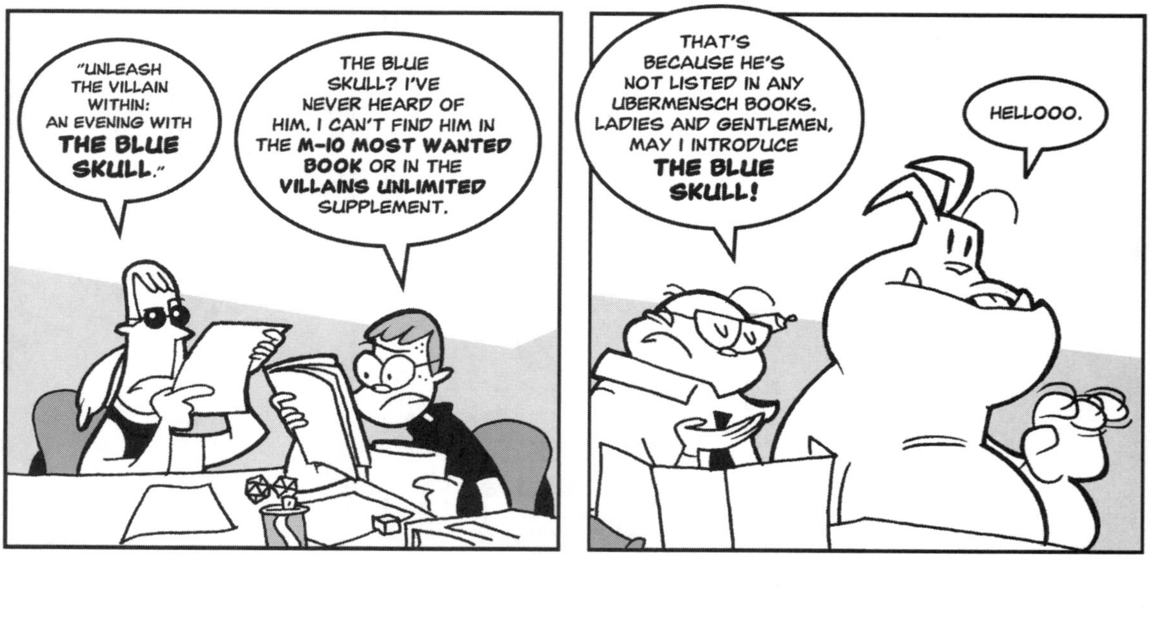
"UNLEASH THE VILLAIN WITHIN: AN EVENING WITH THE BLUE SKULL."
THE BLUE SKULL? I'VE NEVER HEARD OF HIM. I CAN'T FIND HIM IN THE M-10 MOST WANTED BOOK OR IN THE VILLAINS UNLIMITED SUPPLEMENT.
THAT'S BECAUSE HE'S NOT LISTED IN ANY UBERMENSCH BOOKS. LADIES AND GENTLEMEN, MAY I INTRODUCE THE BLUE SKULL!
HELLOOO.

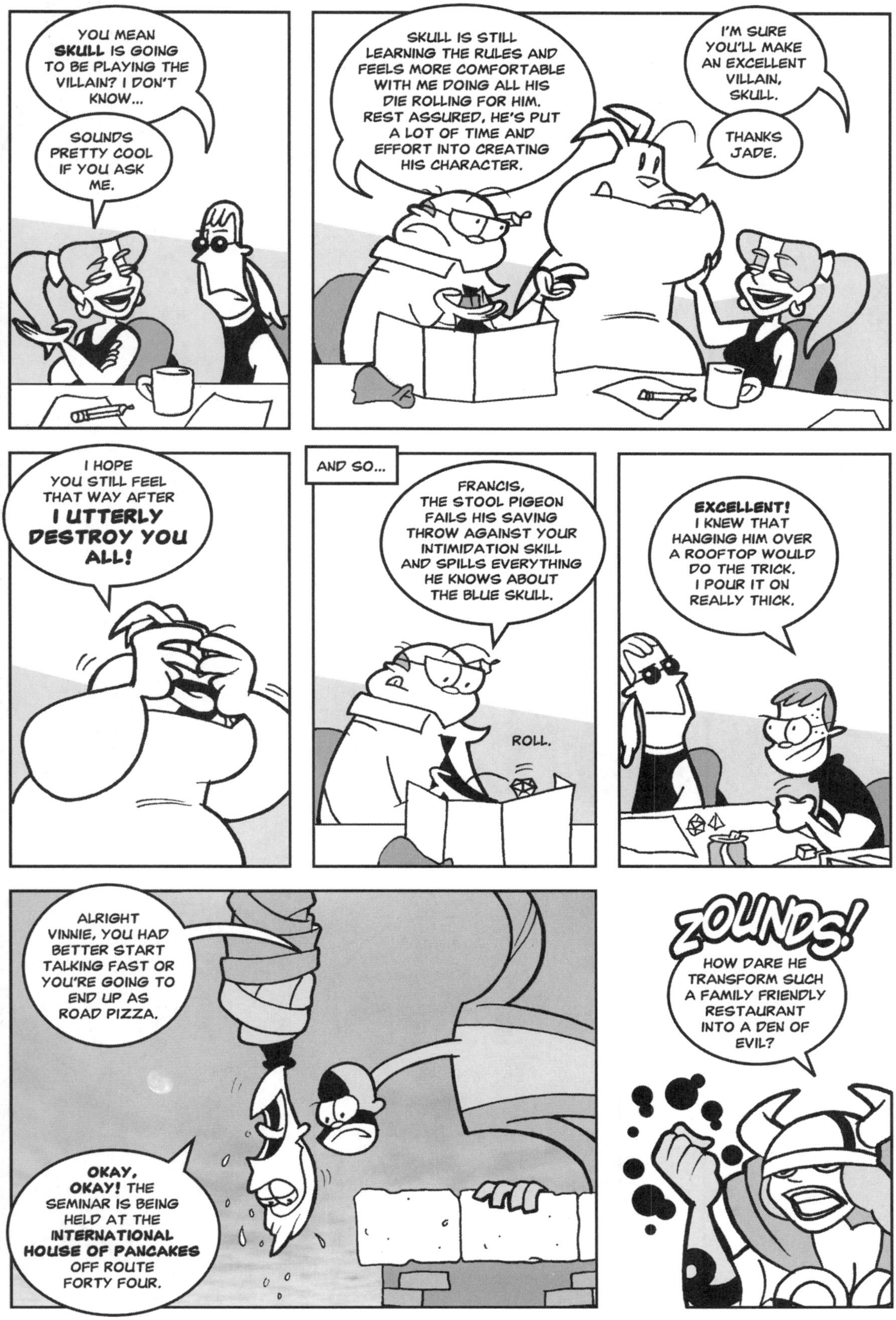

YOU MEAN SKULL IS GOING TO BE PLAYING THE VILLAIN? I DON'T KNOW...
SOUNDS PRETTY COOL IF YOU ASK ME.
SKULL IS STILL LEARNING THE RULES AND FEELS MORE COMFORTABLE WITH ME DOING ALL HIS DIE ROLLING FOR HIM. REST ASSURED, HE'S PUT A LOT OF TIME AND EFFORT INTO CREATING HIS CHARACTER.
I'M SURE YOU'LL MAKE AN EXCELLENT VILLAIN, SKULL.
THANKS JADE.
I HOPE YOU STILL FEEL THAT WAY AFTER I UTTERLY DESTROY YOU ALL!
AND SO...
FRANCIS, THE STOOL PIGEON FAILS HIS SAVING THROW AGAINST YOUR INTIMIDATION SKILL AND SPILLS EVERYTHING HE KNOWS ABOUT THE BLUE SKULL.
ROLL.
EXCELLENT! I KNEW THAT HANGING HIM OVER A ROOFTOP WOULD DO THE TRICK. I POUR IT ON REALLY THICK.
ALRIGHT VINNIE, YOU HAD BETTER START TALKING FAST OR YOU'RE GOING TO END UP AS ROAD PIZZA.
OKAY, OKAY! THE SEMINAR IS BEING HELD AT THE INTERNATIONAL HOUSE OF PANCAKES OFF ROUTE FORTY FOUR.
ZOUNDS!
HOW DARE HE TRANSFORM SUCH A FAMILY FRIENDLY RESTAURANT INTO A DEN OF EVIL?

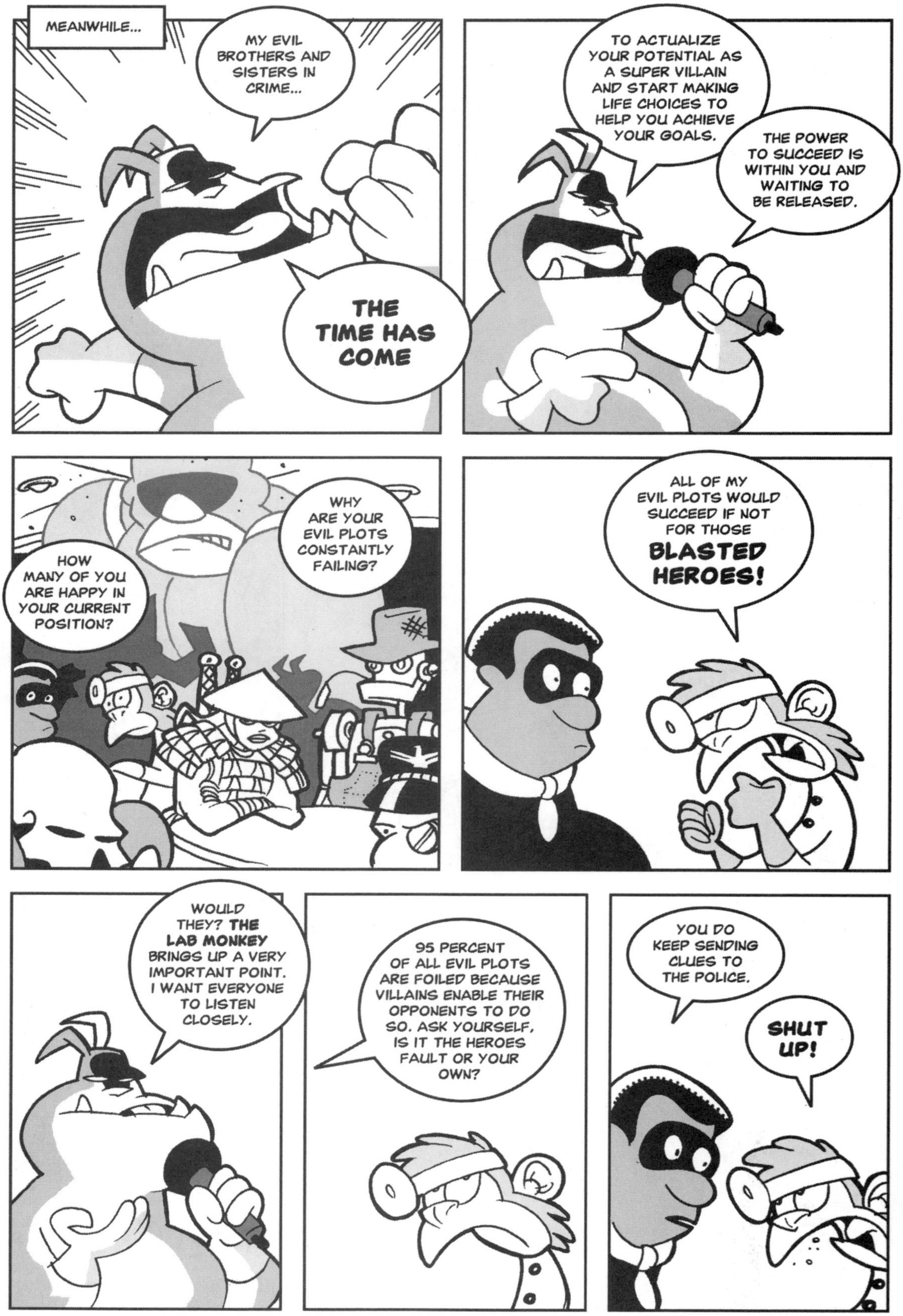

MEANWHILE...
MY EVIL BROTHERS AND SISTERS IN CRIME...
THE TIME HAS COME
TO ACTUALIZE YOUR POTENTIAL AS A SUPER VILLAIN AND START MAKING LIFE CHOICES TO HELP YOU ACHIEVE YOUR GOALS.
THE POWER TO SUCCEED IS WITHIN YOU AND WAITING TO BE RELEASED.
HOW MANY OF YOU ARE HAPPY IN YOUR CURRENT POSITION?
WHY ARE YOUR EVIL PLOTS CONSTANTLY FAILING?
ALL OF MY EVIL PLOTS WOULD SUCCEED IF NOT FOR THOSE BLASTED HEROES!
WOULD THEY? THE LAB MONKEY BRINGS UP A VERY IMPORTANT POINT. I WANT EVERYONE TO LISTEN CLOSELY.
95 PERCENT OF ALL EVIL PLOTS ARE FOILED BECAUSE VILLAINS ENABLE THEIR OPPONENTS TO DO SO. ASK YOURSELF, IS IT THE HEROES FAULT OR YOUR OWN?
YOU DO KEEP SENDING CLUES TO THE POLICE.
SHUT UP!

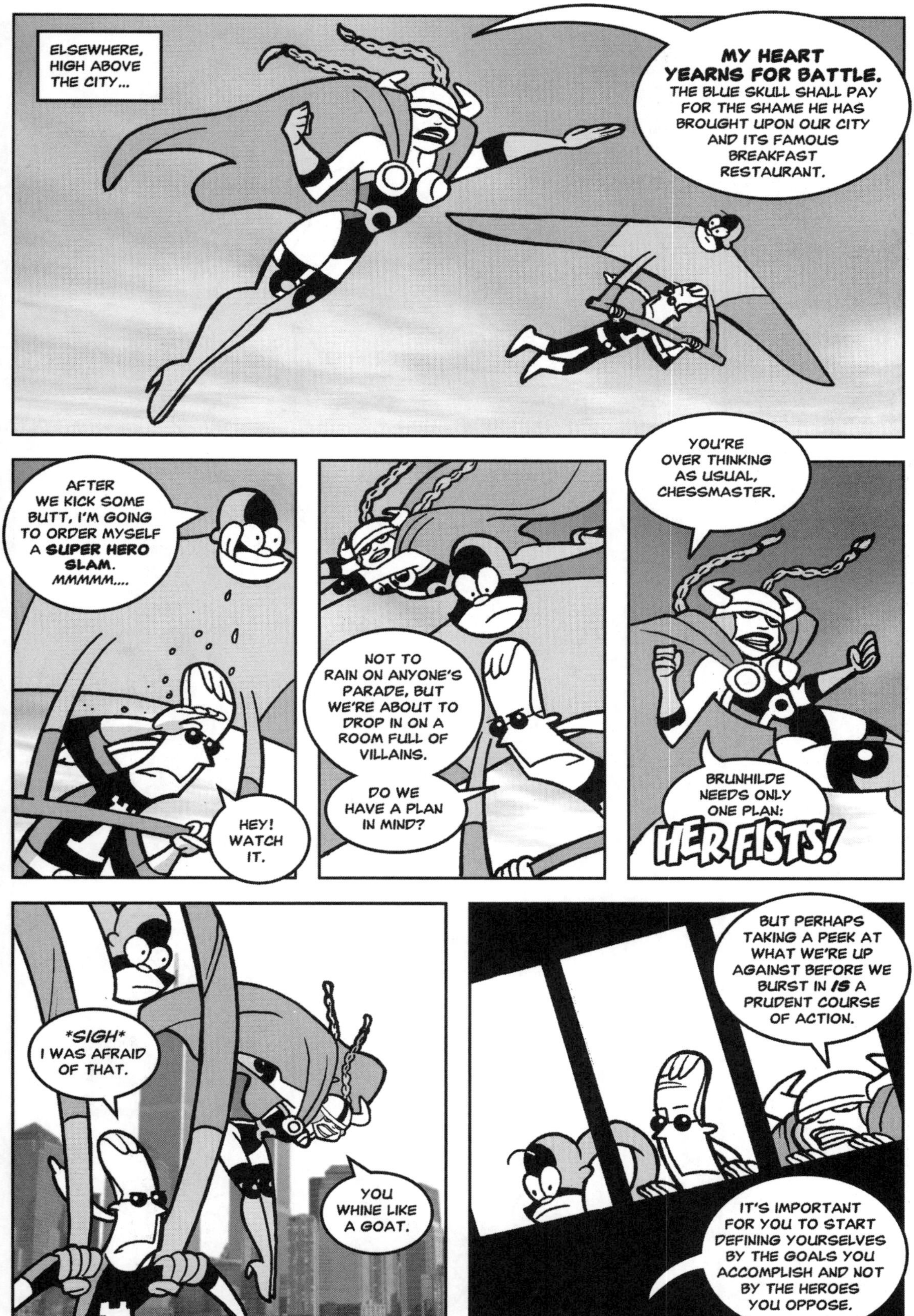

ELSEWHERE, HIGH ABOVE THE CITY...
MY HEART YEARNS FOR BATTLE. THE BLUE SKULL SHALL PAY FOR THE SHAME HE HAS BROUGHT UPON OUR CITY AND ITS FAMOUS BREAKFAST RESTAURANT.
AFTER WE KICK SOME BUTT, I'M GOING TO ORDER MYSELF A SUPER HERO SLAM. MMMMM....
HEY! WATCH IT.
NOT TO RAIN ON ANYONE'S PARADE, BUT WE'RE ABOUT TO DROP IN ON A ROOM FULL OF VILLAINS.
DO WE HAVE A PLAN IN MIND?
YOU'RE OVER THINKING AS USUAL, CHESSMASTER.
BRUNHILDE NEEDS ONLY ONE PLAN:
HER FISTS!
SIGH I WAS AFRAID OF THAT.
YOU WHINE LIKE A GOAT.
BUT PERHAPS TAKING A PEEK AT WHAT WE'RE UP AGAINST BEFORE WE BURST IN IS A PRUDENT COURSE OF ACTION.
IT'S IMPORTANT FOR YOU TO START DEFINING YOURSELVES BY THE GOALS YOU ACCOMPLISH AND NOT BY THE HEROES YOU OPPOSE.

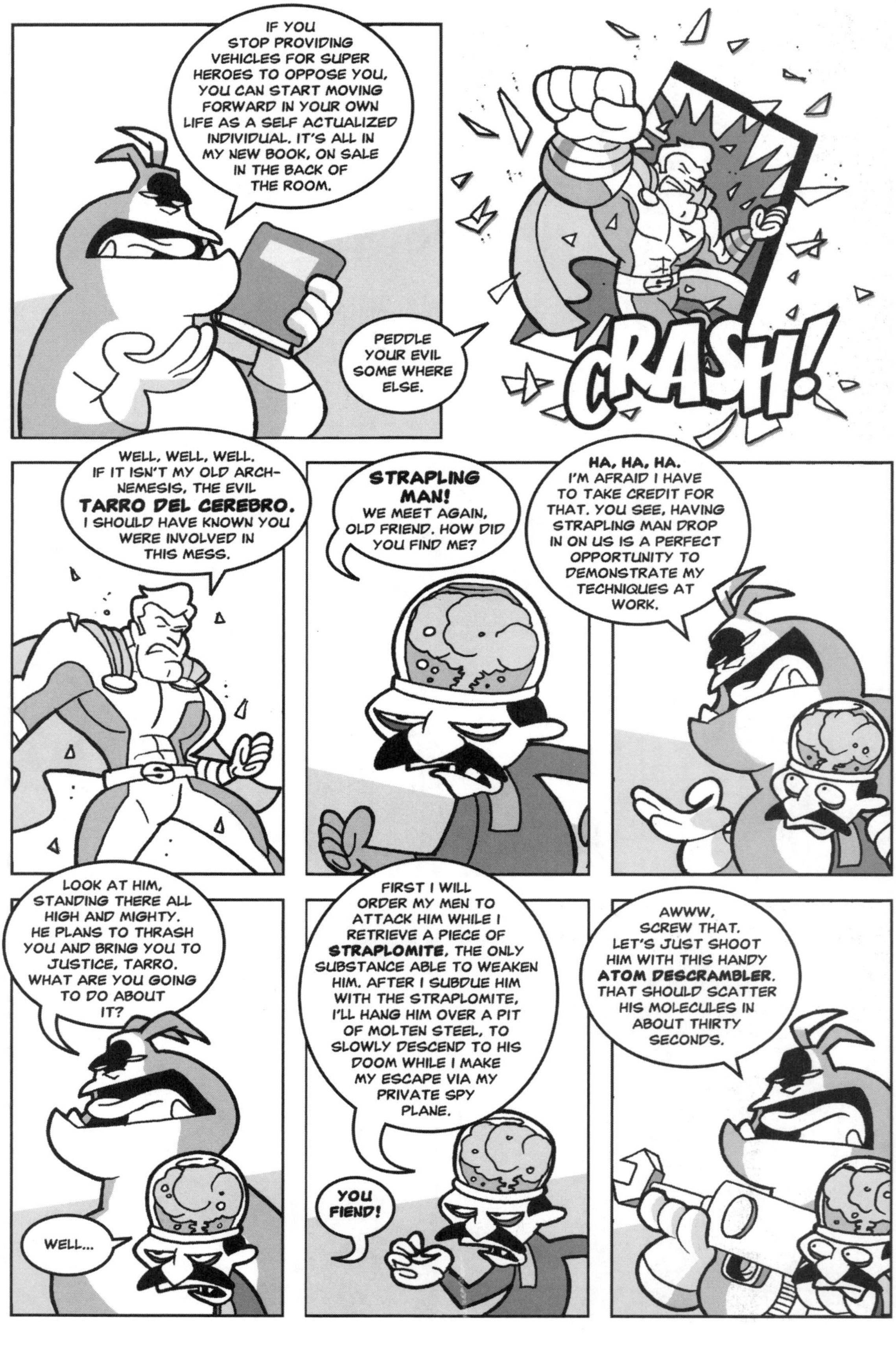
IF YOU STOP PROVIDING VEHICLES FOR SUPER HEROES TO OPPOSE YOU, YOU CAN START MOVING FORWARD IN YOUR OWN LIFE AS A SELF ACTUALIZED INDIVIDUAL. IT'S ALL IN MY NEW BOOK, ON SALE IN THE BACK OF THE ROOM.
PEDDLE YOUR EVIL SOME WHERE ELSE.
CRASH!
WELL, WELL, WELL. IF IT ISN'T MY OLD ARCH-NEMESIS, THE EVIL **TARRO DEL CEREBRO.** I SHOULD HAVE KNOWN YOU WERE INVOLVED IN THIS MESS.
STRAPLING MAN! WE MEET AGAIN, OLD FRIEND. HOW DID YOU FIND ME?
HA, HA, HA. I'M AFRAID I HAVE TO TAKE CREDIT FOR THAT. YOU SEE, HAVING STRAPLING MAN DROP IN ON US IS A PERFECT OPPORTUNITY TO DEMONSTRATE MY TECHNIQUES AT WORK.
LOOK AT HIM, STANDING THERE ALL HIGH AND MIGHTY. HE PLANS TO THRASH YOU AND BRING YOU TO JUSTICE, TARRO. WHAT ARE YOU GOING TO DO ABOUT IT?
WELL...
FIRST I WILL ORDER MY MEN TO ATTACK HIM WHILE I RETRIEVE A PIECE OF **STRAPLOMITE**, THE ONLY SUBSTANCE ABLE TO WEAKEN HIM. AFTER I SUBDUE HIM WITH THE STRAPLOMITE, I'LL HANG HIM OVER A PIT OF MOLTEN STEEL, TO SLOWLY DESCEND TO HIS DOOM WHILE I MAKE MY ESCAPE VIA MY PRIVATE SPY PLANE.
YOU FIEND!
AWWW, SCREW THAT. LET'S JUST SHOOT HIM WITH THIS HANDY **ATOM DESCRAMBLER**. THAT SHOULD SCATTER HIS MOLECULES IN ABOUT THIRTY SECONDS.

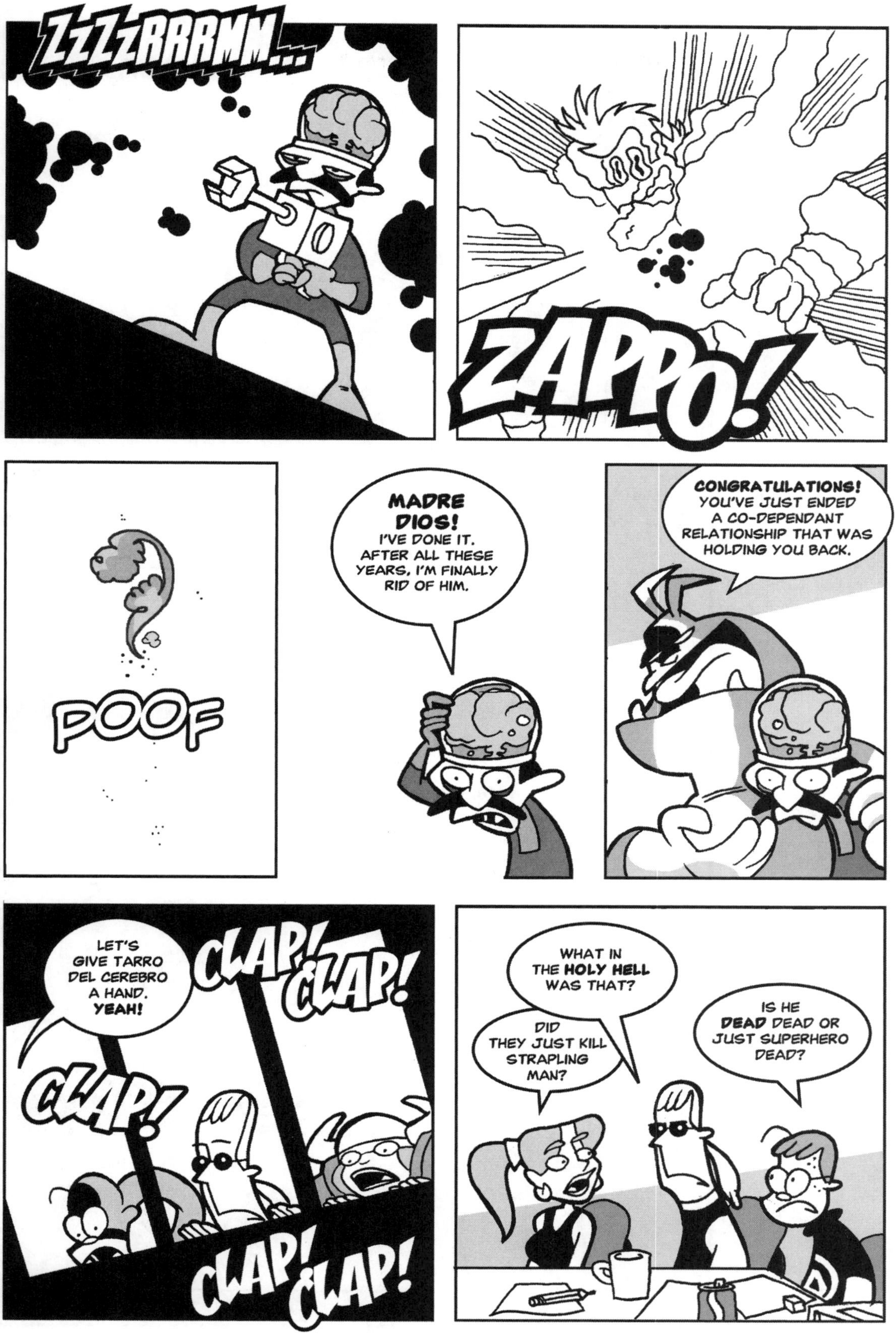
ZzZzRRRMM...
ZAPPO!
POOF
MADRE DIOS! I'VE DONE IT. AFTER ALL THESE YEARS, I'M FINALLY RID OF HIM.
CONGRATULATIONS! YOU'VE JUST ENDED A CO-DEPENDANT RELATIONSHIP THAT WAS HOLDING YOU BACK.
LET'S GIVE TARRO DEL CEREBRO A HAND. YEAH!
CLAP! CLAP!
CLAP!
CLAP! CLAP!
WHAT IN THE HOLY HELL WAS THAT?
DID THEY JUST KILL STRAPLING MAN?
IS HE DEAD DEAD OR JUST SUPERHERO DEAD?

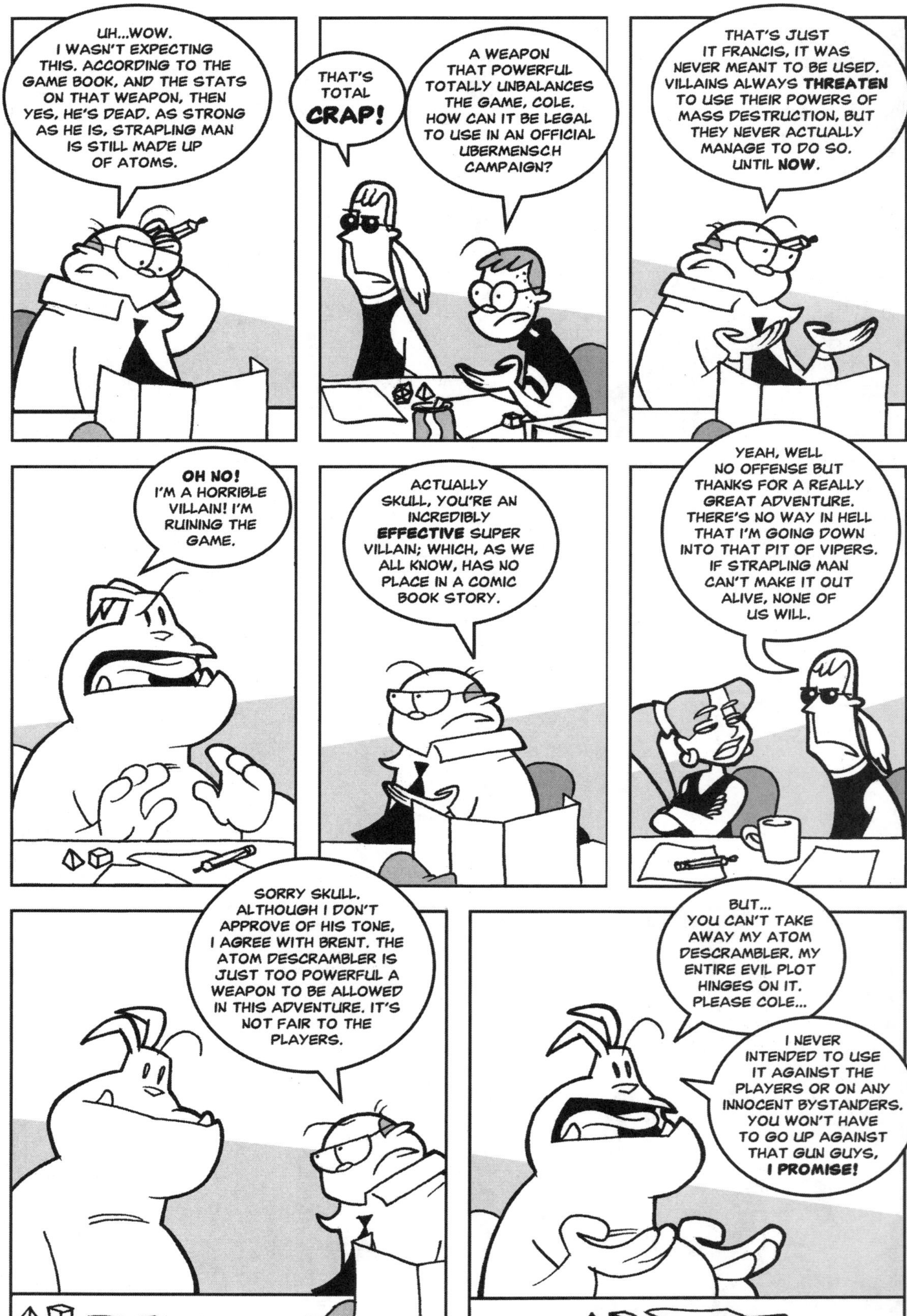
UH...WOW. I WASN'T EXPECTING THIS. ACCORDING TO THE GAME BOOK, AND THE STATS ON THAT WEAPON, THEN YES, HE'S DEAD. AS STRONG AS HE IS, STRAPLING MAN IS STILL MADE UP OF ATOMS.
THAT'S TOTAL **CRAP!**
A WEAPON THAT POWERFUL TOTALLY UNBALANCES THE GAME, COLE. HOW CAN IT BE LEGAL TO USE IN AN OFFICIAL UBERMENSCH CAMPAIGN?
THAT'S JUST IT FRANCIS, IT WAS NEVER MEANT TO BE USED. VILLAINS ALWAYS **THREATEN** TO USE THEIR POWERS OF MASS DESTRUCTION, BUT THEY NEVER ACTUALLY MANAGE TO DO SO. UNTIL **NOW**.
OH NO! I'M A HORRIBLE VILLAIN! I'M RUINING THE GAME.
ACTUALLY SKULL, YOU'RE AN INCREDIBLY **EFFECTIVE** SUPER VILLAIN; WHICH, AS WE ALL KNOW, HAS NO PLACE IN A COMIC BOOK STORY.
YEAH, WELL NO OFFENSE BUT THANKS FOR A REALLY GREAT ADVENTURE. THERE'S NO WAY IN HELL THAT I'M GOING DOWN INTO THAT PIT OF VIPERS. IF STRAPLING MAN CAN'T MAKE IT OUT ALIVE, NONE OF US WILL.
SORRY SKULL. ALTHOUGH I DON'T APPROVE OF HIS TONE, I AGREE WITH BRENT. THE ATOM DESCRAMBLER IS JUST TOO POWERFUL A WEAPON TO BE ALLOWED IN THIS ADVENTURE. IT'S NOT FAIR TO THE PLAYERS.
BUT... YOU CAN'T TAKE AWAY MY ATOM DESCRAMBLER. MY ENTIRE EVIL PLOT HINGES ON IT. PLEASE COLE...
I NEVER INTENDED TO USE IT AGAINST THE PLAYERS OR ON ANY INNOCENT BYSTANDERS. YOU WON'T HAVE TO GO UP AGAINST THAT GUN GUYS, **I PROMISE!**

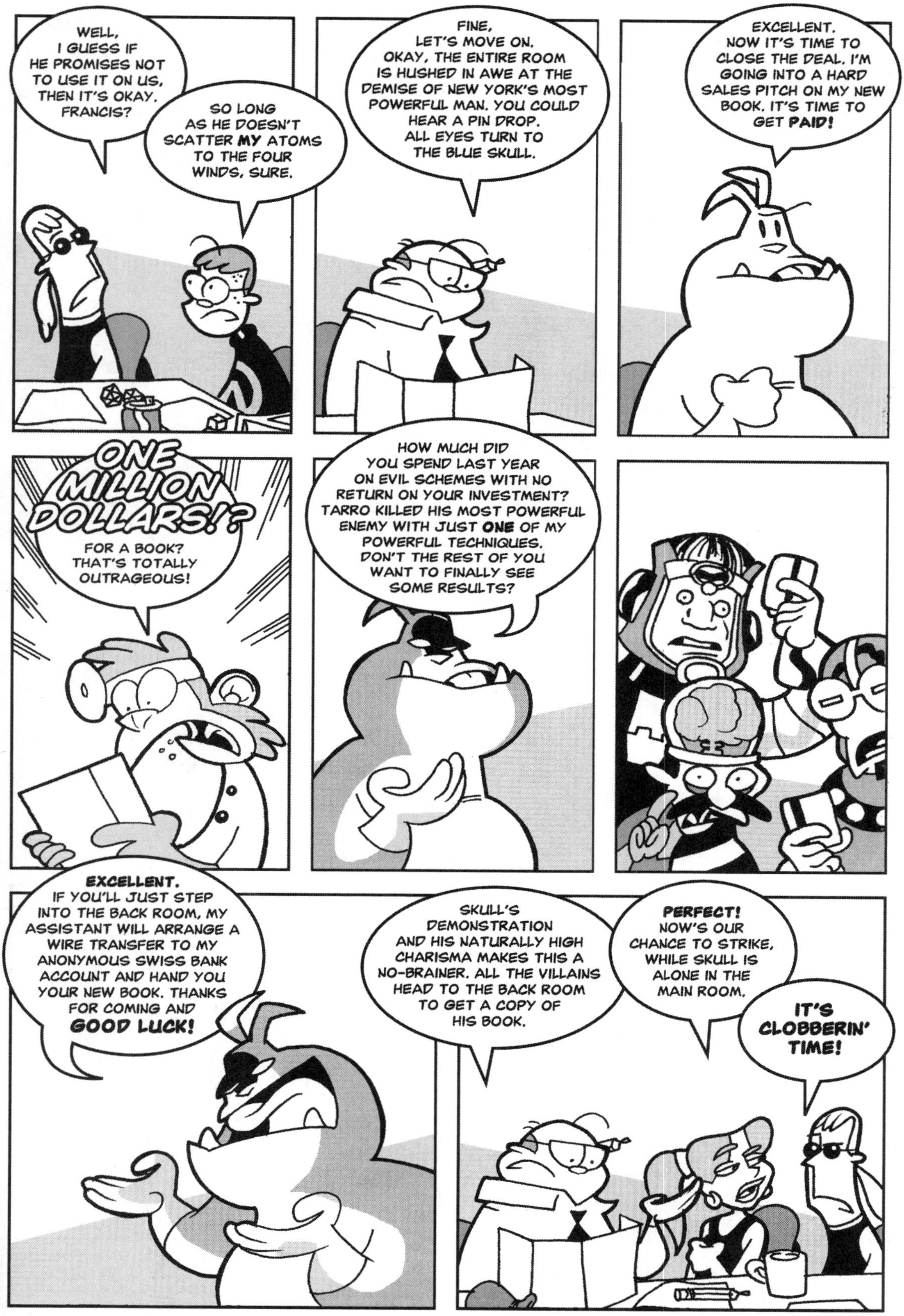
WELL, I GUESS IF HE PROMISES NOT TO USE IT ON US, THEN IT'S OKAY. FRANCIS?
SO LONG AS HE DOESN'T SCATTER MY ATOMS TO THE FOUR WINDS, SURE.
FINE, LET'S MOVE ON. OKAY, THE ENTIRE ROOM IS HUSHED IN AWE AT THE DEMISE OF NEW YORK'S MOST POWERFUL MAN. YOU COULD HEAR A PIN DROP. ALL EYES TURN TO THE BLUE SKULL.
EXCELLENT. NOW IT'S TIME TO CLOSE THE DEAL. I'M GOING INTO A HARD SALES PITCH ON MY NEW BOOK. IT'S TIME TO GET PAID!
ONE MILLION DOLLARS!? FOR A BOOK? THAT'S TOTALLY OUTRAGEOUS!
HOW MUCH DID YOU SPEND LAST YEAR ON EVIL SCHEMES WITH NO RETURN ON YOUR INVESTMENT? TARRO KILLED HIS MOST POWERFUL ENEMY WITH JUST ONE OF MY POWERFUL TECHNIQUES. DON'T THE REST OF YOU WANT TO FINALLY SEE SOME RESULTS?
EXCELLENT. IF YOU'LL JUST STEP INTO THE BACK ROOM, MY ASSISTANT WILL ARRANGE A WIRE TRANSFER TO MY ANONYMOUS SWISS BANK ACCOUNT AND HAND YOU YOUR NEW BOOK. THANKS FOR COMING AND GOOD LUCK!
SKULL'S DEMONSTRATION AND HIS NATURALLY HIGH CHARISMA MAKES THIS A NO-BRAINER. ALL THE VILLAINS HEAD TO THE BACK ROOM TO GET A COPY OF HIS BOOK.
PERFECT! NOW'S OUR CHANCE TO STRIKE, WHILE SKULL IS ALONE IN THE MAIN ROOM.
IT'S CLOBBERIN' TIME!

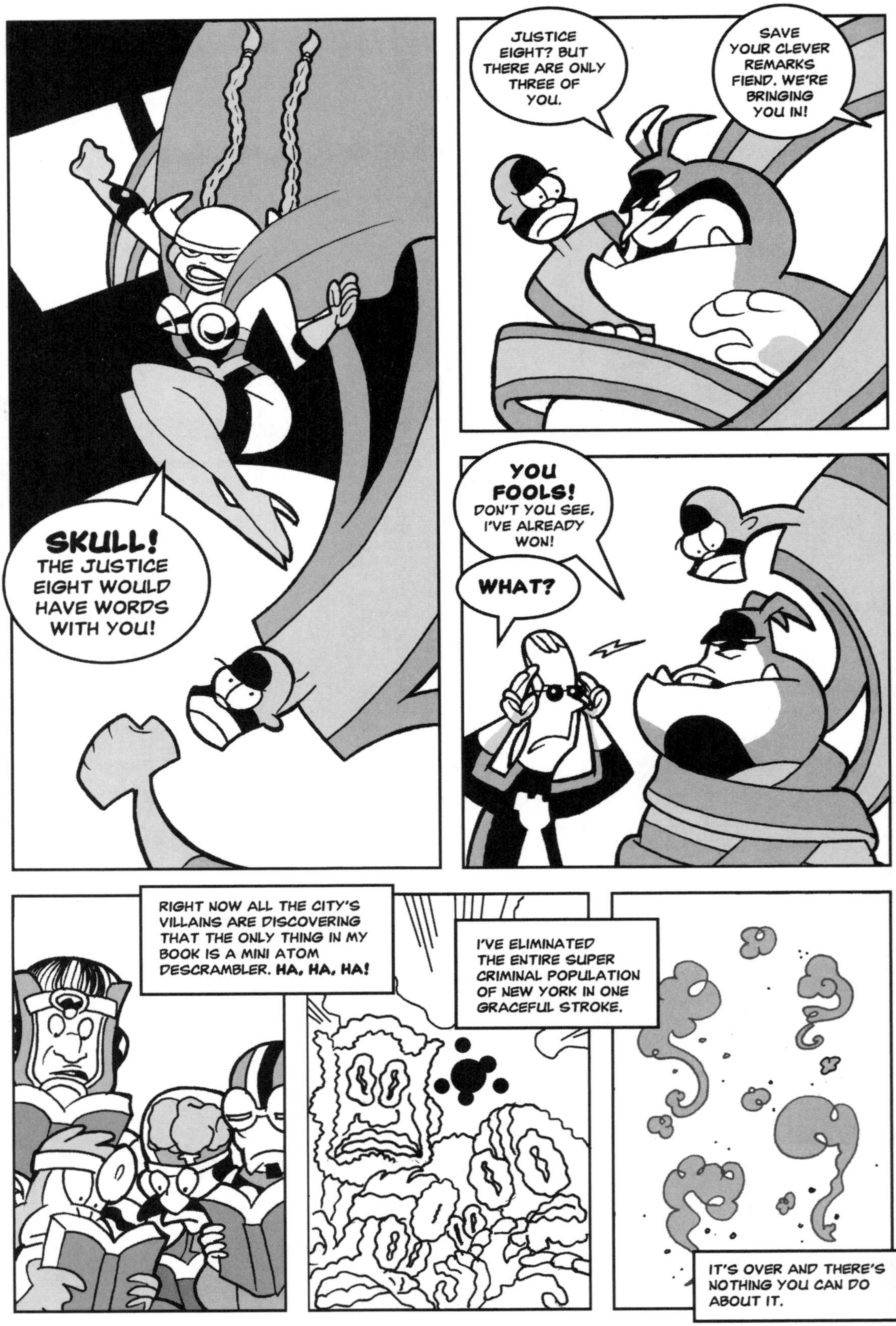
SKULL! THE JUSTICE EIGHT WOULD HAVE WORDS WITH YOU!
JUSTICE EIGHT? BUT THERE ARE ONLY THREE OF YOU.
SAVE YOUR CLEVER REMARKS FIEND. WE'RE BRINGING YOU IN!
YOU FOOLS! DON'T YOU SEE, I'VE ALREADY WON!
WHAT?
RIGHT NOW ALL THE CITY'S VILLAINS ARE DISCOVERING THAT THE ONLY THING IN MY BOOK IS A MINI ATOM DESCRAMBLER. HA, HA, HA!
I'VE ELIMINATED THE ENTIRE SUPER CRIMINAL POPULATION OF NEW YORK IN ONE GRACEFUL STROKE.
IT'S OVER AND THERE'S NOTHING YOU CAN DO ABOUT IT.

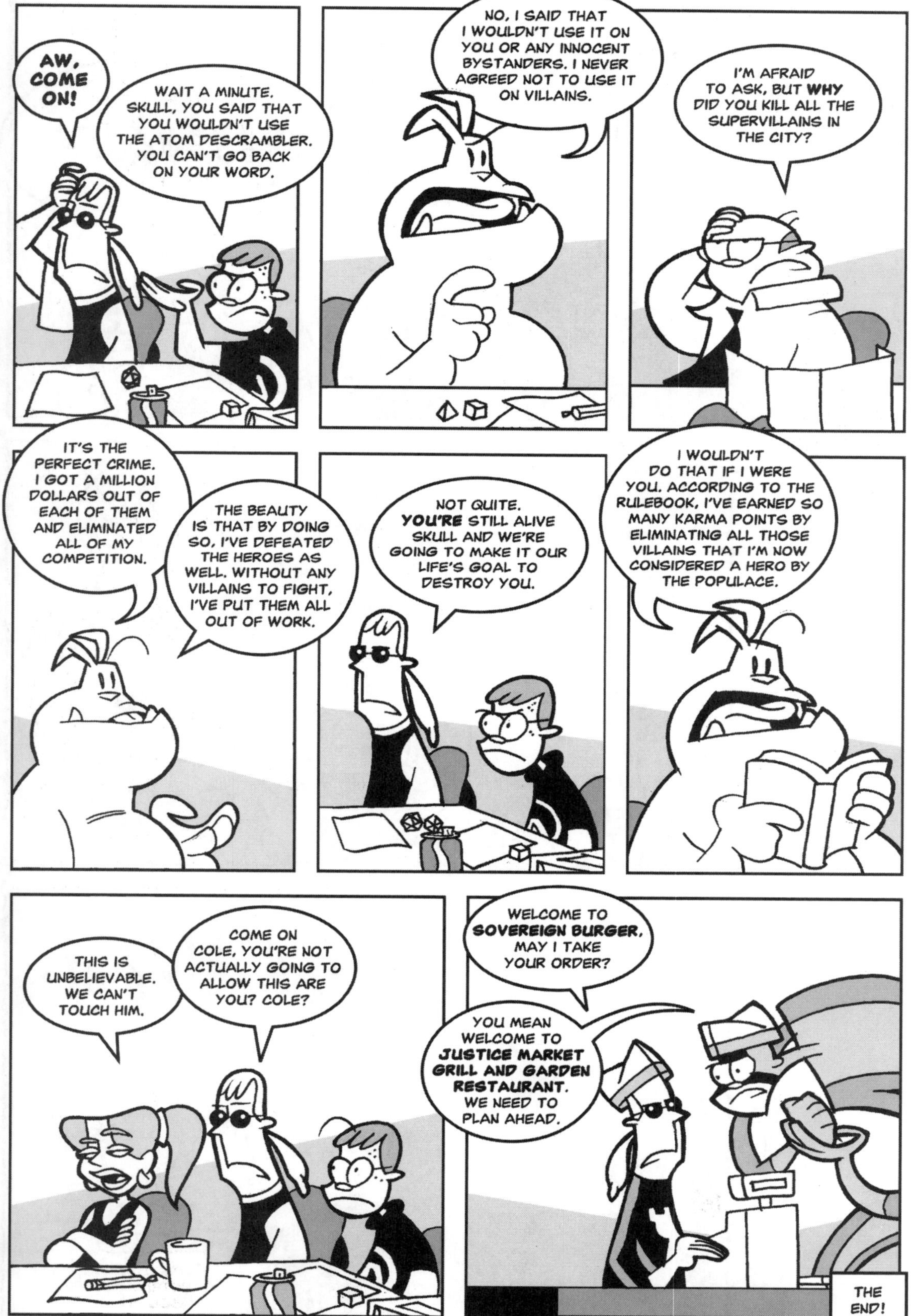

AW, COME ON!
WAIT A MINUTE. SKULL, YOU SAID THAT YOU WOULDN'T USE THE ATOM DESCRAMBLER. YOU CAN'T GO BACK ON YOUR WORD.
NO, I SAID THAT I WOULDN'T USE IT ON YOU OR ANY INNOCENT BYSTANDERS. I NEVER AGREED NOT TO USE IT ON VILLAINS.
I'M AFRAID TO ASK, BUT WHY DID YOU KILL ALL THE SUPERVILLAINS IN THE CITY?
IT'S THE PERFECT CRIME. I GOT A MILLION DOLLARS OUT OF EACH OF THEM AND ELIMINATED ALL OF MY COMPETITION.
THE BEAUTY IS THAT BY DOING SO, I'VE DEFEATED THE HEROES AS WELL. WITHOUT ANY VILLAINS TO FIGHT, I'VE PUT THEM ALL OUT OF WORK.
NOT QUITE. YOU'RE STILL ALIVE SKULL AND WE'RE GOING TO MAKE IT OUR LIFE'S GOAL TO DESTROY YOU.
I WOULDN'T DO THAT IF I WERE YOU. ACCORDING TO THE RULEBOOK, I'VE EARNED SO MANY KARMA POINTS BY ELIMINATING ALL THOSE VILLAINS THAT I'M NOW CONSIDERED A HERO BY THE POPULACE.
THIS IS UNBELIEVABLE. WE CAN'T TOUCH HIM.
COME ON COLE, YOU'RE NOT ACTUALLY GOING TO ALLOW THIS ARE YOU? COLE?
WELCOME TO SOVEREIGN BURGER, MAY I TAKE YOUR ORDER?
YOU MEAN WELCOME TO JUSTICE MARKET GRILL AND GARDEN RESTAURANT. WE NEED TO PLAN AHEAD.
THE END!

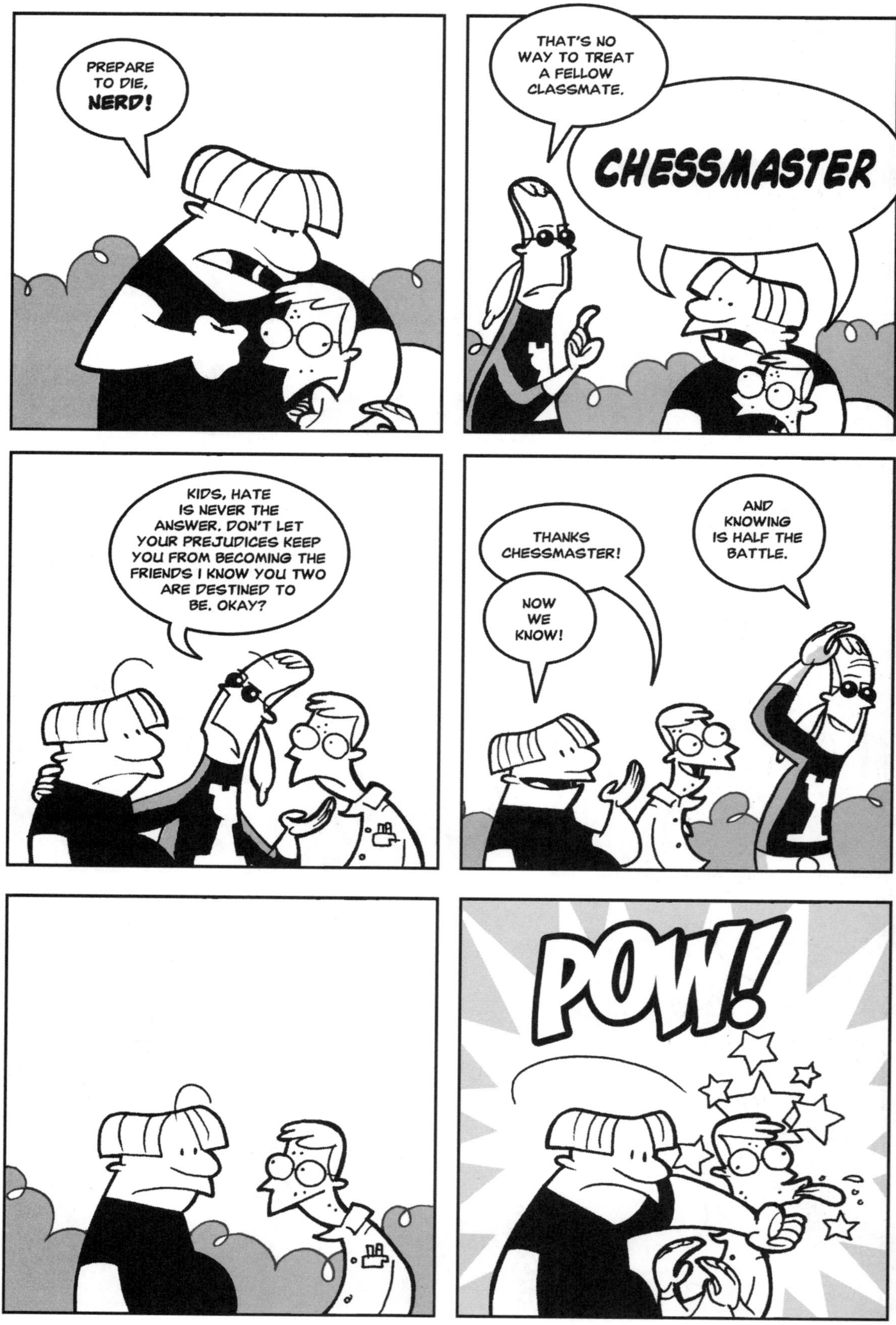
PREPARE TO DIE, **NERD!**
THAT'S NO WAY TO TREAT A FELLOW CLASSMATE.
CHESSMASTER
KIDS, HATE IS NEVER THE ANSWER. DON'T LET YOUR PREJUDICES KEEP YOU FROM BECOMING THE FRIENDS I KNOW YOU TWO ARE DESTINED TO BE. OKAY?
THANKS CHESSMASTER!
NOW WE KNOW!
AND KNOWING IS HALF THE BATTLE.
POW!

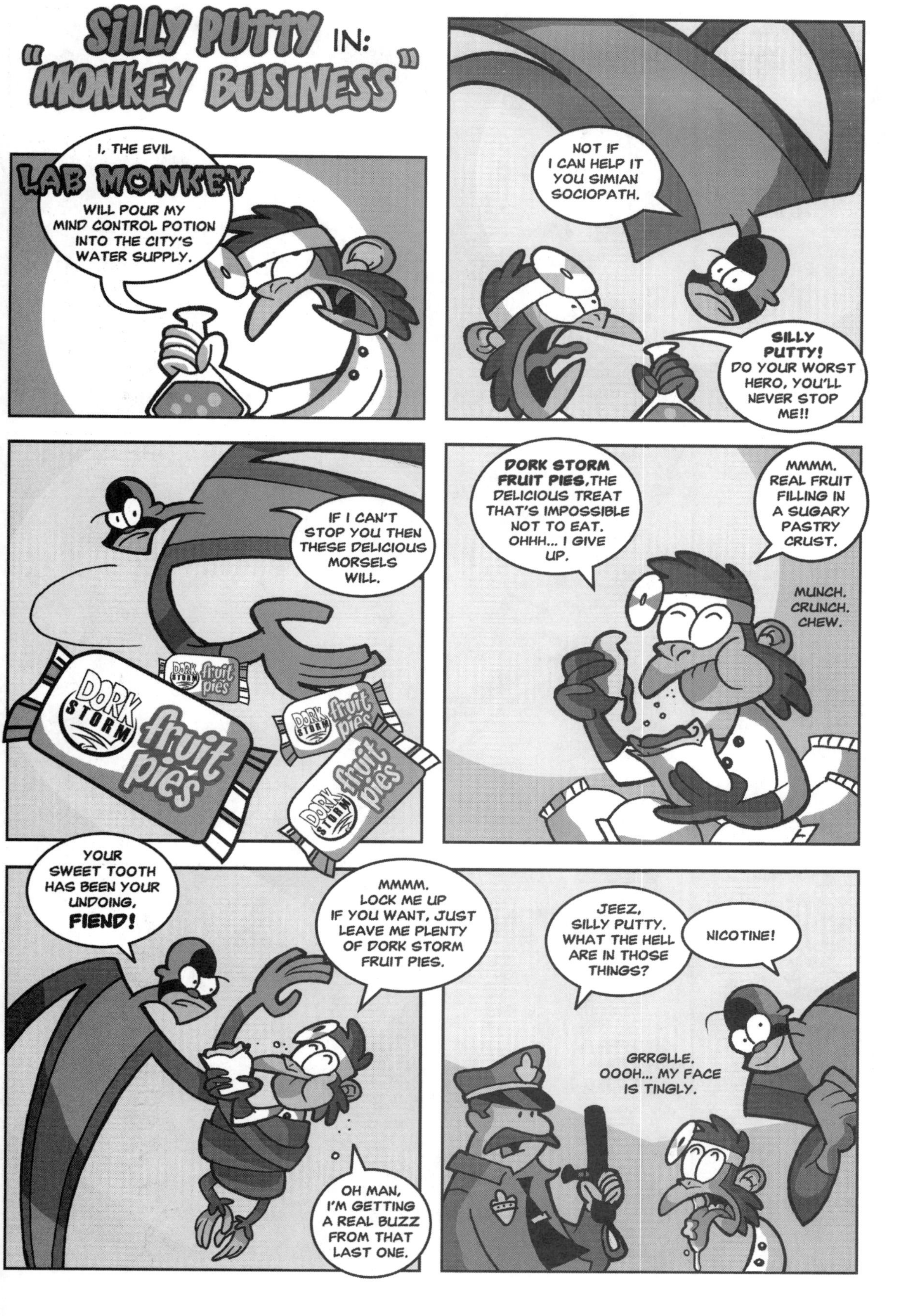

SILLY PUTTY IN:
"MONKEY BUSINESS"
I, THE EVIL LAB MONKEY WILL POUR MY MIND CONTROL POTION INTO THE CITY'S WATER SUPPLY.
NOT IF I CAN HELP IT YOU SIMIAN SOCIOPATH.
SILLY PUTTY! DO YOUR WORST HERO, YOU'LL NEVER STOP ME!!
IF I CAN'T STOP YOU THEN THESE DELICIOUS MORSELS WILL.
DORK STORM fruit pies
DORK STORM FRUIT PIES, THE DELICIOUS TREAT THAT'S IMPOSSIBLE NOT TO EAT. OHHH... I GIVE UP.
MMMM. REAL FRUIT FILLING IN A SUGARY PASTRY CRUST.
MUNCH. CRUNCH. CHEW.
YOUR SWEET TOOTH HAS BEEN YOUR UNDOING, FIEND!
MMMM. LOCK ME UP IF YOU WANT, JUST LEAVE ME PLENTY OF DORK STORM FRUIT PIES.
OH MAN, I'M GETTING A REAL BUZZ FROM THAT LAST ONE.
JEEZ, SILLY PUTTY. WHAT THE HELL ARE IN THOSE THINGS?
NICOTINE!
GRRGLLE. OOOH... MY FACE IS TINGLY.

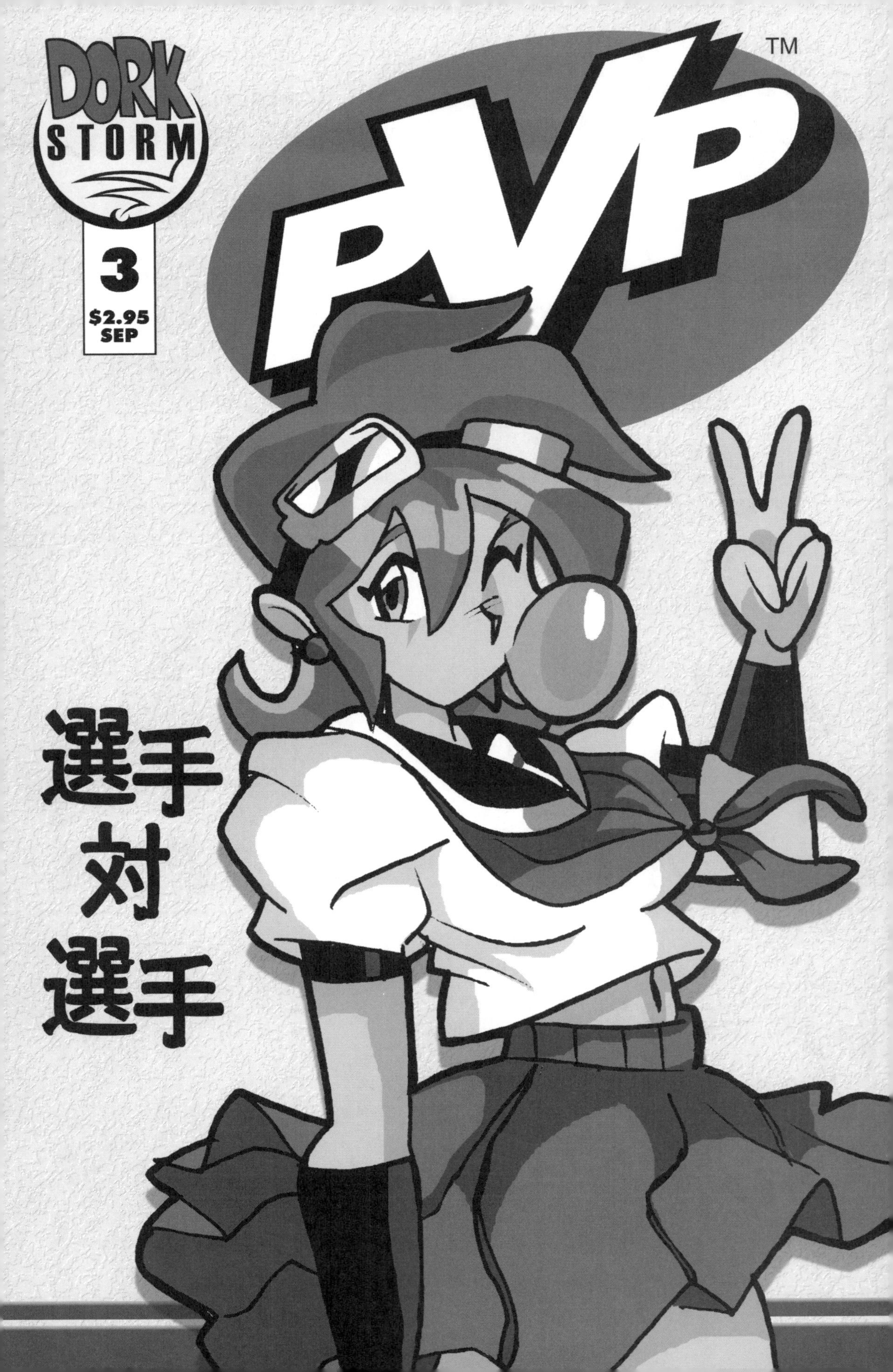
DORK STORM
3
$2.95
SEP
PVP™
選手
対
選手

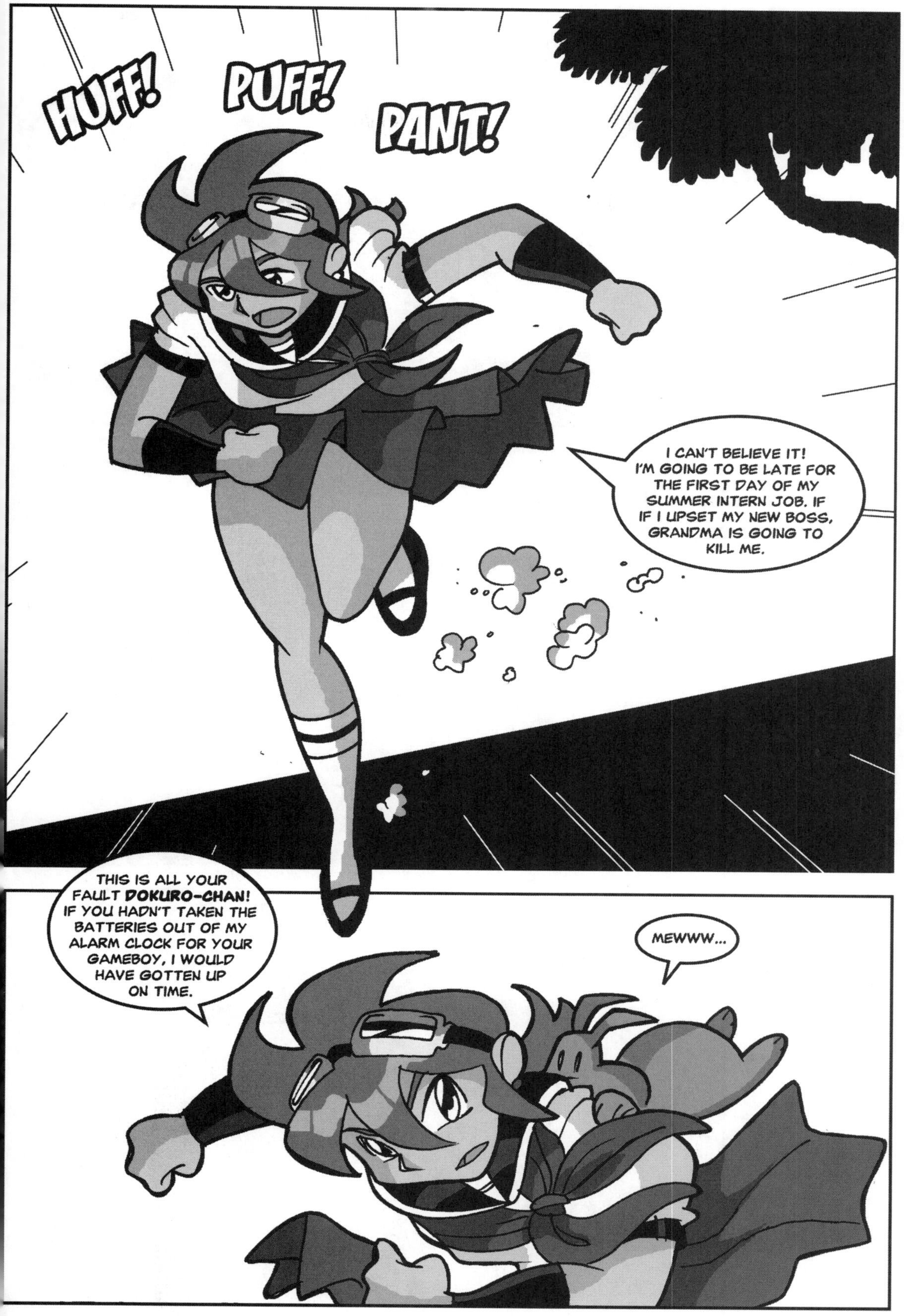
HUFF! PUFF! PANT!
I CAN'T BELIEVE IT! I'M GOING TO BE LATE FOR THE FIRST DAY OF MY SUMMER INTERN JOB. IF IF I UPSET MY NEW BOSS, GRANDMA IS GOING TO KILL ME.
THIS IS ALL YOUR FAULT DOKURO-CHAN! IF YOU HADN'T TAKEN THE BATTERIES OUT OF MY ALARM CLOCK FOR YOUR GAMEBOY, I WOULD HAVE GOTTEN UP ON TIME.
MEWWW...

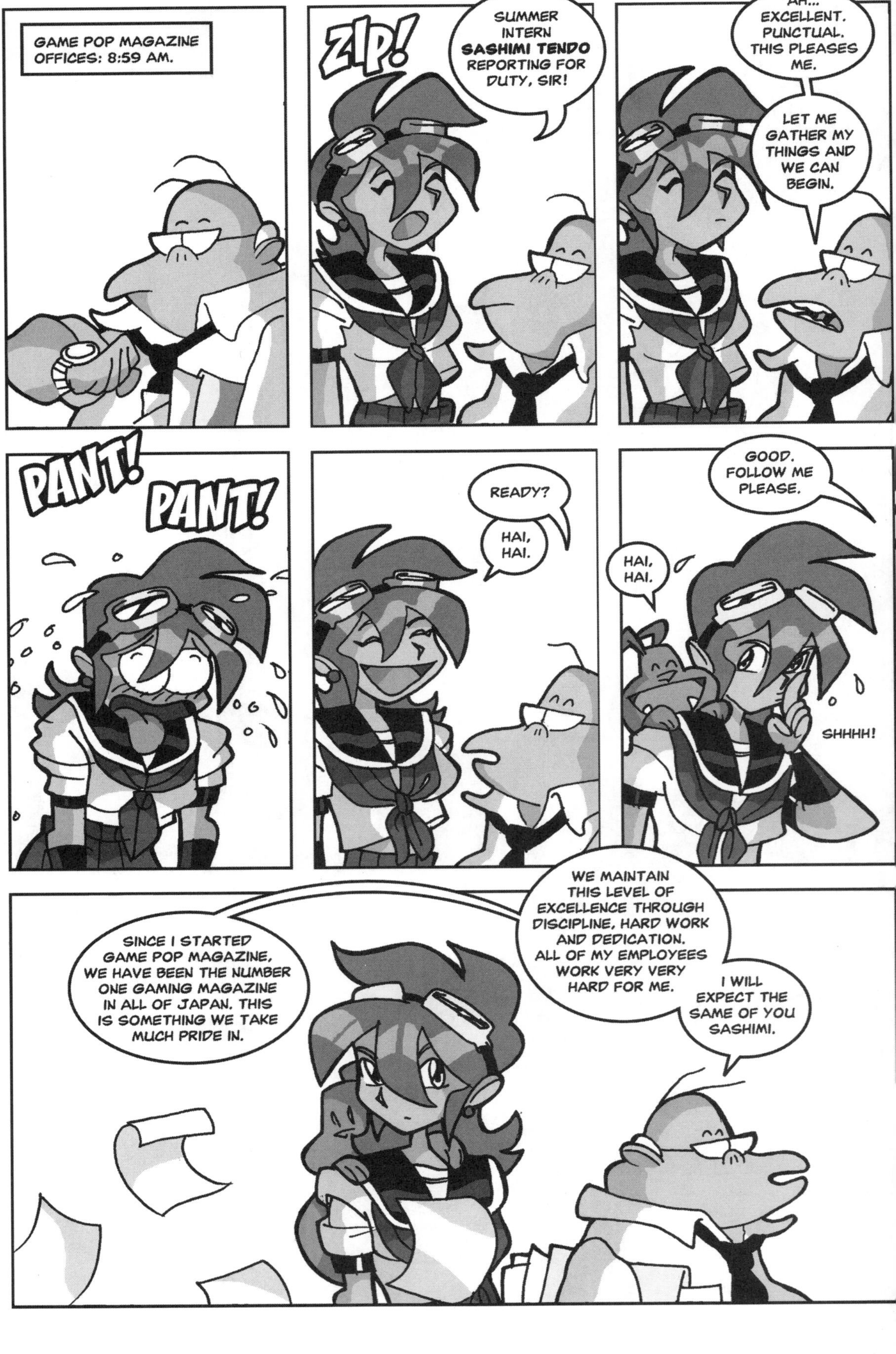
GAME POP MAGAZINE OFFICES: 8:59 AM.
ZIP!
SUMMER INTERN SASHIMI TENDO REPORTING FOR DUTY, SIR!
AH... EXCELLENT. PUNCTUAL. THIS PLEASES ME.
LET ME GATHER MY THINGS AND WE CAN BEGIN.
PANT! PANT!
READY?
HAI, HAI.
GOOD. FOLLOW ME PLEASE.
HAI, HAI.
SHHHH!
SINCE I STARTED GAME POP MAGAZINE, WE HAVE BEEN THE NUMBER ONE GAMING MAGAZINE IN ALL OF JAPAN. THIS IS SOMETHING WE TAKE MUCH PRIDE IN.
WE MAINTAIN THIS LEVEL OF EXCELLENCE THROUGH DISCIPLINE, HARD WORK AND DEDICATION. ALL OF MY EMPLOYEES WORK VERY VERY HARD FOR ME.
I WILL EXPECT THE SAME OF YOU SASHIMI.

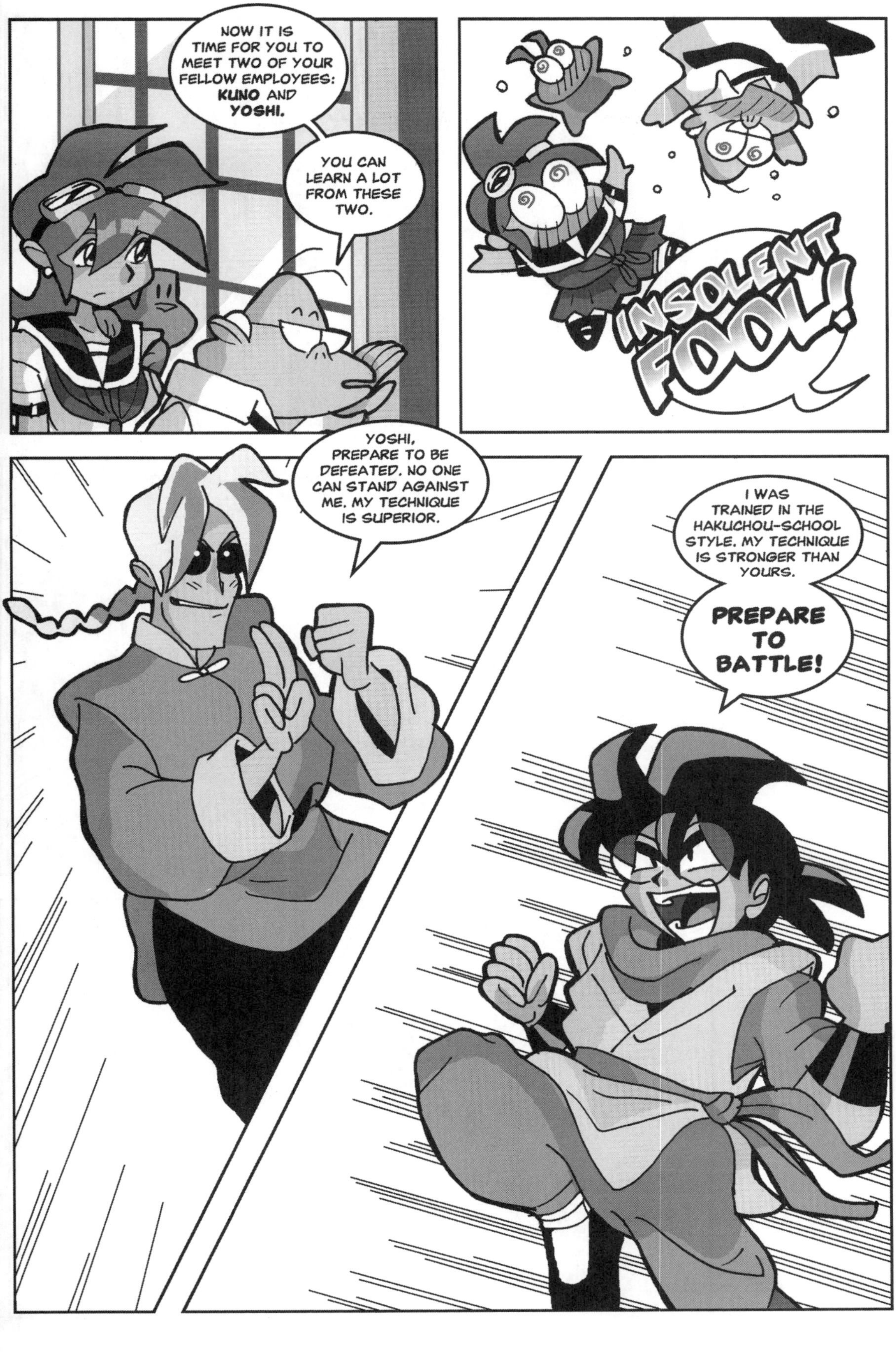
NOW IT IS TIME FOR YOU TO MEET TWO OF YOUR FELLOW EMPLOYEES: **KUNO** AND **YOSHI.**
YOU CAN LEARN A LOT FROM THESE TWO.
INSOLENT FOOL!
YOSHI, PREPARE TO BE DEFEATED. NO ONE CAN STAND AGAINST ME. MY TECHNIQUE IS SUPERIOR.
I WAS TRAINED IN THE HAKUCHOU-SCHOOL STYLE. MY TECHNIQUE IS STRONGER THAN YOURS.
PREPARE TO BATTLE!

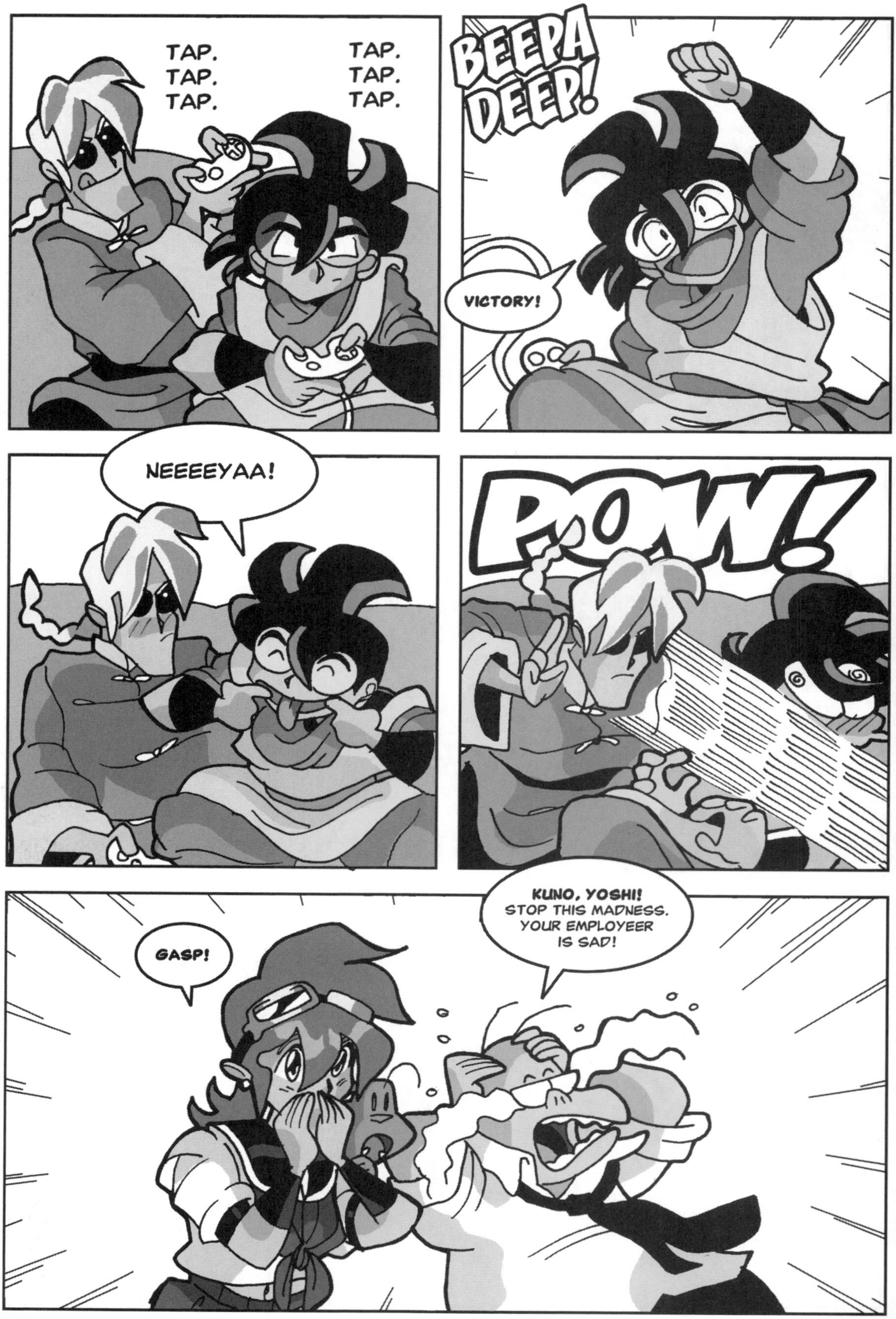
TAP.
TAP.
TAP.
TAP.
TAP.
TAP.
BEEPA DEEP!
VICTORY!
NEEEEYAA!
POW!
GASP!
KUNO, YOSHI!
STOP THIS MADNESS.
YOUR EMPLOYEER
IS SAD!

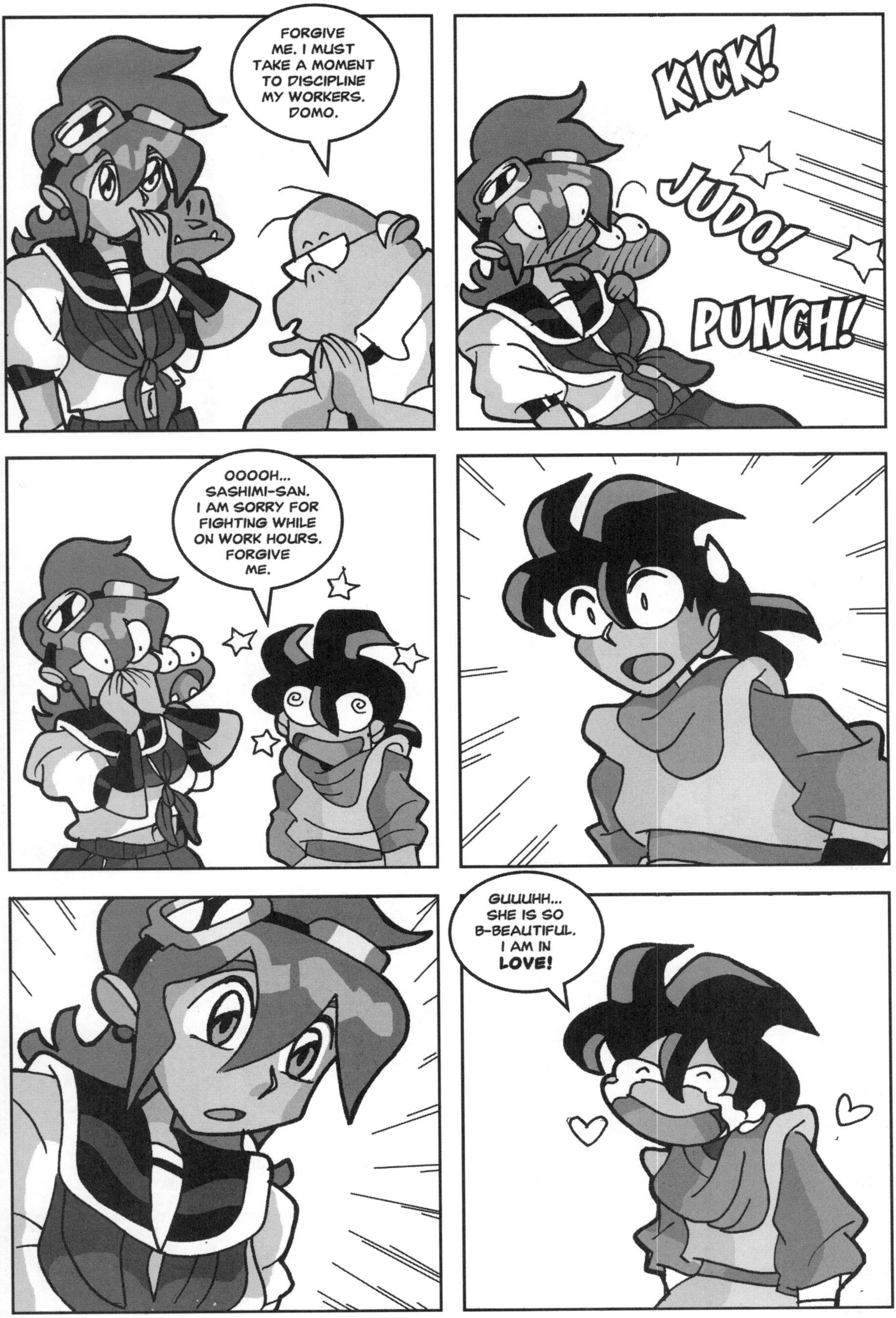
FORGIVE ME. I MUST TAKE A MOMENT TO DISCIPLINE MY WORKERS. DOMO.
KICK!
JUDO!
PUNCH!
OOOOH... SASHIMI-SAN. I AM SORRY FOR FIGHTING WHILE ON WORK HOURS. FORGIVE ME.
GUUUHH... SHE IS SO B-BEAUTIFUL. I AM IN **LOVE!**

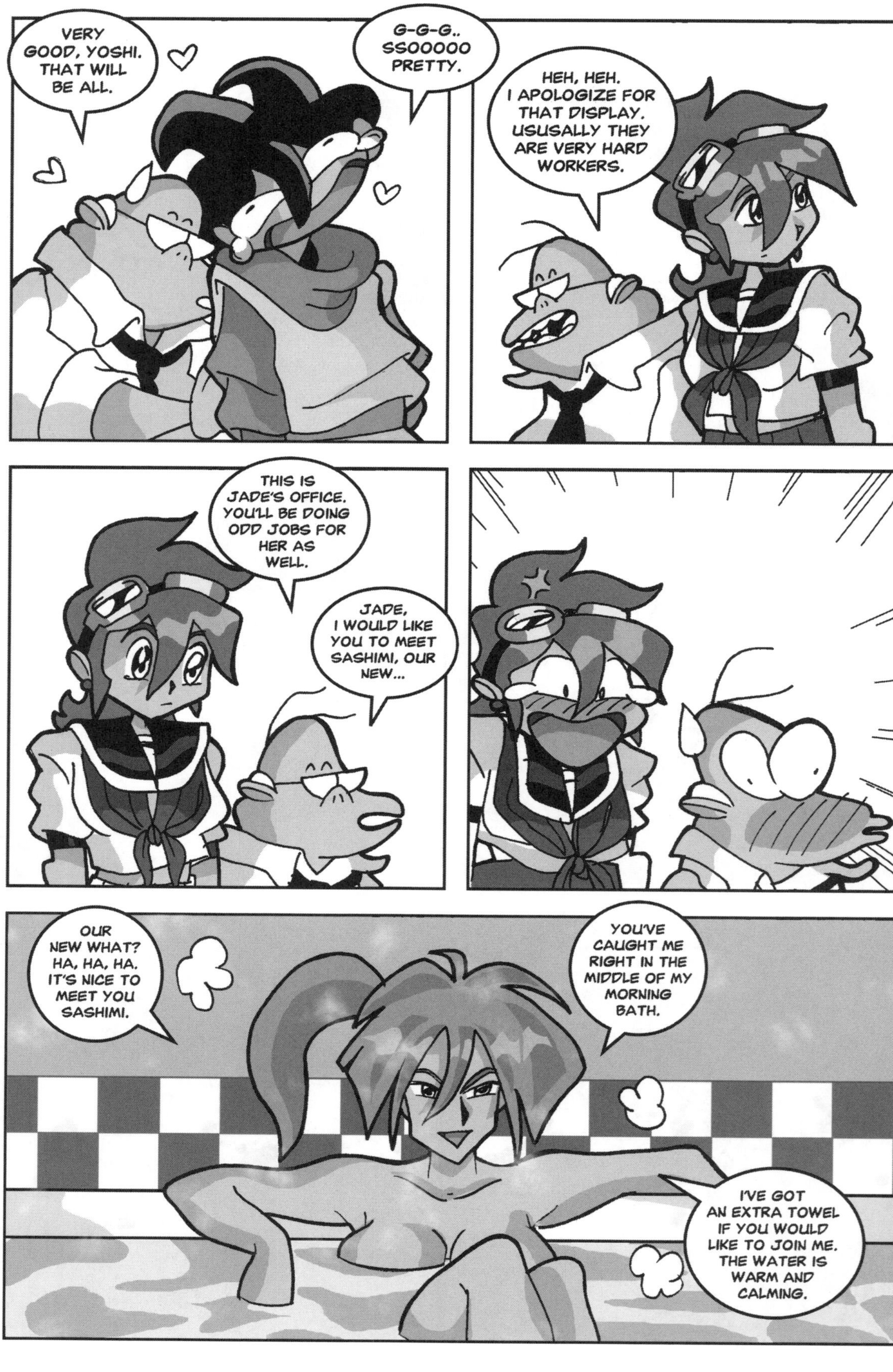
VERY GOOD, YOSHI. THAT WILL BE ALL.
G-G-G.. SSOOOOO PRETTY.
HEH, HEH. I APOLOGIZE FOR THAT DISPLAY. USUSALLY THEY ARE VERY HARD WORKERS.
THIS IS JADE'S OFFICE. YOU'LL BE DOING ODD JOBS FOR HER AS WELL.
JADE, I WOULD LIKE YOU TO MEET SASHIMI, OUR NEW...
OUR NEW WHAT? HA, HA, HA. IT'S NICE TO MEET YOU SASHIMI.
YOU'VE CAUGHT ME RIGHT IN THE MIDDLE OF MY MORNING BATH.
I'VE GOT AN EXTRA TOWEL IF YOU WOULD LIKE TO JOIN ME. THE WATER IS WARM AND CALMING.

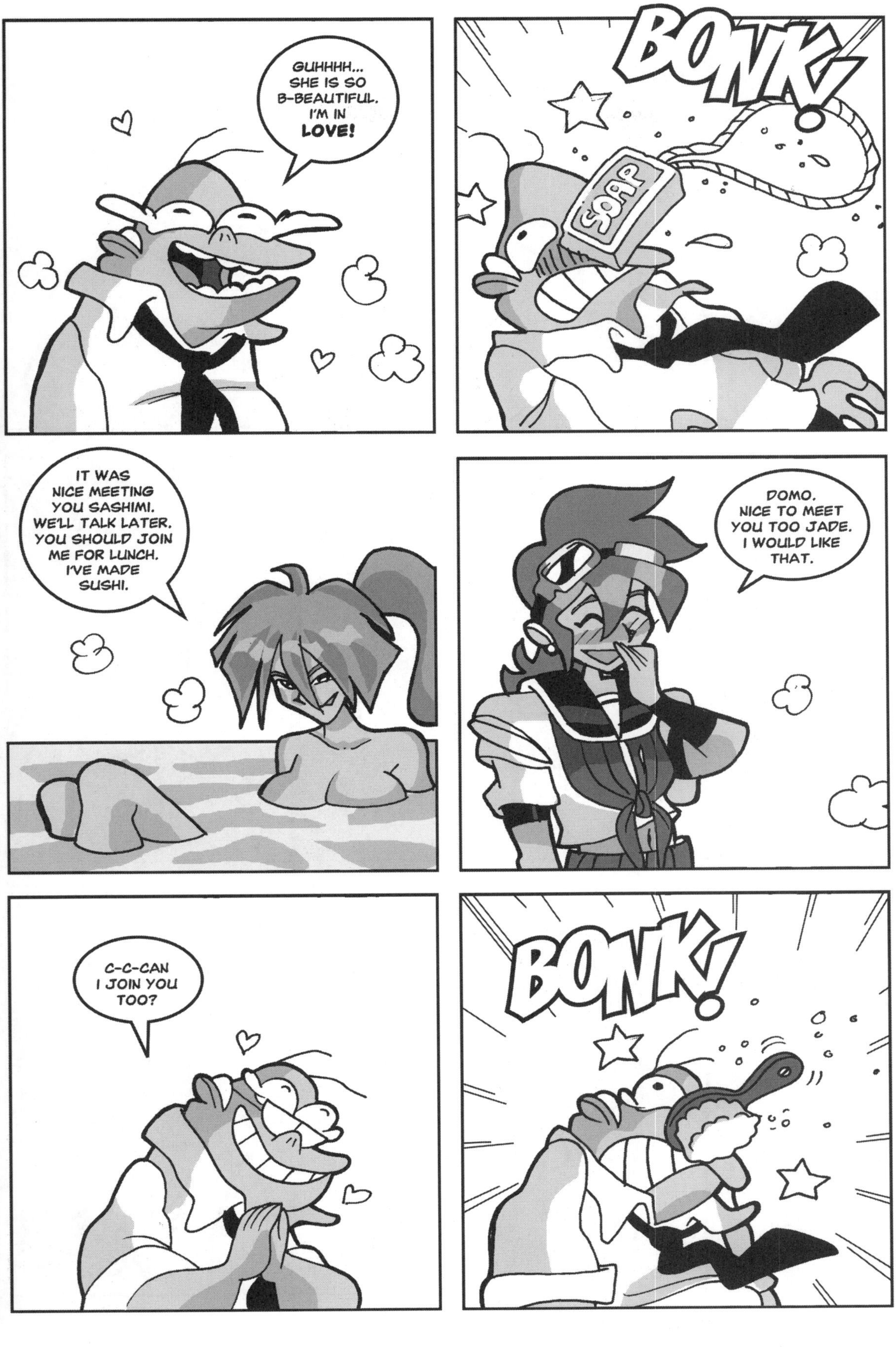
GUHHHH... SHE IS SO B-BEAUTIFUL. I'M IN **LOVE!**
BONK!
SOAP
IT WAS NICE MEETING YOU SASHIMI. WE'LL TALK LATER. YOU SHOULD JOIN ME FOR LUNCH. I'VE MADE SUSHI.
DOMO. NICE TO MEET YOU TOO JADE. I WOULD LIKE THAT.
C-C-CAN I JOIN YOU TOO?
BONK!

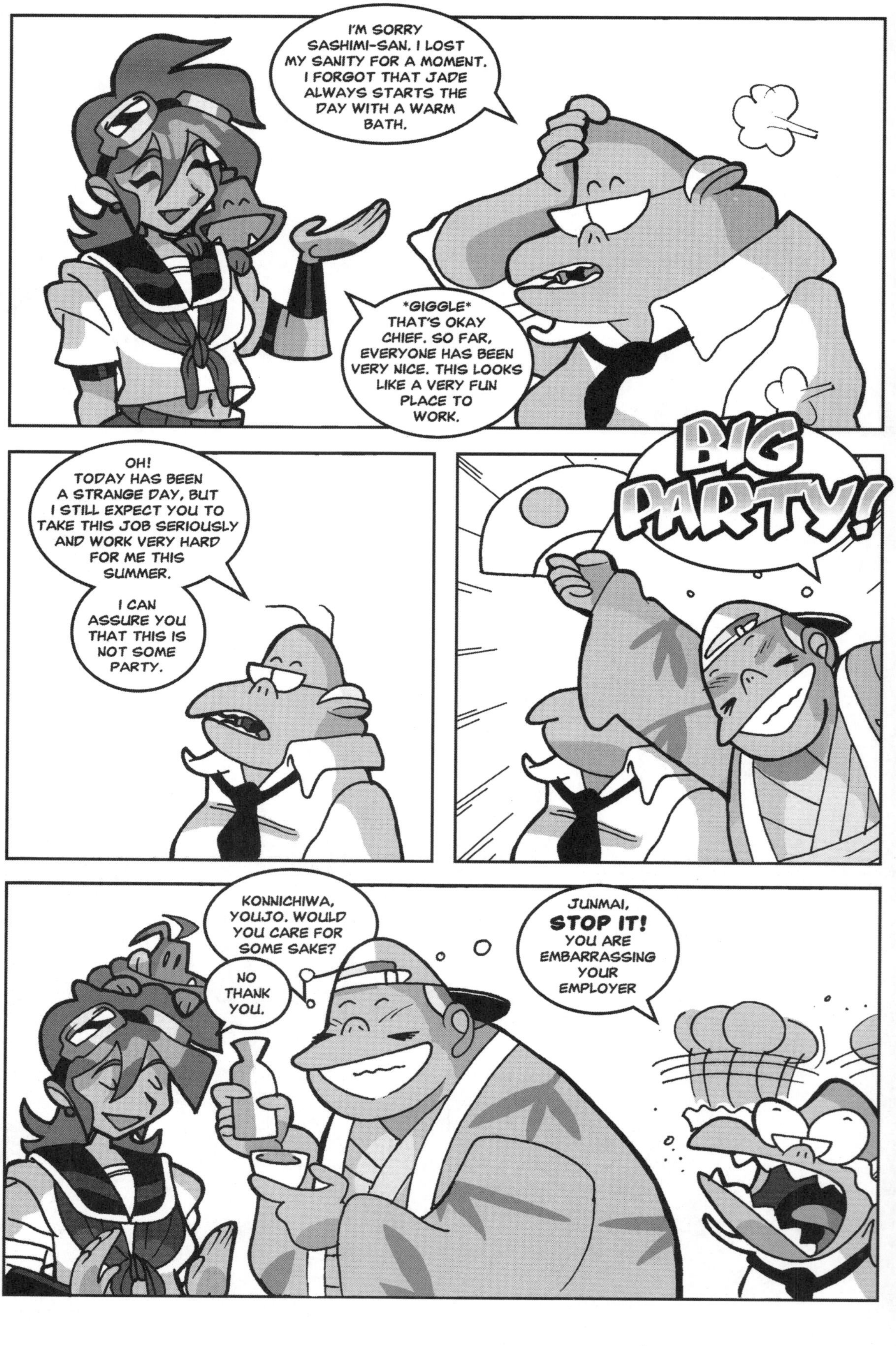
I'M SORRY SASHIMI-SAN. I LOST MY SANITY FOR A MOMENT. I FORGOT THAT JADE ALWAYS STARTS THE DAY WITH A WARM BATH.
GIGGLE THAT'S OKAY CHIEF. SO FAR, EVERYONE HAS BEEN VERY NICE. THIS LOOKS LIKE A VERY FUN PLACE TO WORK.
OH! TODAY HAS BEEN A STRANGE DAY, BUT I STILL EXPECT YOU TO TAKE THIS JOB SERIOUSLY AND WORK VERY HARD FOR ME THIS SUMMER.
I CAN ASSURE YOU THAT THIS IS NOT SOME PARTY.
BIG PARTY!
KONNICHIWA, YOUJO. WOULD YOU CARE FOR SOME SAKE?
NO THANK YOU.
JUNMAI, STOP IT! YOU ARE EMBARRASSING YOUR EMPLOYER

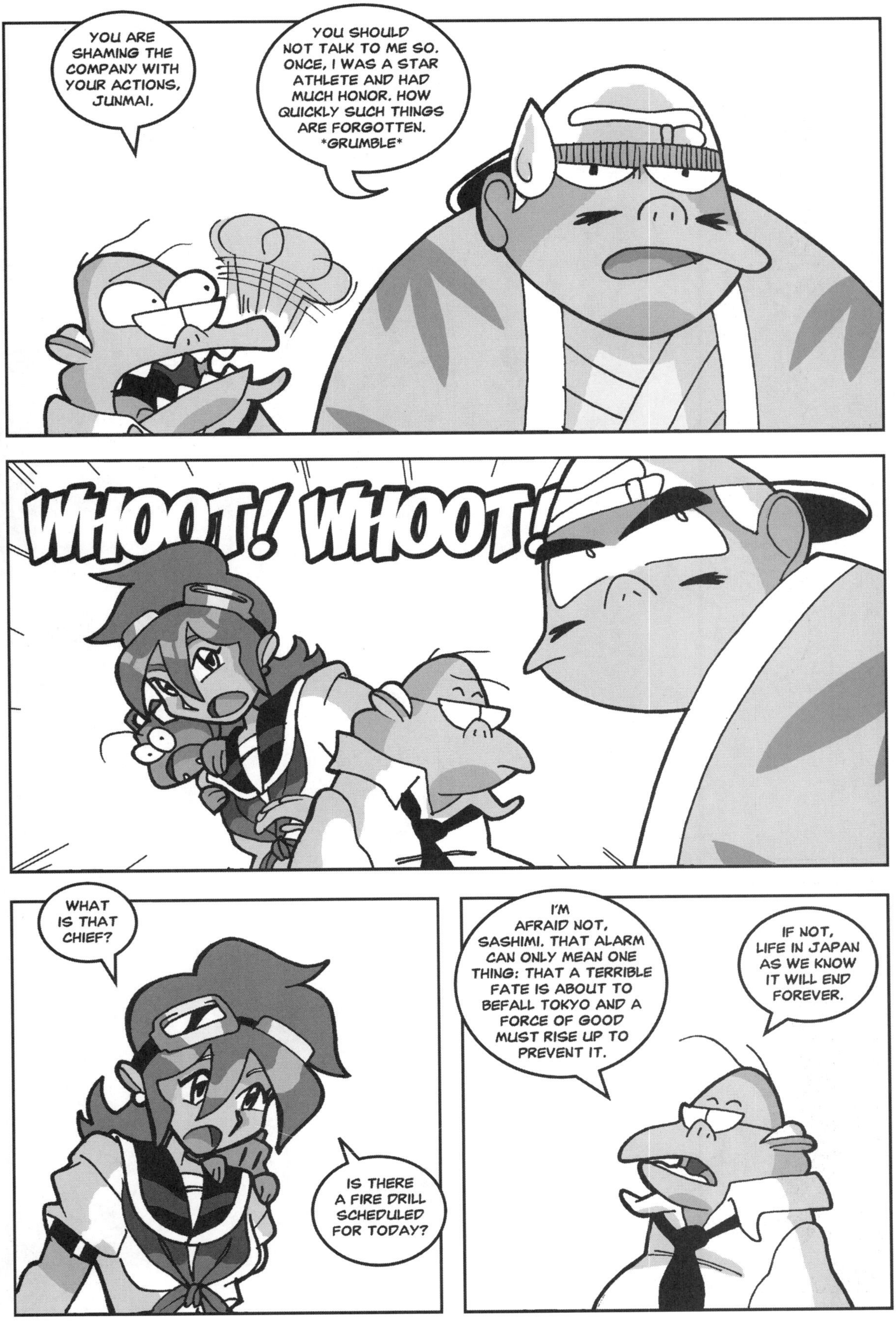
YOU ARE SHAMING THE COMPANY WITH YOUR ACTIONS, JUNMAI.
YOU SHOULD NOT TALK TO ME SO. ONCE, I WAS A STAR ATHLETE AND HAD MUCH HONOR. HOW QUICKLY SUCH THINGS ARE FORGOTTEN. *GRUMBLE*
WHOOT! WHOOT!
WHAT IS THAT CHIEF?
IS THERE A FIRE DRILL SCHEDULED FOR TODAY?
I'M AFRAID NOT, SASHIMI. THAT ALARM CAN ONLY MEAN ONE THING: THAT A TERRIBLE FATE IS ABOUT TO BEFALL TOKYO AND A FORCE OF GOOD MUST RISE UP TO PREVENT IT.
IF NOT, LIFE IN JAPAN AS WE KNOW IT WILL END FOREVER.

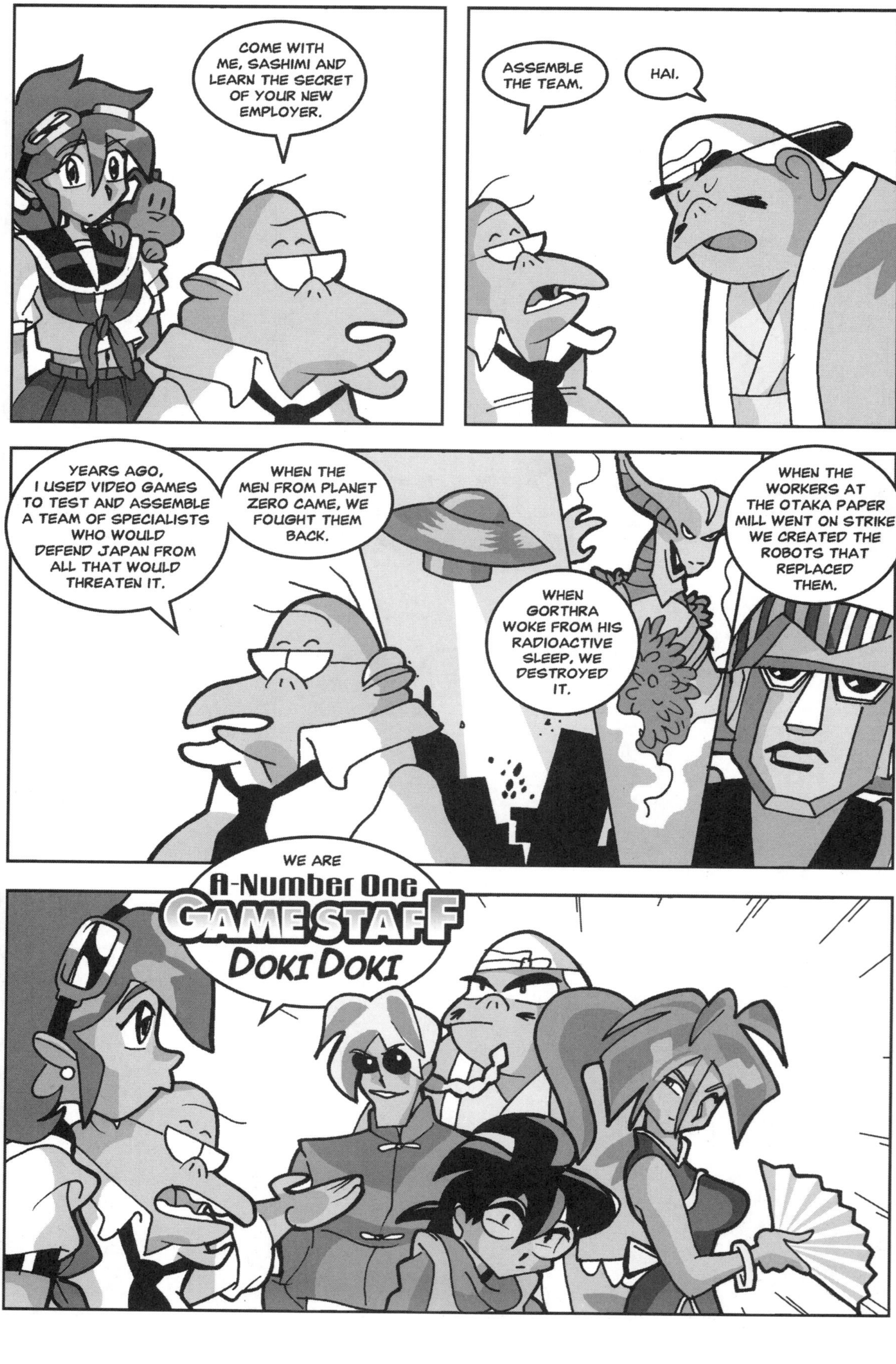
COME WITH ME, SASHIMI AND LEARN THE SECRET OF YOUR NEW EMPLOYER.
ASSEMBLE THE TEAM.
HAI.
YEARS AGO, I USED VIDEO GAMES TO TEST AND ASSEMBLE A TEAM OF SPECIALISTS WHO WOULD DEFEND JAPAN FROM ALL THAT WOULD THREATEN IT.
WHEN THE MEN FROM PLANET ZERO CAME, WE FOUGHT THEM BACK.
WHEN GORTHRA WOKE FROM HIS RADIOACTIVE SLEEP, WE DESTROYED IT.
WHEN THE WORKERS AT THE OTAKA PAPER MILL WENT ON STRIKE WE CREATED THE ROBOTS THAT REPLACED THEM.
WE ARE
A-Number One
GAME STAFF
DOKI DOKI

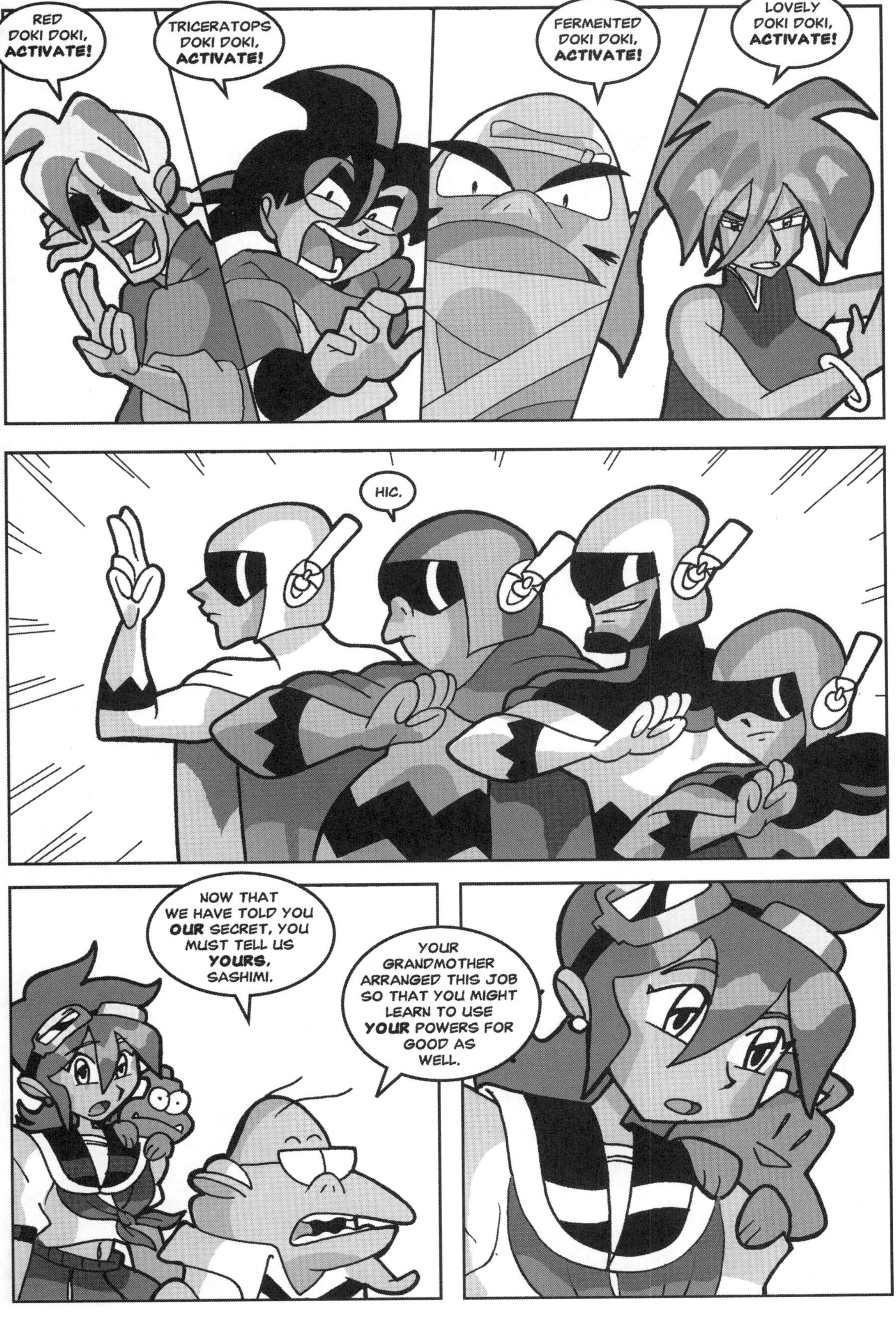
RED DOKI DOKI, ACTIVATE!
TRICERATOPS DOKI DOKI, ACTIVATE!
FERMENTED DOKI DOKI, ACTIVATE!
LOVELY DOKI DOKI, ACTIVATE!
HIC.
NOW THAT WE HAVE TOLD YOU OUR SECRET, YOU MUST TELL US YOURS, SASHIMI.
YOUR GRANDMOTHER ARRANGED THIS JOB SO THAT YOU MIGHT LEARN TO USE YOUR POWERS FOR GOOD AS WELL.

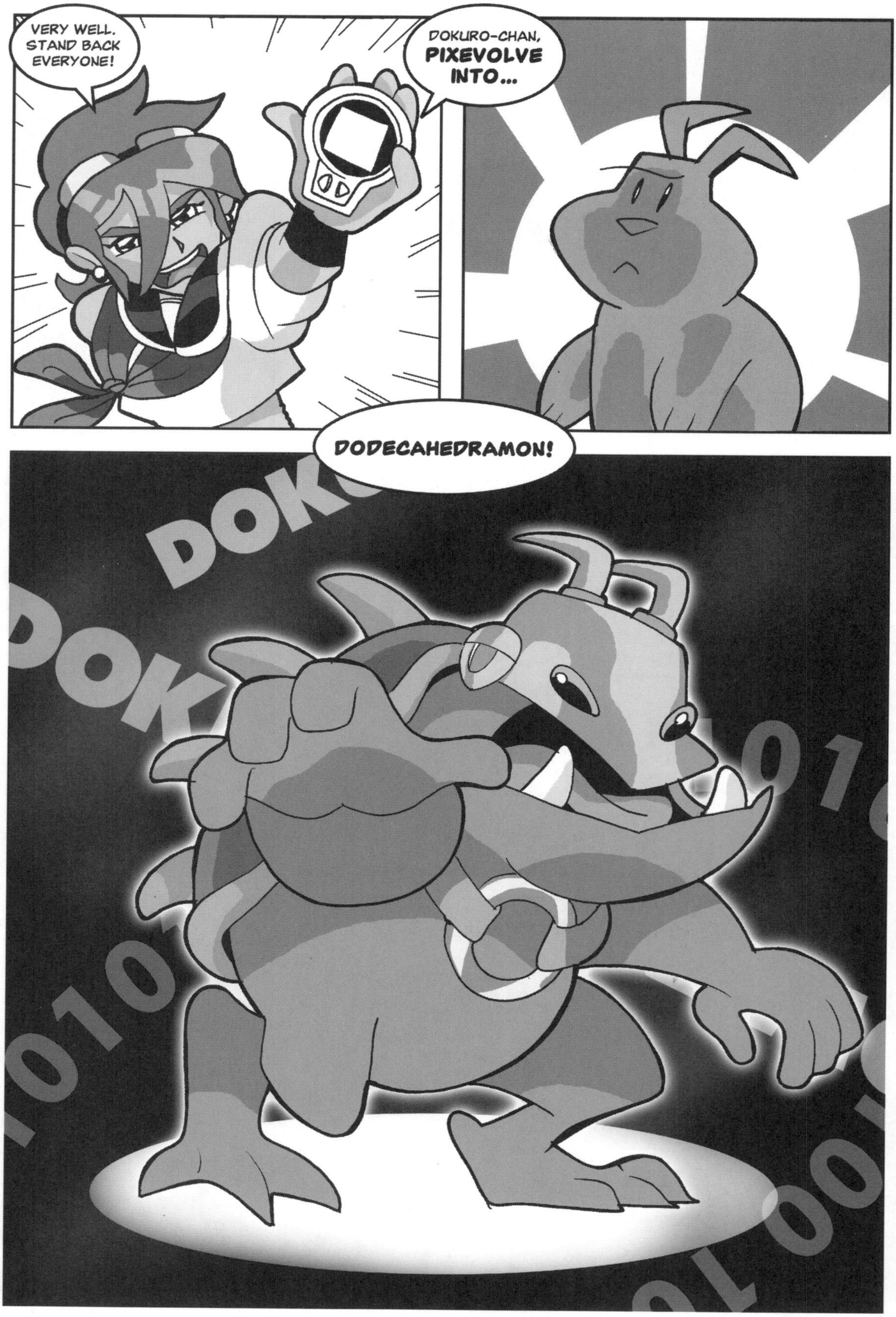
VERY WELL. STAND BACK EVERYONE!
DOKURO-CHAN, PIXEVOLVE INTO...
DODECAHEDRAMON!
DOK
DOK

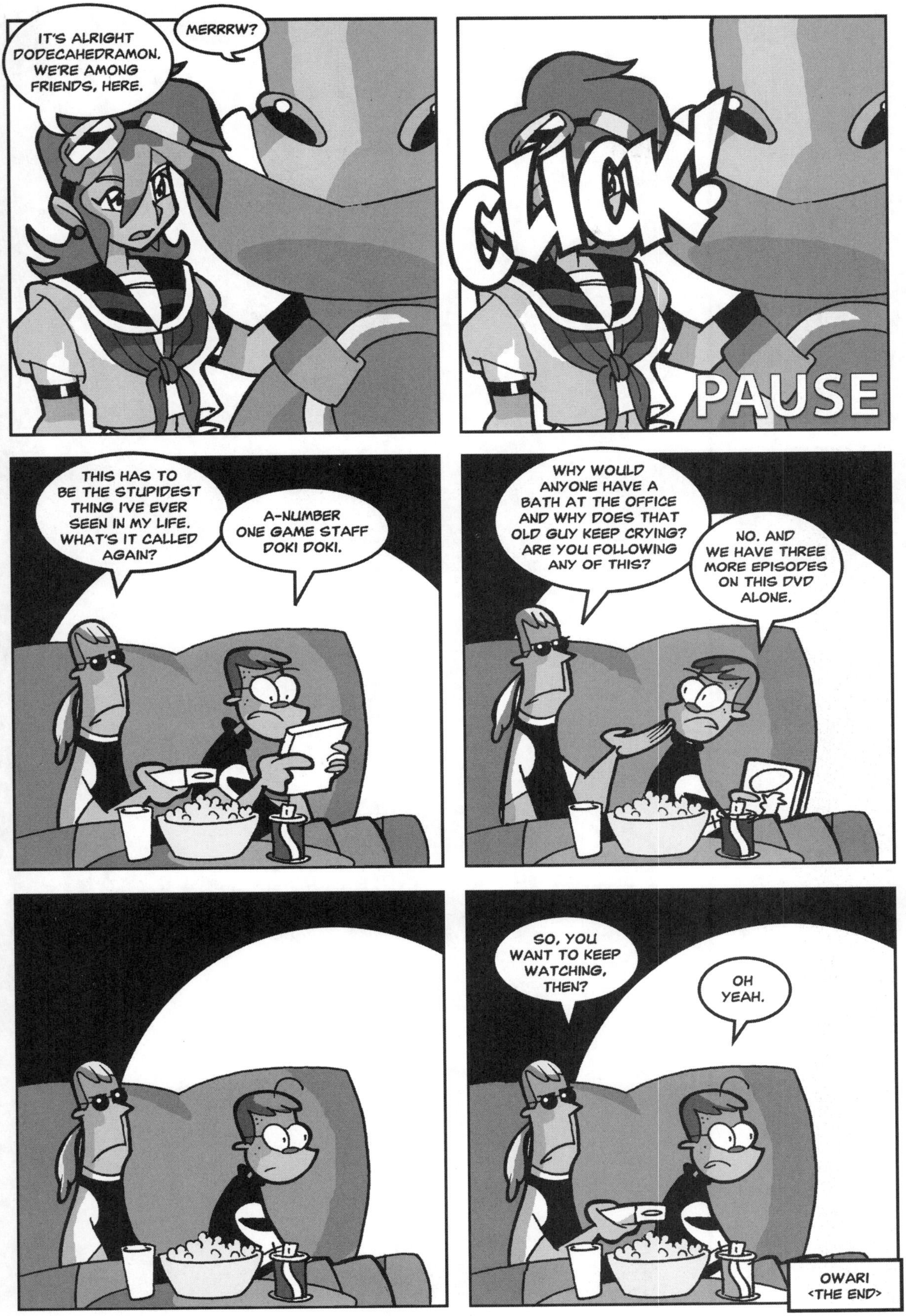
IT'S ALRIGHT DODECAHEDRAMON. WE'RE AMONG FRIENDS, HERE.
MERRRW?
CLICK!
PAUSE
THIS HAS TO BE THE STUPIDEST THING I'VE EVER SEEN IN MY LIFE. WHAT'S IT CALLED AGAIN?
A-NUMBER ONE GAME STAFF DOKI DOKI.
WHY WOULD ANYONE HAVE A BATH AT THE OFFICE AND WHY DOES THAT OLD GUY KEEP CRYING? ARE YOU FOLLOWING ANY OF THIS?
NO. AND WE HAVE THREE MORE EPISODES ON THIS DVD ALONE.
SO, YOU WANT TO KEEP WATCHING, THEN?
OH YEAH.
OWARI
<THE END>

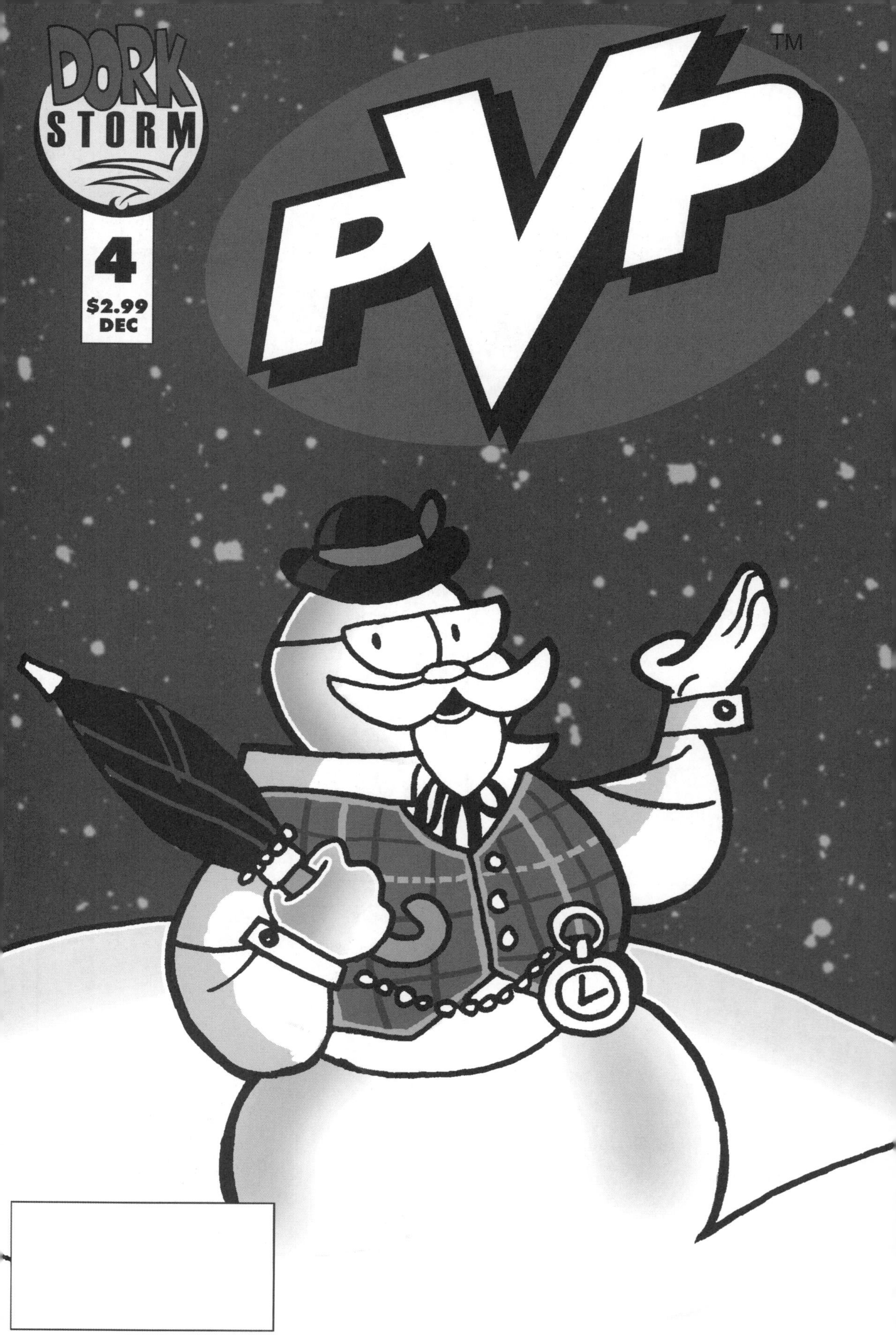
DORK STORM
PVP™
4
$2.99
DEC

www.pvponline.com

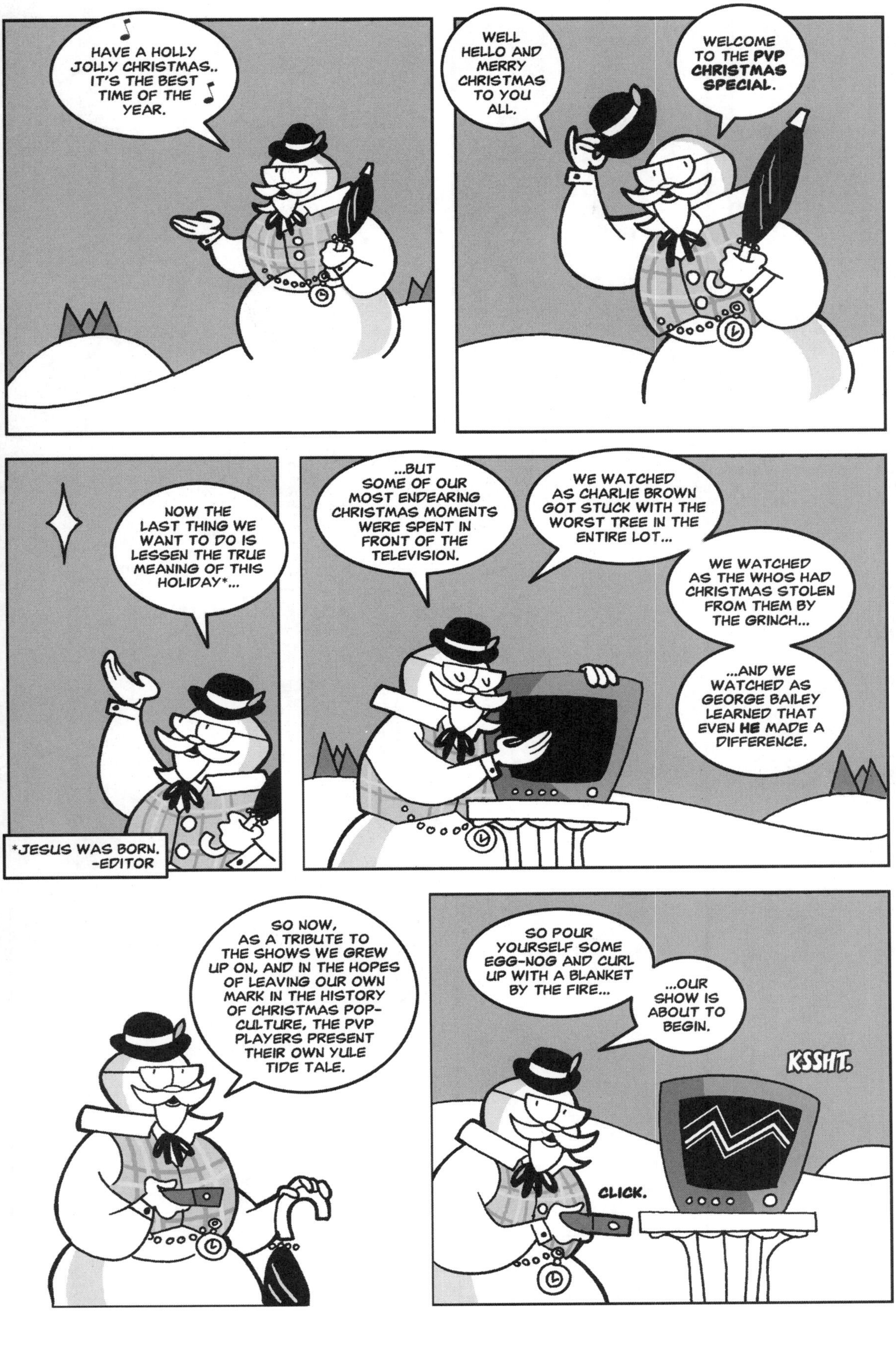
HAVE A HOLLY JOLLY CHRISTMAS.. IT'S THE BEST TIME OF THE YEAR.
WELL HELLO AND MERRY CHRISTMAS TO YOU ALL.
WELCOME TO THE **PVP CHRISTMAS SPECIAL**.
NOW THE LAST THING WE WANT TO DO IS LESSEN THE TRUE MEANING OF THIS HOLIDAY*...
*JESUS WAS BORN. -EDITOR
...BUT SOME OF OUR MOST ENDEARING CHRISTMAS MOMENTS WERE SPENT IN FRONT OF THE TELEVISION.
WE WATCHED AS CHARLIE BROWN GOT STUCK WITH THE WORST TREE IN THE ENTIRE LOT...
WE WATCHED AS THE WHOS HAD CHRISTMAS STOLEN FROM THEM BY THE GRINCH...
...AND WE WATCHED AS GEORGE BAILEY LEARNED THAT EVEN **HE** MADE A DIFFERENCE.
SO NOW, AS A TRIBUTE TO THE SHOWS WE GREW UP ON, AND IN THE HOPES OF LEAVING OUR OWN MARK IN THE HISTORY OF CHRISTMAS POP-CULTURE, THE PVP PLAYERS PRESENT THEIR OWN YULE TIDE TALE.
SO POUR YOURSELF SOME EGG-NOG AND CURL UP WITH A BLANKET BY THE FIRE...
...OUR SHOW IS ABOUT TO BEGIN.
KSSHT.
CLICK.

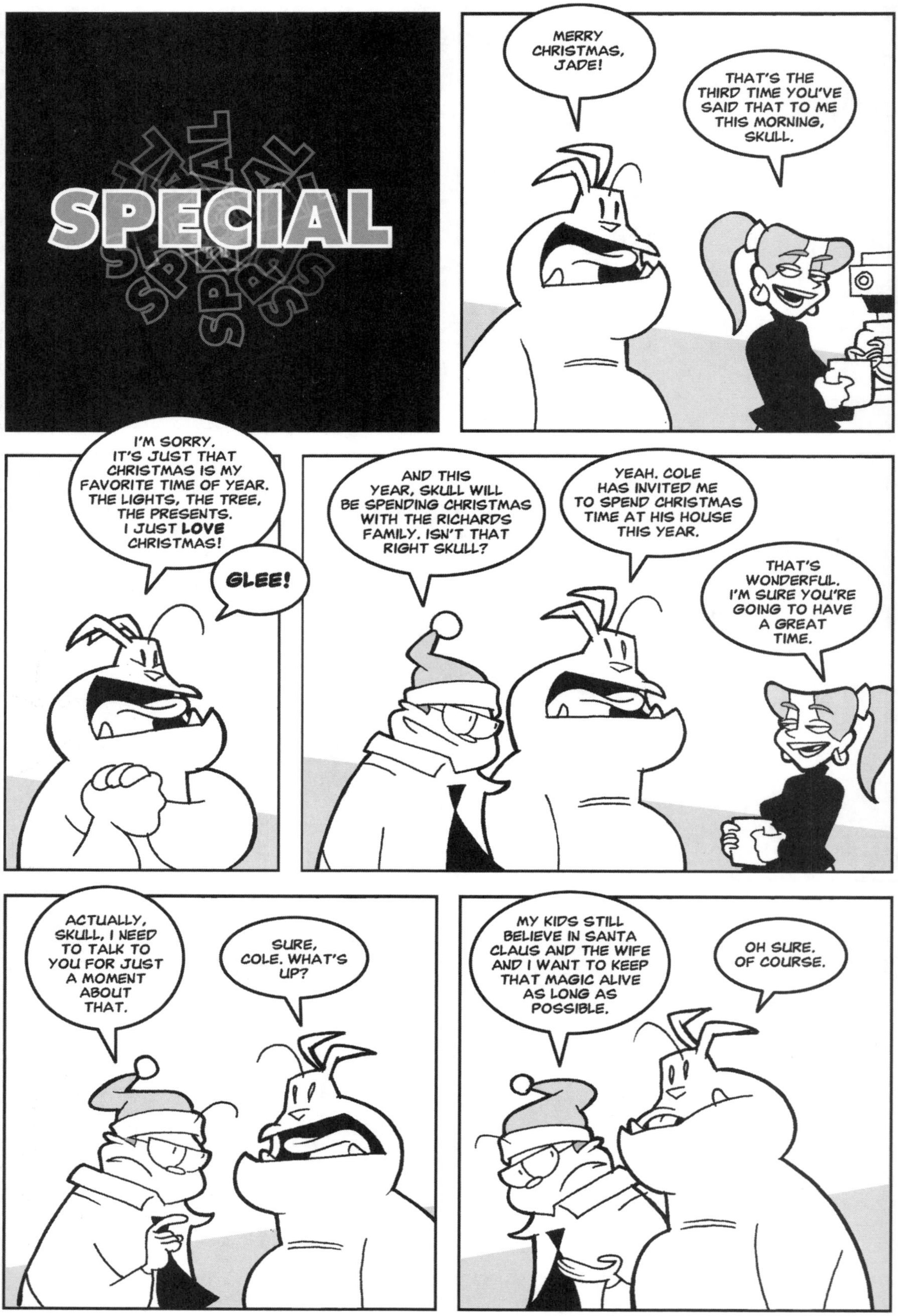
SPECIAL
MERRY CHRISTMAS, JADE!
THAT'S THE THIRD TIME YOU'VE SAID THAT TO ME THIS MORNING, SKULL.
I'M SORRY. IT'S JUST THAT CHRISTMAS IS MY FAVORITE TIME OF YEAR. THE LIGHTS, THE TREE, THE PRESENTS. I JUST **LOVE** CHRISTMAS!
GLEE!
AND THIS YEAR, SKULL WILL BE SPENDING CHRISTMAS WITH THE RICHARDS FAMILY. ISN'T THAT RIGHT SKULL?
YEAH. COLE HAS INVITED ME TO SPEND CHRISTMAS TIME AT HIS HOUSE THIS YEAR.
THAT'S WONDERFUL. I'M SURE YOU'RE GOING TO HAVE A GREAT TIME.
ACTUALLY, SKULL, I NEED TO TALK TO YOU FOR JUST A MOMENT ABOUT THAT.
SURE, COLE. WHAT'S UP?
MY KIDS STILL BELIEVE IN SANTA CLAUS AND THE WIFE AND I WANT TO KEEP THAT MAGIC ALIVE AS LONG AS POSSIBLE.
OH SURE. OF COURSE.

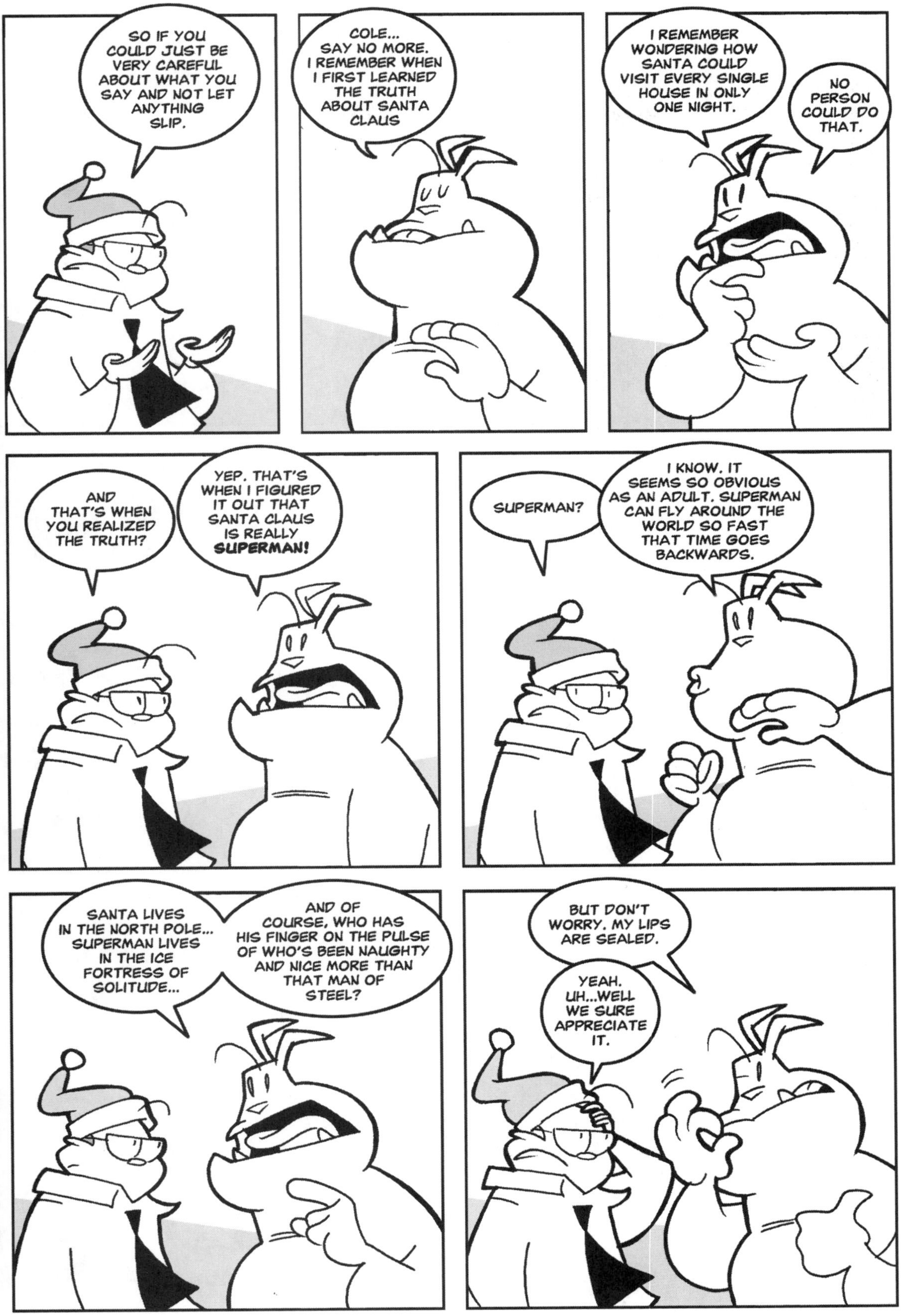
SO IF YOU COULD JUST BE VERY CAREFUL ABOUT WHAT YOU SAY AND NOT LET ANYTHING SLIP.
COLE... SAY NO MORE. I REMEMBER WHEN I FIRST LEARNED THE TRUTH ABOUT SANTA CLAUS
I REMEMBER WONDERING HOW SANTA COULD VISIT EVERY SINGLE HOUSE IN ONLY ONE NIGHT.
NO PERSON COULD DO THAT.
AND THAT'S WHEN YOU REALIZED THE TRUTH?
YEP. THAT'S WHEN I FIGURED IT OUT THAT SANTA CLAUS IS REALLY **SUPERMAN!**
SUPERMAN?
I KNOW. IT SEEMS SO OBVIOUS AS AN ADULT. SUPERMAN CAN FLY AROUND THE WORLD SO FAST THAT TIME GOES BACKWARDS.
SANTA LIVES IN THE NORTH POLE... SUPERMAN LIVES IN THE ICE FORTRESS OF SOLITUDE...
AND OF COURSE, WHO HAS HIS FINGER ON THE PULSE OF WHO'S BEEN NAUGHTY AND NICE MORE THAN THAT MAN OF STEEL?
BUT DON'T WORRY. MY LIPS ARE SEALED.
YEAH. UH...WELL WE SURE APPRECIATE IT.

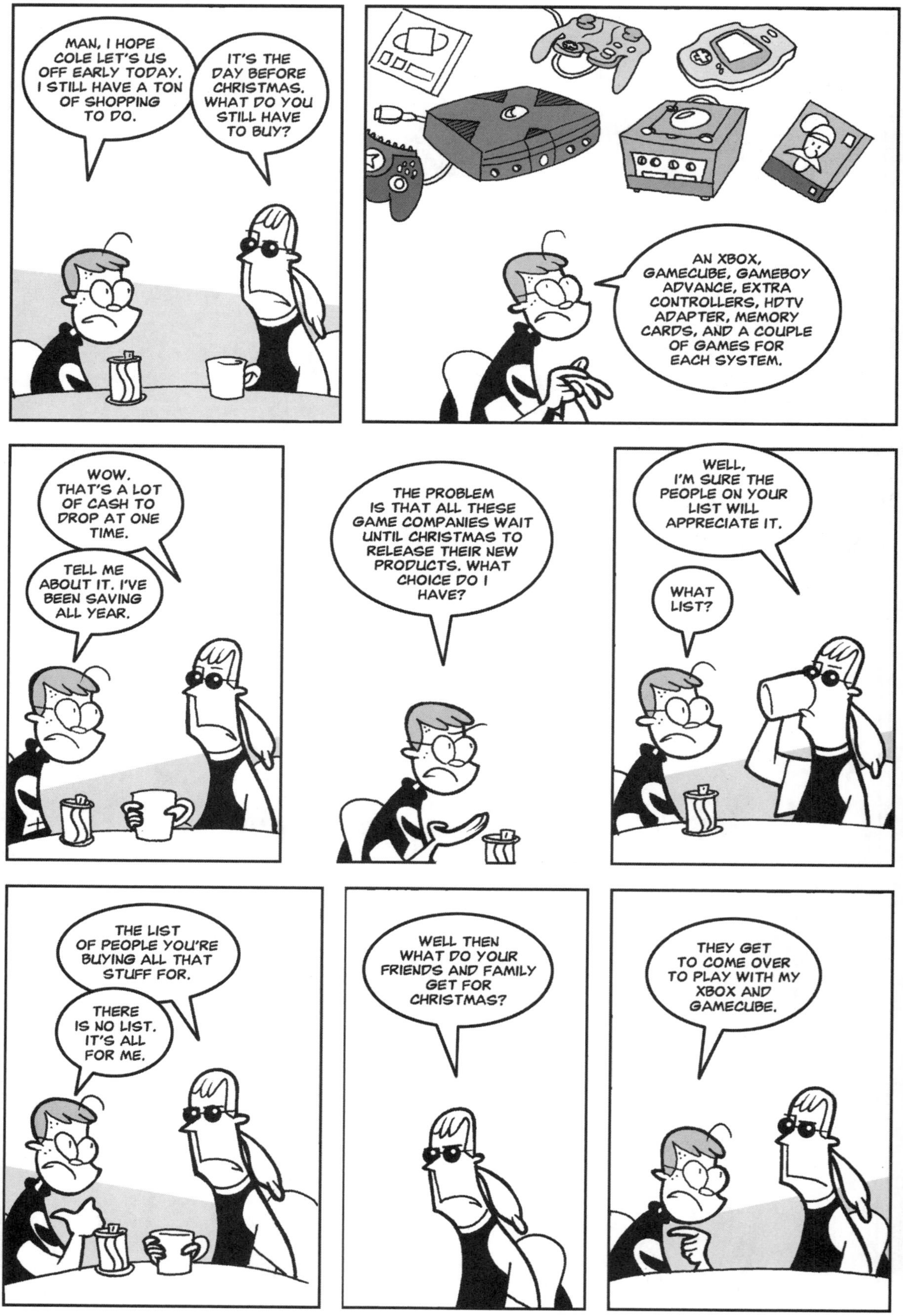
MAN, I HOPE COLE LET'S US OFF EARLY TODAY. I STILL HAVE A TON OF SHOPPING TO DO.
IT'S THE DAY BEFORE CHRISTMAS. WHAT DO YOU STILL HAVE TO BUY?
AN XBOX, GAMECUBE, GAMEBOY ADVANCE, EXTRA CONTROLLERS, HDTV ADAPTER, MEMORY CARDS, AND A COUPLE OF GAMES FOR EACH SYSTEM.
WOW. THAT'S A LOT OF CASH TO DROP AT ONE TIME.
TELL ME ABOUT IT. I'VE BEEN SAVING ALL YEAR.
THE PROBLEM IS THAT ALL THESE GAME COMPANIES WAIT UNTIL CHRISTMAS TO RELEASE THEIR NEW PRODUCTS. WHAT CHOICE DO I HAVE?
WELL, I'M SURE THE PEOPLE ON YOUR LIST WILL APPRECIATE IT.
WHAT LIST?
THE LIST OF PEOPLE YOU'RE BUYING ALL THAT STUFF FOR.
THERE IS NO LIST. IT'S ALL FOR ME.
WELL THEN WHAT DO YOUR FRIENDS AND FAMILY GET FOR CHRISTMAS?
THEY GET TO COME OVER TO PLAY WITH MY XBOX AND GAMECUBE.

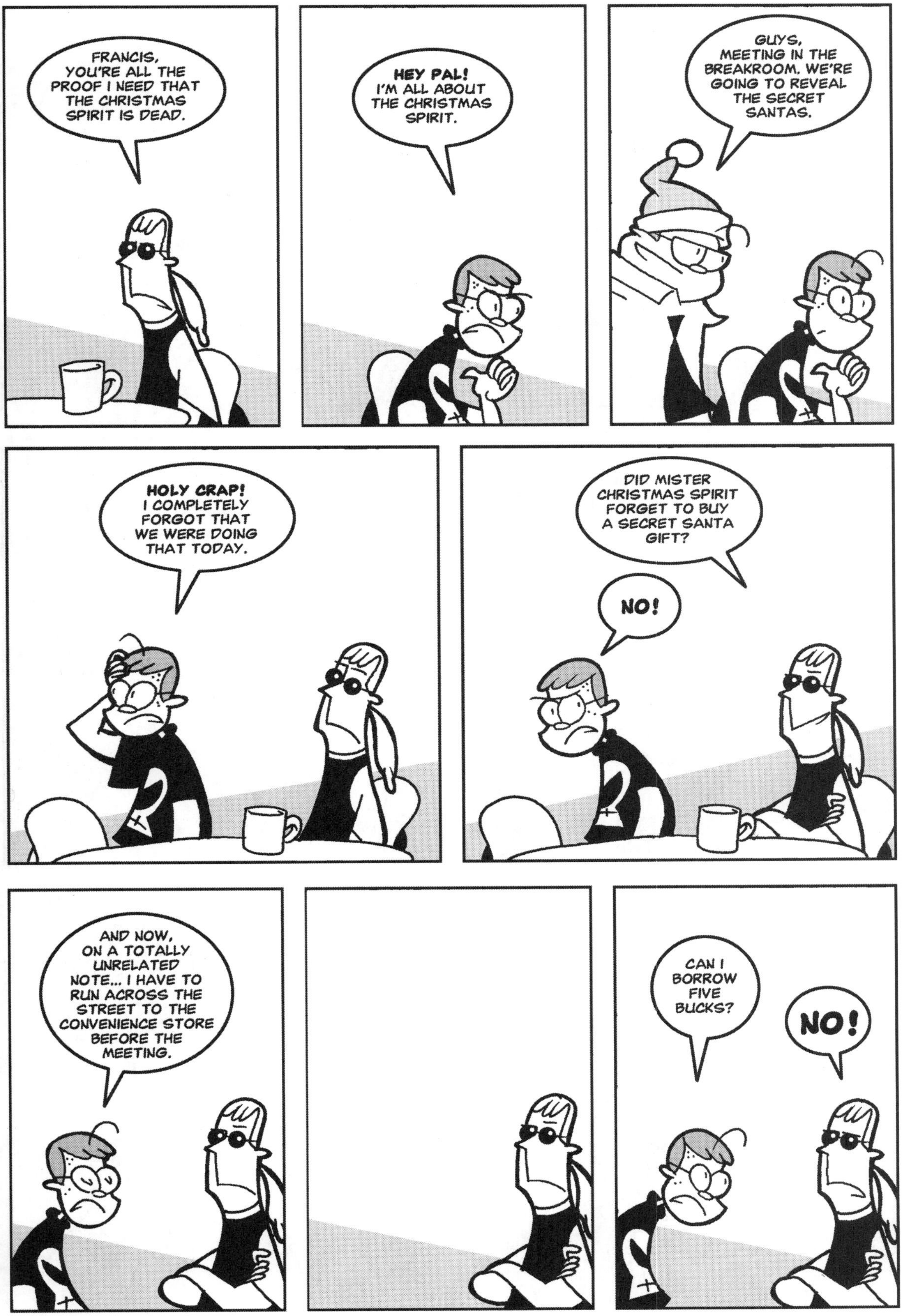
FRANCIS, YOU'RE ALL THE PROOF I NEED THAT THE CHRISTMAS SPIRIT IS DEAD.
HEY PAL! I'M ALL ABOUT THE CHRISTMAS SPIRIT.
GUYS, MEETING IN THE BREAKROOM. WE'RE GOING TO REVEAL THE SECRET SANTAS.
HOLY CRAP! I COMPLETELY FORGOT THAT WE WERE DOING THAT TODAY.
DID MISTER CHRISTMAS SPIRIT FORGET TO BUY A SECRET SANTA GIFT?
NO!
AND NOW, ON A TOTALLY UNRELATED NOTE... I HAVE TO RUN ACROSS THE STREET TO THE CONVENIENCE STORE BEFORE THE MEETING.
CAN I BORROW FIVE BUCKS?
NO!

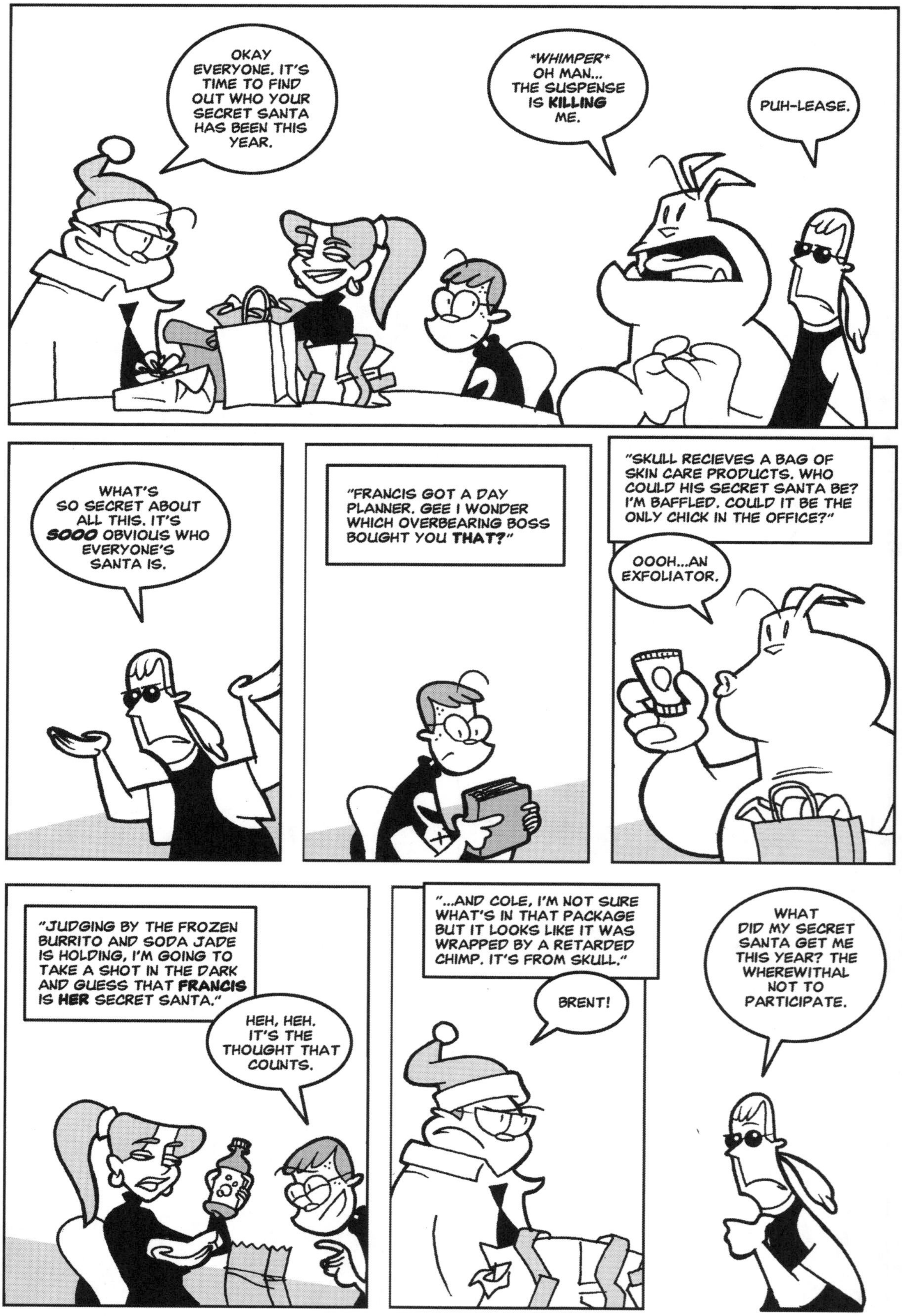
OKAY EVERYONE. IT'S TIME TO FIND OUT WHO YOUR SECRET SANTA HAS BEEN THIS YEAR.
WHIMPER OH MAN... THE SUSPENSE IS **KILLING** ME.
PUH-LEASE.
WHAT'S SO SECRET ABOUT ALL THIS. IT'S **SOOO** OBVIOUS WHO EVERYONE'S SANTA IS.
"FRANCIS GOT A DAY PLANNER. GEE I WONDER WHICH OVERBEARING BOSS BOUGHT YOU **THAT?**"
"SKULL RECIEVES A BAG OF SKIN CARE PRODUCTS. WHO COULD HIS SECRET SANTA BE? I'M BAFFLED. COULD IT BE THE ONLY CHICK IN THE OFFICE?"
OOOH...AN EXFOLIATOR.
"JUDGING BY THE FROZEN BURRITO AND SODA JADE IS HOLDING, I'M GOING TO TAKE A SHOT IN THE DARK AND GUESS THAT **FRANCIS** IS **HER** SECRET SANTA."
HEH, HEH. IT'S THE THOUGHT THAT COUNTS.
"...AND COLE, I'M NOT SURE WHAT'S IN THAT PACKAGE BUT IT LOOKS LIKE IT WAS WRAPPED BY A RETARDED CHIMP. IT'S FROM SKULL."
BRENT!
WHAT DID MY SECRET SANTA GET ME THIS YEAR? THE WHEREWITHAL NOT TO PARTICIPATE.

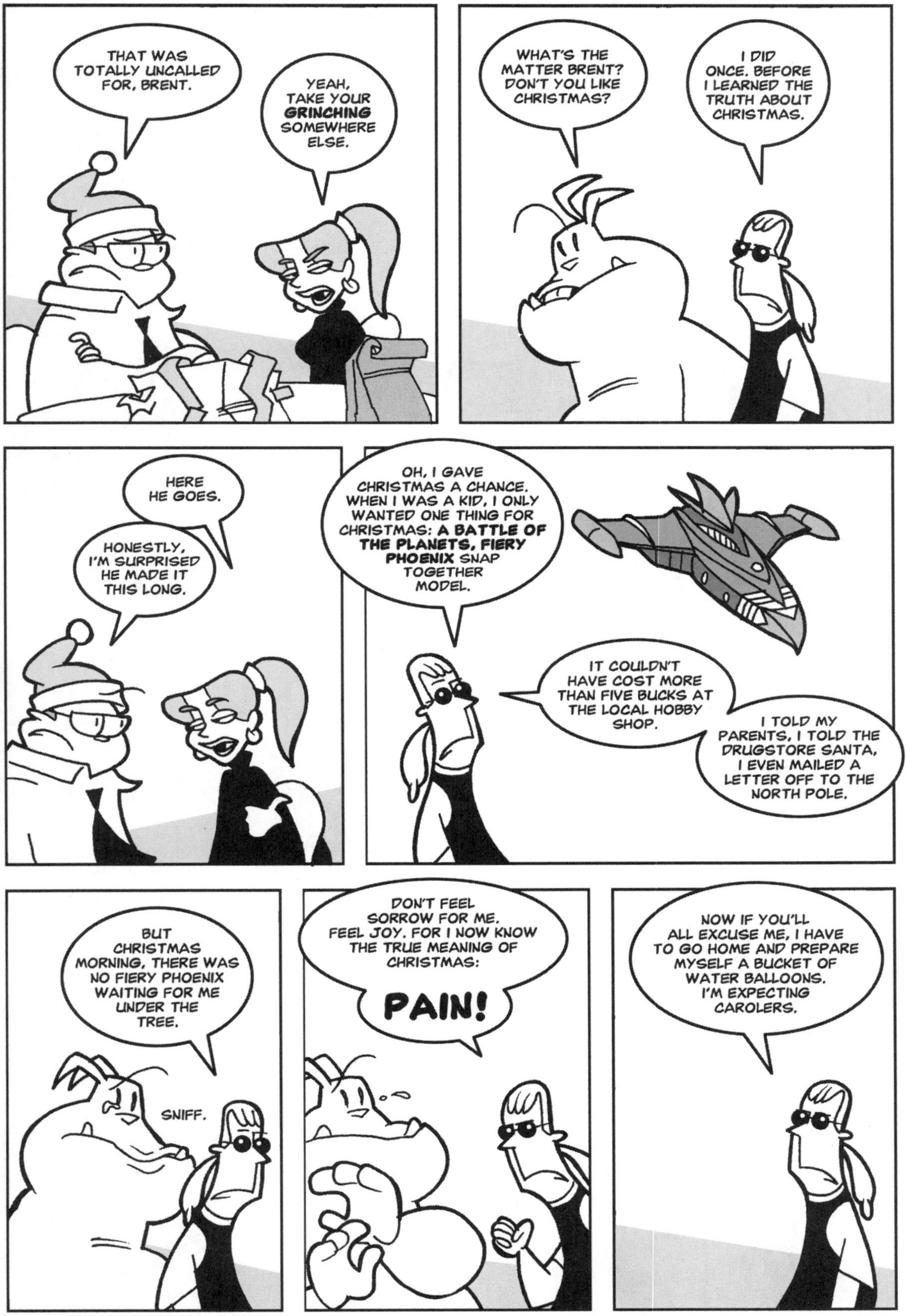
THAT WAS TOTALLY UNCALLED FOR, BRENT.
YEAH, TAKE YOUR **GRINCHING** SOMEWHERE ELSE.
WHAT'S THE MATTER BRENT? DON'T YOU LIKE CHRISTMAS?
I DID ONCE. BEFORE I LEARNED THE TRUTH ABOUT CHRISTMAS.
HERE HE GOES.
HONESTLY, I'M SURPRISED HE MADE IT THIS LONG.
OH, I GAVE CHRISTMAS A CHANCE. WHEN I WAS A KID, I ONLY WANTED ONE THING FOR CHRISTMAS: **A BATTLE OF THE PLANETS, FIERY PHOENIX** SNAP TOGETHER MODEL.
IT COULDN'T HAVE COST MORE THAN FIVE BUCKS AT THE LOCAL HOBBY SHOP.
I TOLD MY PARENTS, I TOLD THE DRUGSTORE SANTA, I EVEN MAILED A LETTER OFF TO THE NORTH POLE.
BUT CHRISTMAS MORNING, THERE WAS NO FIERY PHOENIX WAITING FOR ME UNDER THE TREE.
SNIFF.
DON'T FEEL SORROW FOR ME. FEEL JOY. FOR I NOW KNOW THE TRUE MEANING OF CHRISTMAS:
PAIN!
NOW IF YOU'LL ALL EXCUSE ME, I HAVE TO GO HOME AND PREPARE MYSELF A BUCKET OF WATER BALLOONS. I'M EXPECTING CAROLERS.

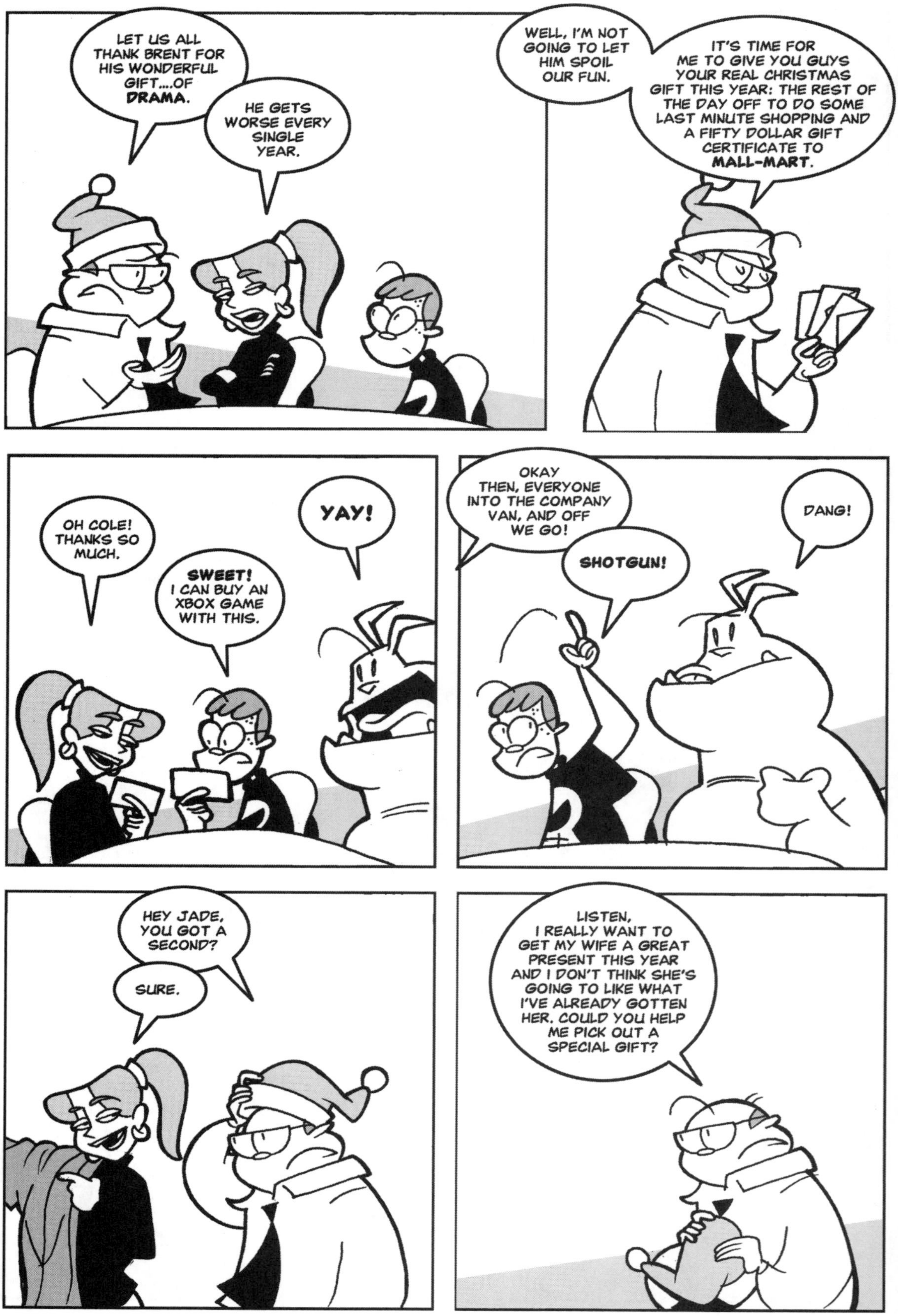
LET US ALL THANK BRENT FOR HIS WONDERFUL GIFT....OF **DRAMA**.
HE GETS WORSE EVERY SINGLE YEAR.
WELL, I'M NOT GOING TO LET HIM SPOIL OUR FUN.
IT'S TIME FOR ME TO GIVE YOU GUYS YOUR REAL CHRISTMAS GIFT THIS YEAR: THE REST OF THE DAY OFF TO DO SOME LAST MINUTE SHOPPING AND A FIFTY DOLLAR GIFT CERTIFICATE TO **MALL-MART**.
OH COLE! THANKS SO MUCH.
SWEET! I CAN BUY AN XBOX GAME WITH THIS.
YAY!
OKAY THEN, EVERYONE INTO THE COMPANY VAN, AND OFF WE GO!
SHOTGUN!
DANG!
HEY JADE, YOU GOT A SECOND?
SURE.
LISTEN, I REALLY WANT TO GET MY WIFE A GREAT PRESENT THIS YEAR AND I DON'T THINK SHE'S GOING TO LIKE WHAT I'VE ALREADY GOTTEN HER. COULD YOU HELP ME PICK OUT A SPECIAL GIFT?

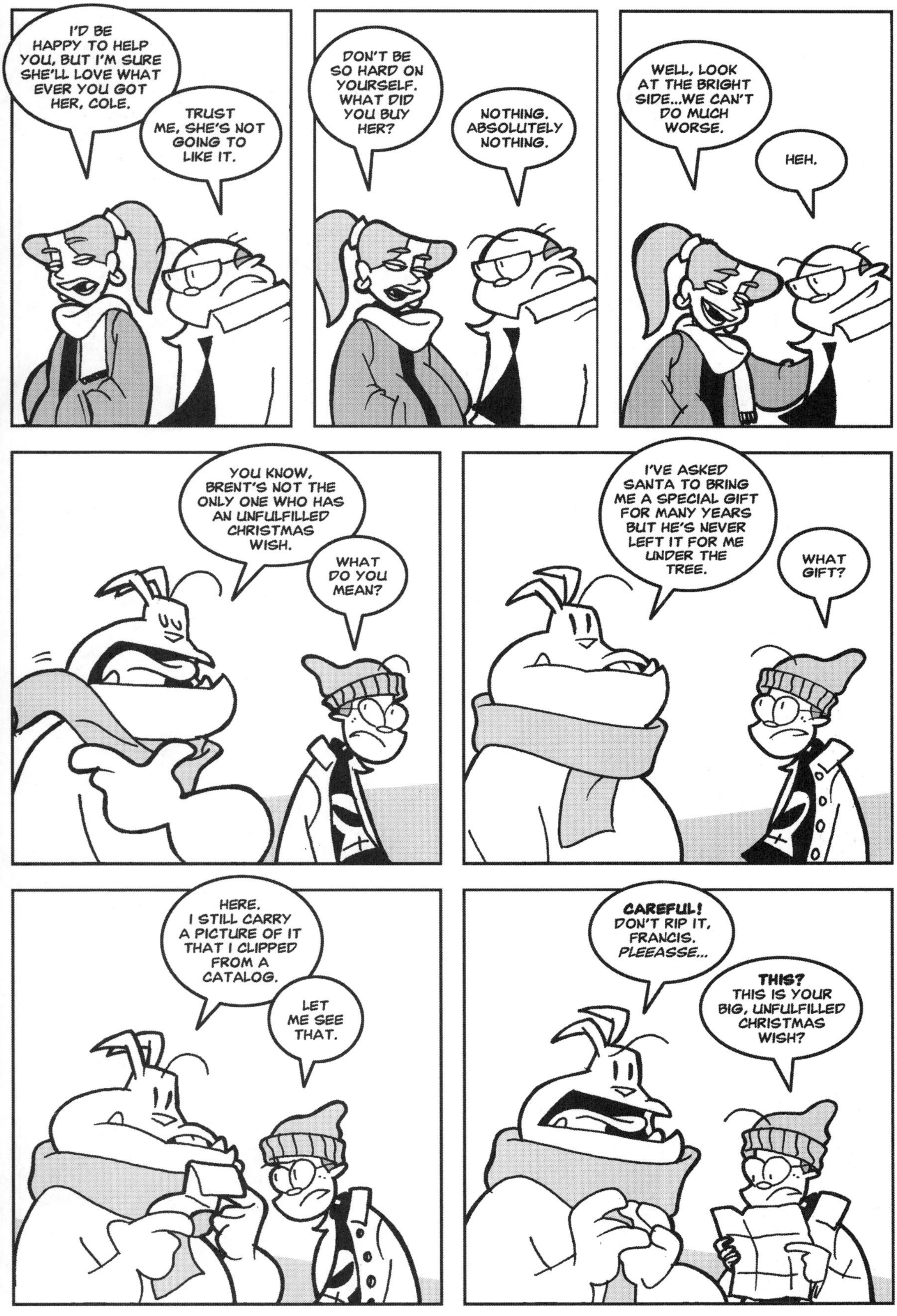
I'D BE HAPPY TO HELP YOU, BUT I'M SURE SHE'LL LOVE WHAT EVER YOU GOT HER, COLE.
TRUST ME, SHE'S NOT GOING TO LIKE IT.
DON'T BE SO HARD ON YOURSELF. WHAT DID YOU BUY HER?
NOTHING. ABSOLUTELY NOTHING.
WELL, LOOK AT THE BRIGHT SIDE...WE CAN'T DO MUCH WORSE.
HEH.
YOU KNOW, BRENT'S NOT THE ONLY ONE WHO HAS AN UNFULFILLED CHRISTMAS WISH.
WHAT DO YOU MEAN?
I'VE ASKED SANTA TO BRING ME A SPECIAL GIFT FOR MANY YEARS BUT HE'S NEVER LEFT IT FOR ME UNDER THE TREE.
WHAT GIFT?
HERE. I STILL CARRY A PICTURE OF IT THAT I CLIPPED FROM A CATALOG.
LET ME SEE THAT.
CAREFUL! DON'T RIP IT, FRANCIS. PLEEASSE...
THIS? THIS IS YOUR BIG, UNFULFILLED CHRISTMAS WISH?

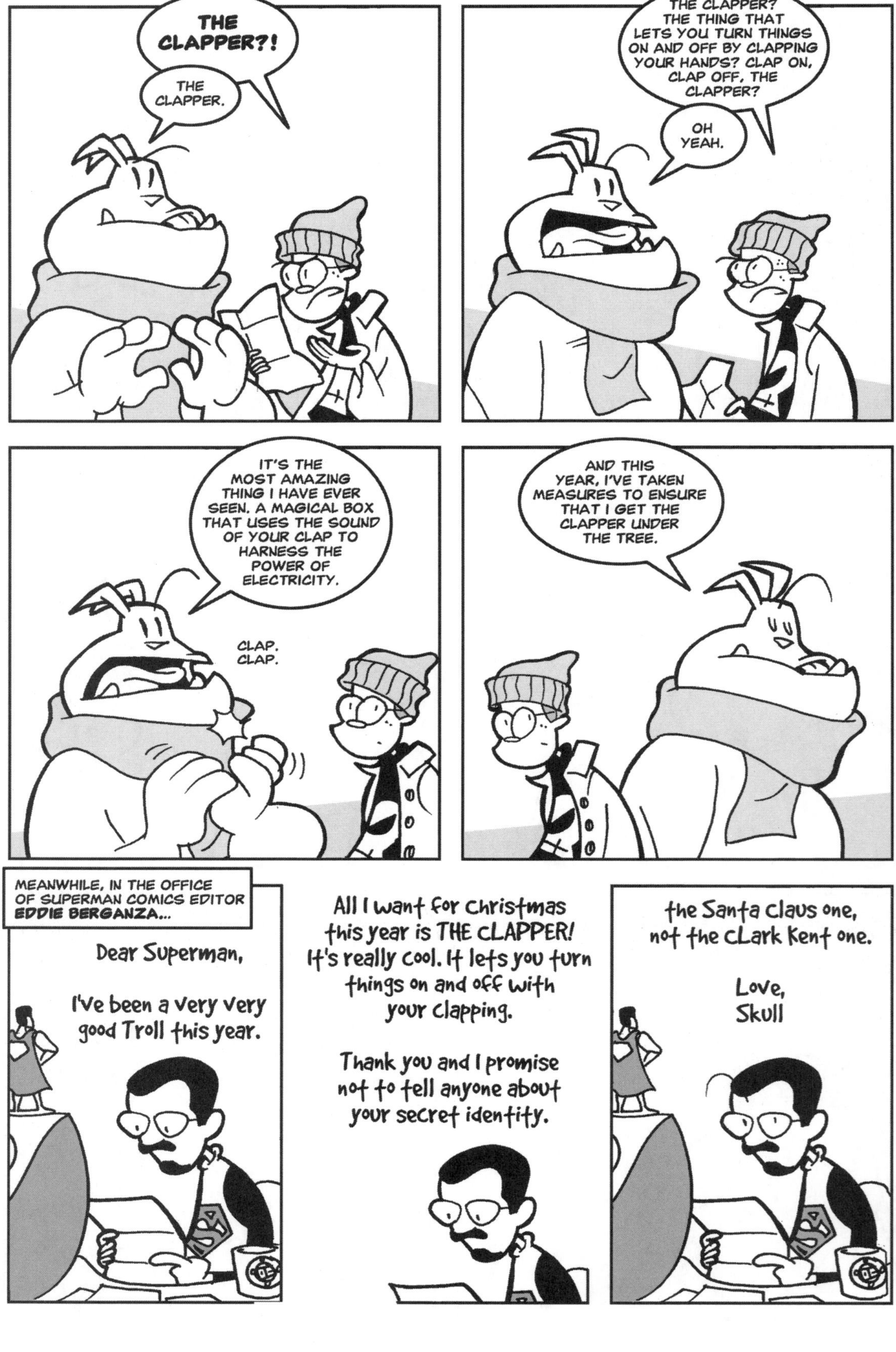
THE CLAPPER?!
THE CLAPPER.
THE CLAPPER? THE THING THAT LETS YOU TURN THINGS ON AND OFF BY CLAPPING YOUR HANDS? CLAP ON, CLAP OFF, THE CLAPPER?
OH YEAH.
IT'S THE MOST AMAZING THING I HAVE EVER SEEN. A MAGICAL BOX THAT USES THE SOUND OF YOUR CLAP TO HARNESS THE POWER OF ELECTRICITY.
CLAP. CLAP.
AND THIS YEAR, I'VE TAKEN MEASURES TO ENSURE THAT I GET THE CLAPPER UNDER THE TREE.
MEANWHILE, IN THE OFFICE OF SUPERMAN COMICS EDITOR EDDIE BERGANZA...
Dear Superman,
I've been a very very good Troll this year.
All I want for christmas this year is THE CLAPPER! It's really cool. It lets you turn things on and off with your clapping.
Thank you and I promise not to tell anyone about your secret identity.
the Santa claus one, not the clark Kent one.
Love, Skull

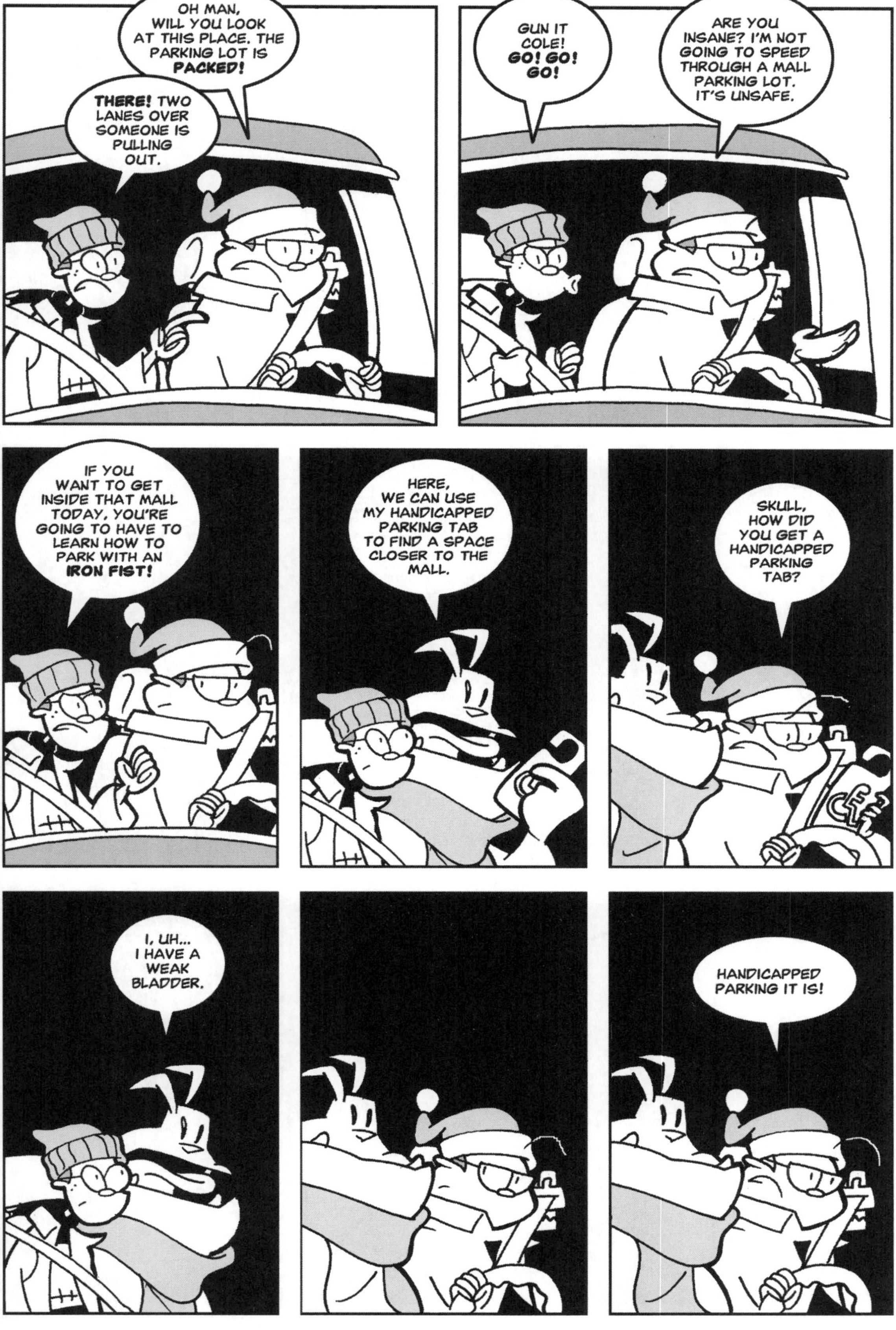
OH MAN, WILL YOU LOOK AT THIS PLACE. THE PARKING LOT IS **PACKED!**
THERE! TWO LANES OVER SOMEONE IS PULLING OUT.
GUN IT COLE! **GO! GO! GO!**
ARE YOU INSANE? I'M NOT GOING TO SPEED THROUGH A MALL PARKING LOT. IT'S UNSAFE.
IF YOU WANT TO GET INSIDE THAT MALL TODAY, YOU'RE GOING TO HAVE TO LEARN HOW TO PARK WITH AN **IRON FIST!**
HERE, WE CAN USE MY HANDICAPPED PARKING TAB TO FIND A SPACE CLOSER TO THE MALL.
SKULL, HOW DID YOU GET A HANDICAPPED PARKING TAB?
I, UH... I HAVE A WEAK BLADDER.
HANDICAPPED PARKING IT IS!

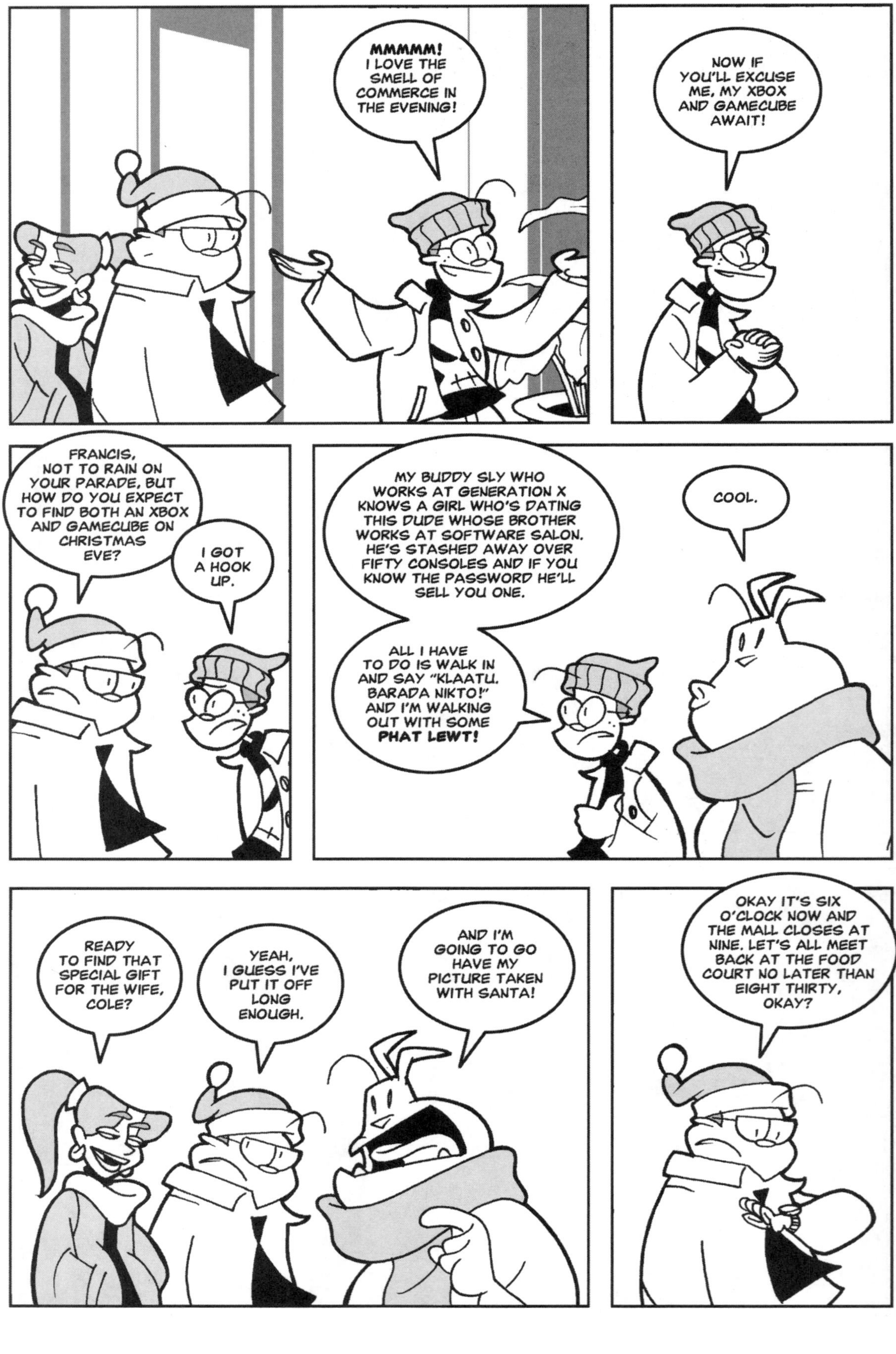
MMMMM! I LOVE THE SMELL OF COMMERCE IN THE EVENING!
NOW IF YOU'LL EXCUSE ME, MY XBOX AND GAMECUBE AWAIT!
FRANCIS, NOT TO RAIN ON YOUR PARADE, BUT HOW DO YOU EXPECT TO FIND BOTH AN XBOX AND GAMECUBE ON CHRISTMAS EVE?
I GOT A HOOK UP.
MY BUDDY SLY WHO WORKS AT GENERATION X KNOWS A GIRL WHO'S DATING THIS DUDE WHOSE BROTHER WORKS AT SOFTWARE SALON. HE'S STASHED AWAY OVER FIFTY CONSOLES AND IF YOU KNOW THE PASSWORD HE'LL SELL YOU ONE.
ALL I HAVE TO DO IS WALK IN AND SAY "KLAATU. BARADA NIKTO!" AND I'M WALKING OUT WITH SOME **PHAT LEWT!**
COOL.
READY TO FIND THAT SPECIAL GIFT FOR THE WIFE, COLE?
YEAH, I GUESS I'VE PUT IT OFF LONG ENOUGH.
AND I'M GOING TO GO HAVE MY PICTURE TAKEN WITH SANTA!
OKAY IT'S SIX O'CLOCK NOW AND THE MALL CLOSES AT NINE. LET'S ALL MEET BACK AT THE FOOD COURT NO LATER THAN EIGHT THIRTY, OKAY?

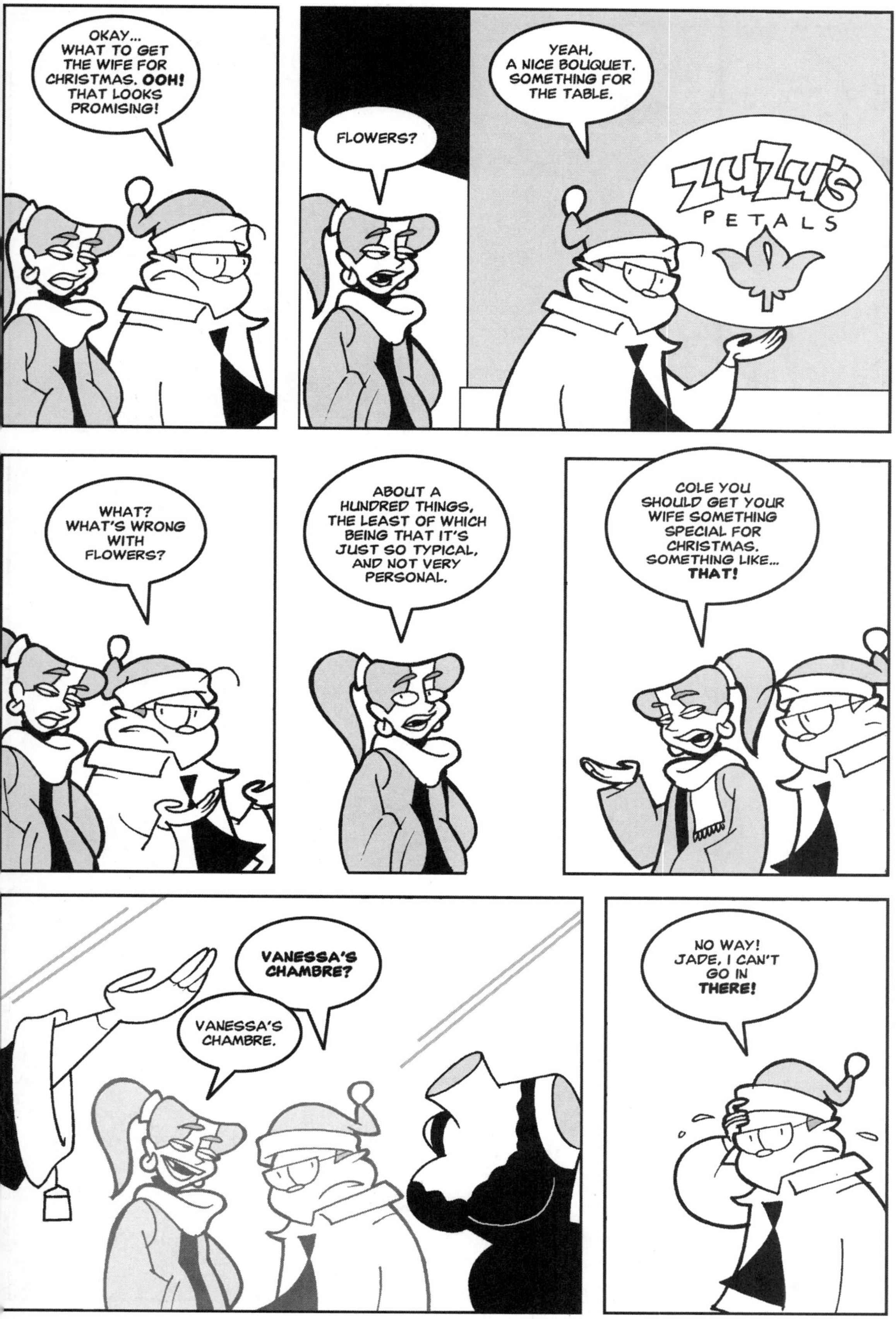
OKAY... WHAT TO GET THE WIFE FOR CHRISTMAS. OOH! THAT LOOKS PROMISING!
FLOWERS?
YEAH, A NICE BOUQUET. SOMETHING FOR THE TABLE.
ZUZU'S PETALS
WHAT? WHAT'S WRONG WITH FLOWERS?
ABOUT A HUNDRED THINGS, THE LEAST OF WHICH BEING THAT IT'S JUST SO TYPICAL, AND NOT VERY PERSONAL.
COLE YOU SHOULD GET YOUR WIFE SOMETHING SPECIAL FOR CHRISTMAS. SOMETHING LIKE... THAT!
VANESSA'S CHAMBRE.
VANESSA'S CHAMBRE?
NO WAY! JADE, I CAN'T GO IN THERE!

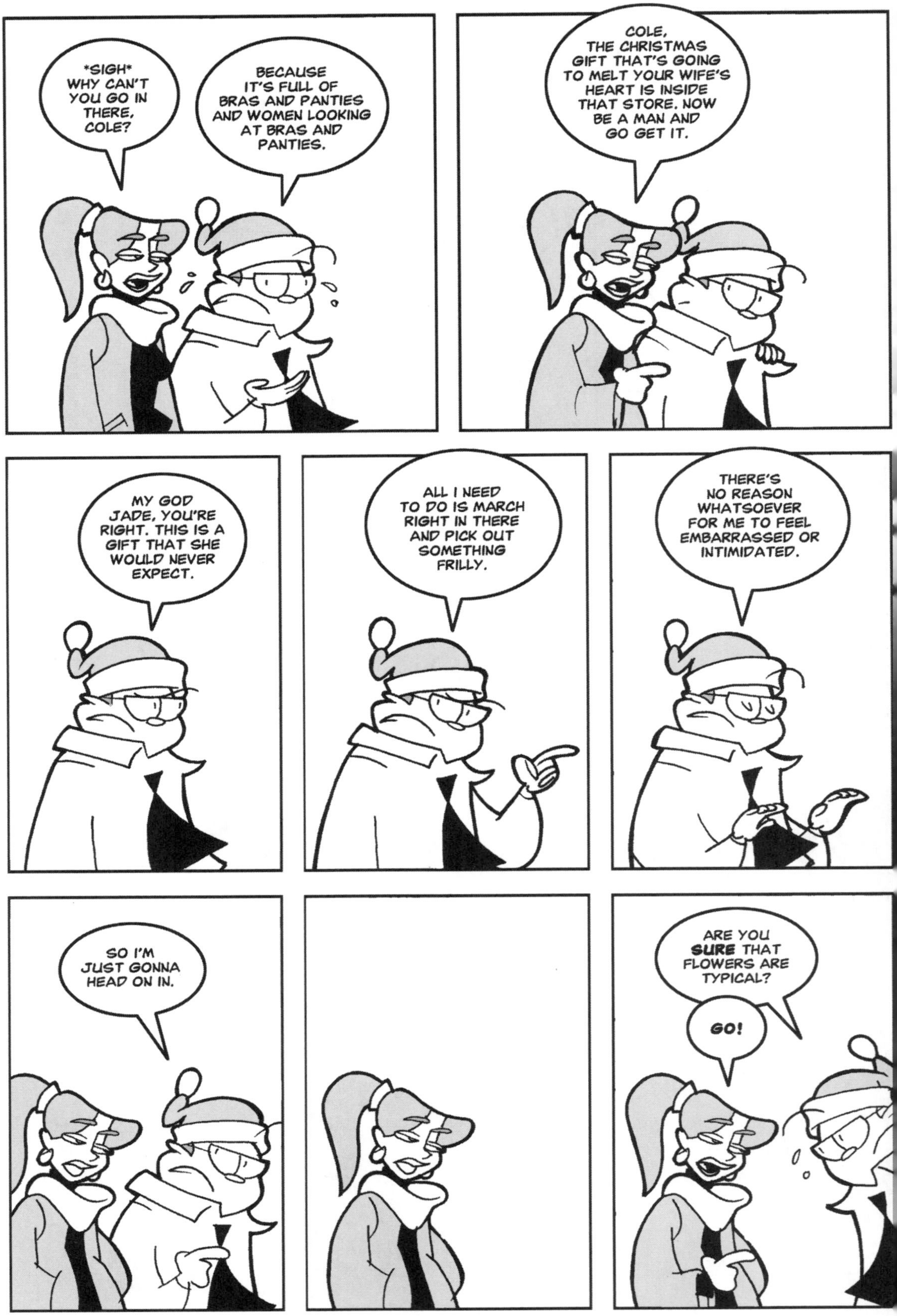
SIGH WHY CAN'T YOU GO IN THERE, COLE?
BECAUSE IT'S FULL OF BRAS AND PANTIES AND WOMEN LOOKING AT BRAS AND PANTIES.
COLE, THE CHRISTMAS GIFT THAT'S GOING TO MELT YOUR WIFE'S HEART IS INSIDE THAT STORE. NOW BE A MAN AND GO GET IT.
MY GOD JADE, YOU'RE RIGHT. THIS IS A GIFT THAT SHE WOULD NEVER EXPECT.
ALL I NEED TO DO IS MARCH RIGHT IN THERE AND PICK OUT SOMETHING FRILLY.
THERE'S NO REASON WHATSOEVER FOR ME TO FEEL EMBARRASSED OR INTIMIDATED.
SO I'M JUST GONNA HEAD ON IN.
ARE YOU **SURE** THAT FLOWERS ARE TYPICAL?
GO!

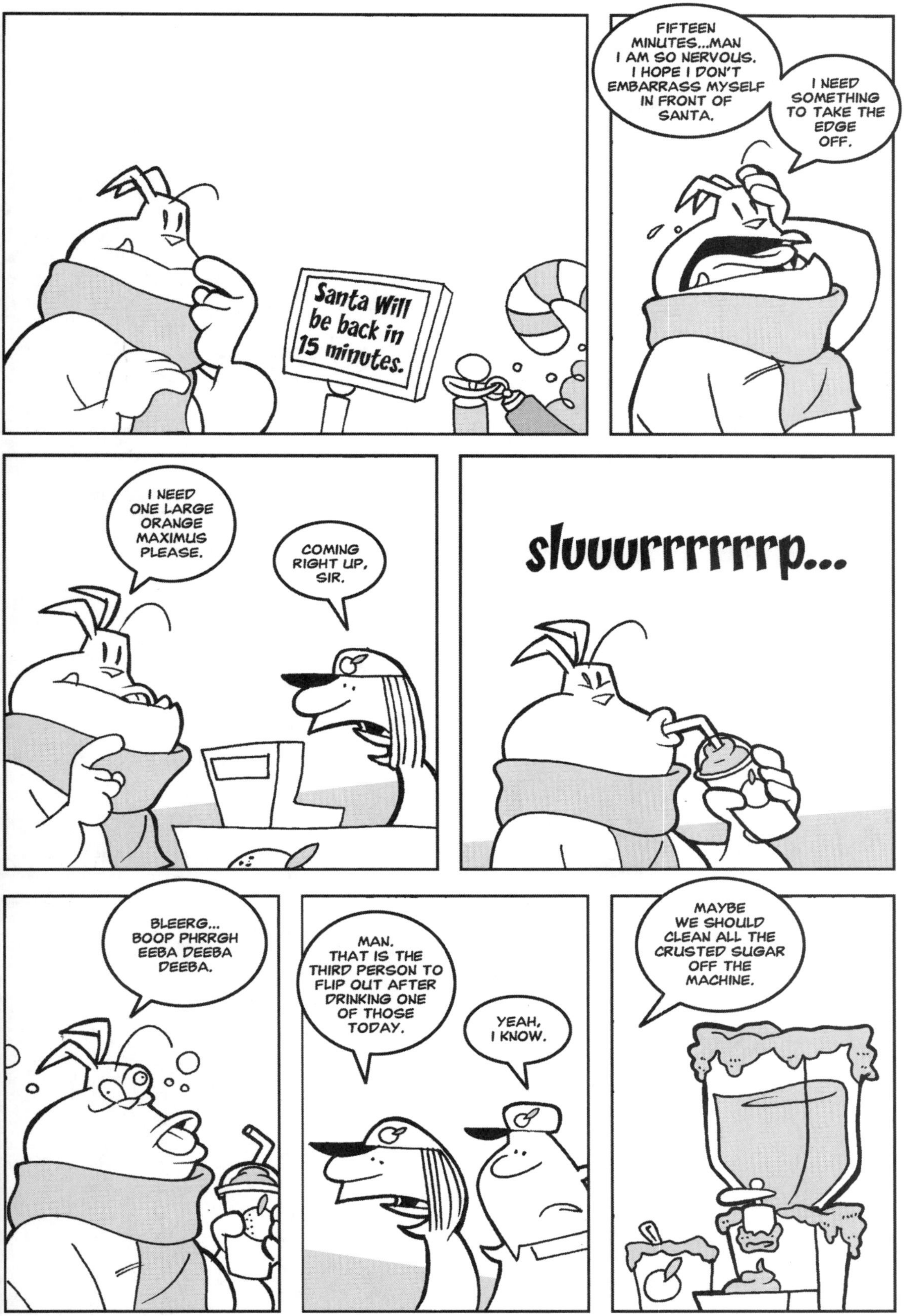
Santa Will be back in 15 minutes.
FIFTEEN MINUTES...MAN I AM SO NERVOUS. I HOPE I DON'T EMBARRASS MYSELF IN FRONT OF SANTA.
I NEED SOMETHING TO TAKE THE EDGE OFF.
I NEED ONE LARGE ORANGE MAXIMUS PLEASE.
COMING RIGHT UP, SIR.
sluuurrrrrrp...
BLEERG... BOOP PHRRGH EEBA DEEBA DEEBA.
MAN. THAT IS THE THIRD PERSON TO FLIP OUT AFTER DRINKING ONE OF THOSE TODAY.
YEAH, I KNOW.
MAYBE WE SHOULD CLEAN ALL THE CRUSTED SUGAR OFF THE MACHINE.

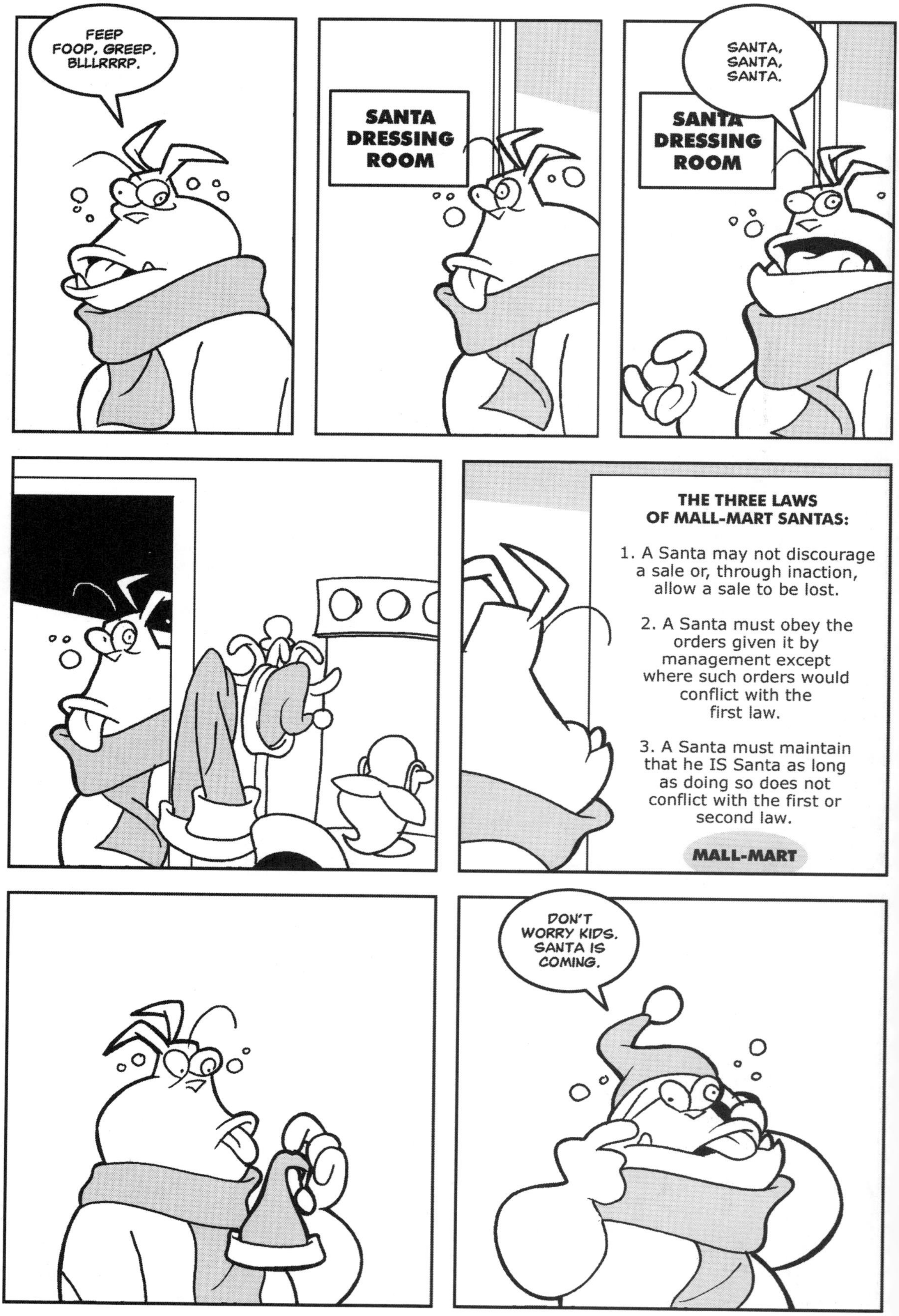
FEEP FOOP, GREEP. BLLLRRRP.
SANTA DRESSING ROOM
SANTA, SANTA, SANTA.
SANTA DRESSING ROOM
THE THREE LAWS OF MALL-MART SANTAS:
1. A Santa may not discourage a sale or, through inaction, allow a sale to be lost.
2. A Santa must obey the orders given it by management except where such orders would conflict with the first law.
3. A Santa must maintain that he IS Santa as long as doing so does not conflict with the first or second law.
MALL-MART
DON'T WORRY KIDS. SANTA IS COMING.

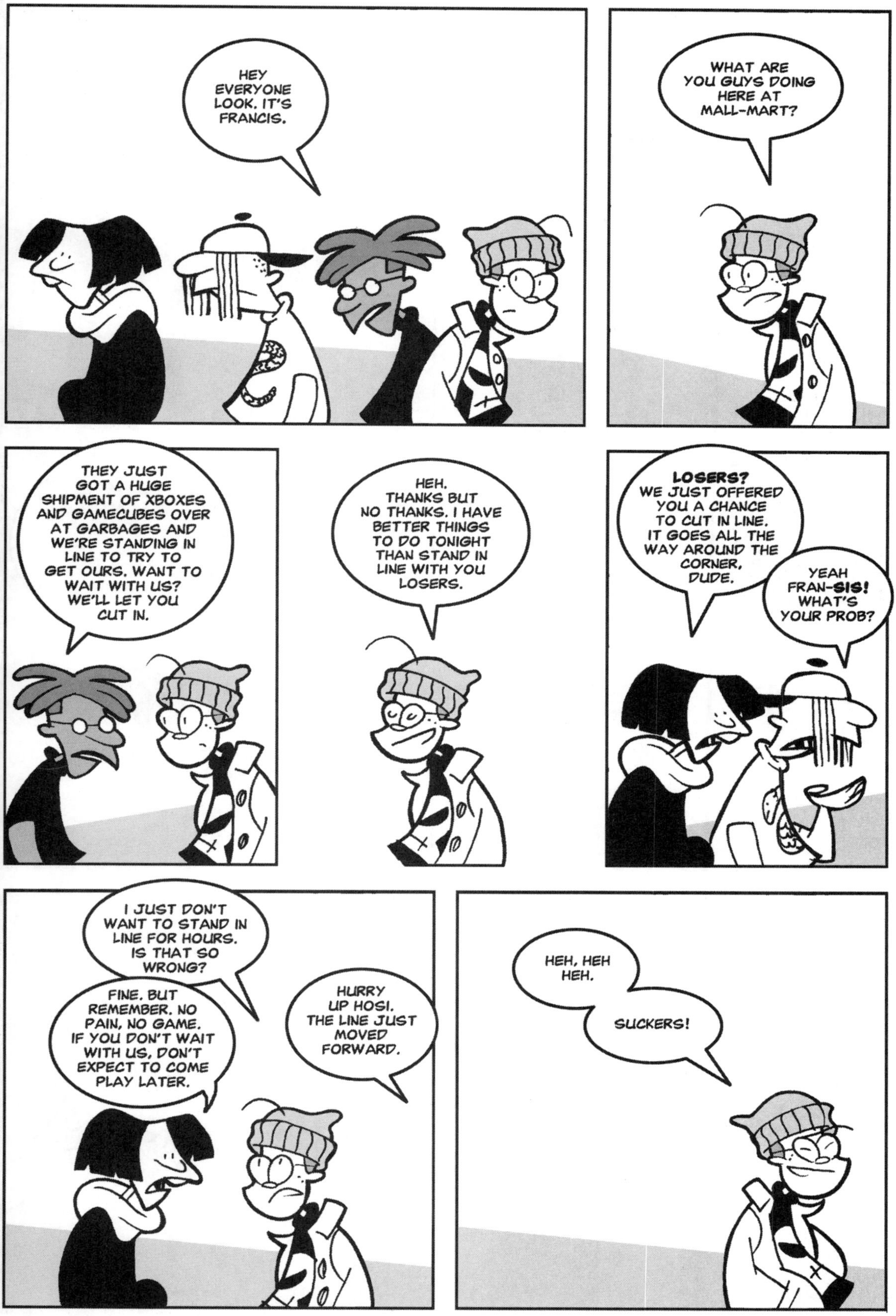
HEY EVERYONE LOOK. IT'S FRANCIS.
WHAT ARE YOU GUYS DOING HERE AT MALL-MART?
THEY JUST GOT A HUGE SHIPMENT OF XBOXES AND GAMECUBES OVER AT GARBAGES AND WE'RE STANDING IN LINE TO TRY TO GET OURS. WANT TO WAIT WITH US? WE'LL LET YOU CUT IN.
HEH. THANKS BUT NO THANKS. I HAVE BETTER THINGS TO DO TONIGHT THAN STAND IN LINE WITH YOU LOSERS.
LOSERS? WE JUST OFFERED YOU A CHANCE TO CUT IN LINE. IT GOES ALL THE WAY AROUND THE CORNER, DUDE.
YEAH FRAN-**SIS!** WHAT'S YOUR PROB?
I JUST DON'T WANT TO STAND IN LINE FOR HOURS. IS THAT SO WRONG?
FINE. BUT REMEMBER. NO PAIN, NO GAME. IF YOU DON'T WAIT WITH US, DON'T EXPECT TO COME PLAY LATER.
HURRY UP HOSI. THE LINE JUST MOVED FORWARD.
HEH, HEH HEH.
SUCKERS!

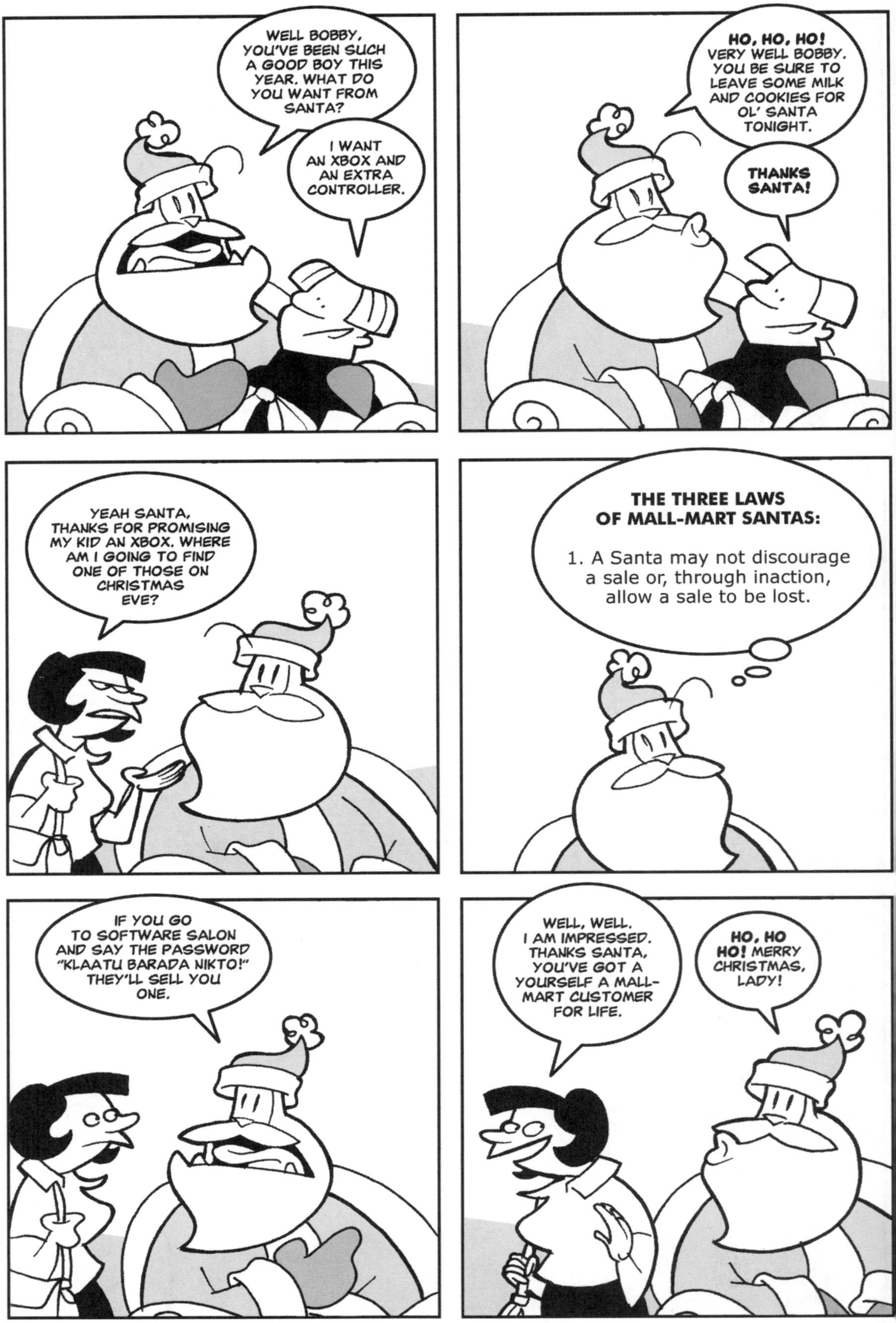
WELL BOBBY, YOU'VE BEEN SUCH A GOOD BOY THIS YEAR. WHAT DO YOU WANT FROM SANTA?
I WANT AN XBOX AND AN EXTRA CONTROLLER.
HO, HO, HO! VERY WELL BOBBY. YOU BE SURE TO LEAVE SOME MILK AND COOKIES FOR OL' SANTA TONIGHT.
THANKS SANTA!
YEAH SANTA, THANKS FOR PROMISING MY KID AN XBOX. WHERE AM I GOING TO FIND ONE OF THOSE ON CHRISTMAS EVE?
THE THREE LAWS OF MALL-MART SANTAS:
1. A Santa may not discourage a sale or, through inaction, allow a sale to be lost.
IF YOU GO TO SOFTWARE SALON AND SAY THE PASSWORD "KLAATU BARADA NIKTO!" THEY'LL SELL YOU ONE.
WELL, WELL. I AM IMPRESSED. THANKS SANTA, YOU'VE GOT A YOURSELF A MALL-MART CUSTOMER FOR LIFE.
HO, HO HO! MERRY CHRISTMAS, LADY!

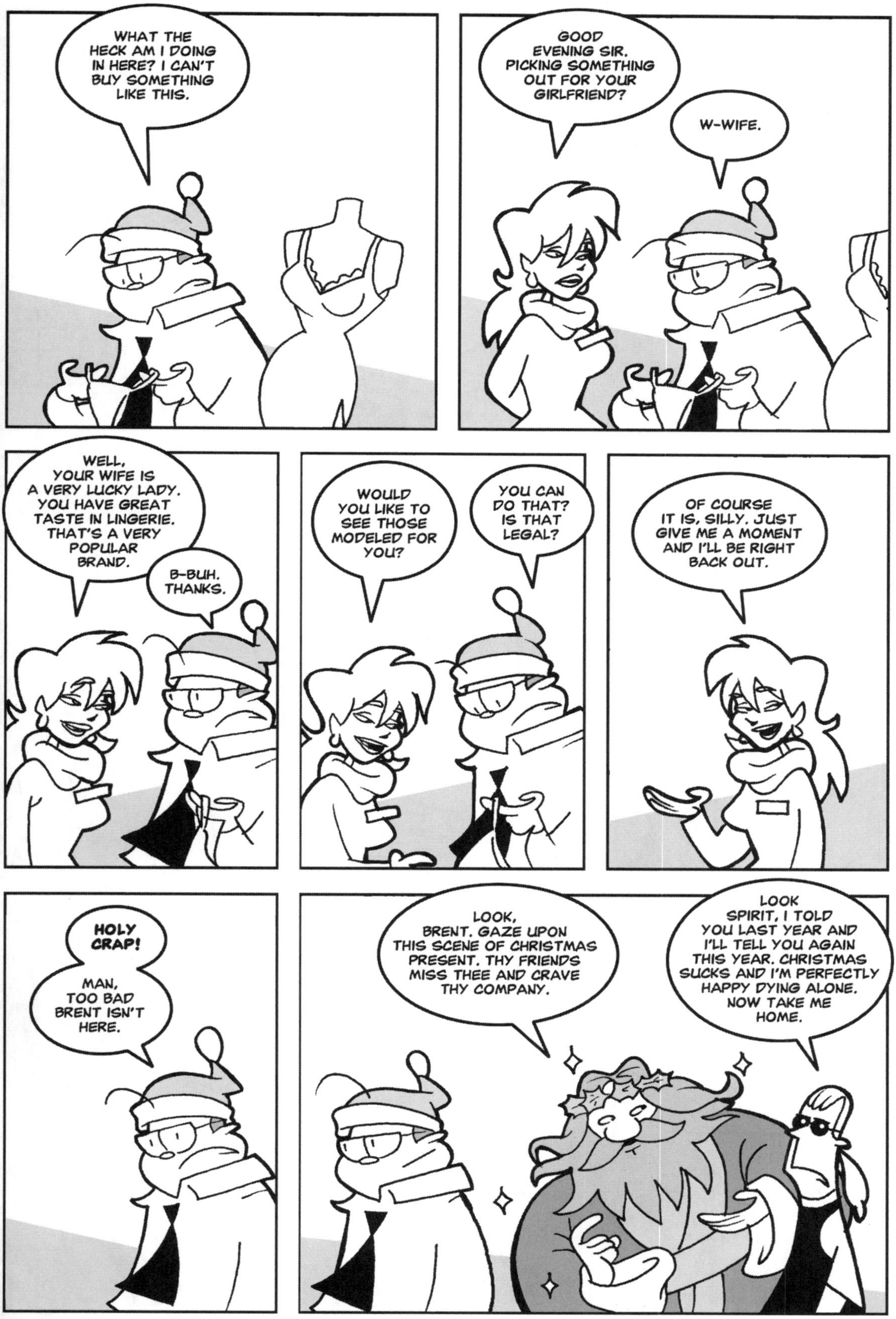

WHAT THE HECK AM I DOING IN HERE? I CAN'T BUY SOMETHING LIKE THIS.
GOOD EVENING SIR. PICKING SOMETHING OUT FOR YOUR GIRLFRIEND?
W-WIFE.
WELL, YOUR WIFE IS A VERY LUCKY LADY. YOU HAVE GREAT TASTE IN LINGERIE. THAT'S A VERY POPULAR BRAND.
B-BUH. THANKS.
WOULD YOU LIKE TO SEE THOSE MODELED FOR YOU?
YOU CAN DO THAT? IS THAT LEGAL?
OF COURSE IT IS, SILLY. JUST GIVE ME A MOMENT AND I'LL BE RIGHT BACK OUT.
HOLY CRAP!
MAN, TOO BAD BRENT ISN'T HERE.
LOOK, BRENT. GAZE UPON THIS SCENE OF CHRISTMAS PRESENT. THY FRIENDS MISS THEE AND CRAVE THY COMPANY.
LOOK SPIRIT, I TOLD YOU LAST YEAR AND I'LL TELL YOU AGAIN THIS YEAR. CHRISTMAS SUCKS AND I'M PERFECTLY HAPPY DYING ALONE. NOW TAKE ME HOME.

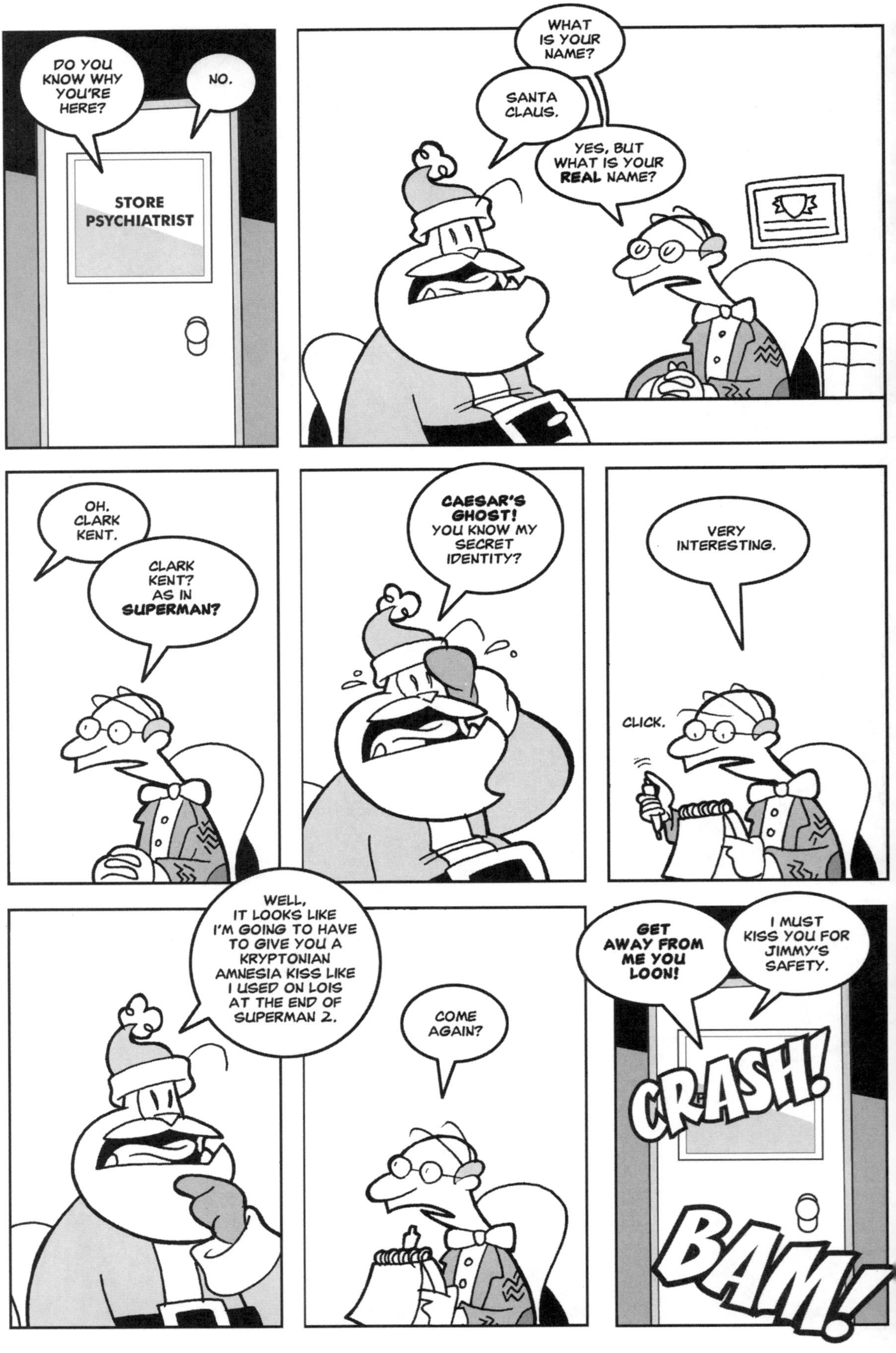
DO YOU KNOW WHY YOU'RE HERE?
NO.
STORE PSYCHIATRIST
WHAT IS YOUR NAME?
SANTA CLAUS.
YES, BUT WHAT IS YOUR REAL NAME?
OH. CLARK KENT.
CLARK KENT? AS IN SUPERMAN?
CAESAR'S GHOST! YOU KNOW MY SECRET IDENTITY?
VERY INTERESTING.
CLICK.
WELL, IT LOOKS LIKE I'M GOING TO HAVE TO GIVE YOU A KRYPTONIAN AMNESIA KISS LIKE I USED ON LOIS AT THE END OF SUPERMAN 2.
COME AGAIN?
GET AWAY FROM ME YOU LOON!
I MUST KISS YOU FOR JIMMY'S SAFETY.
CRASH!
BAM!

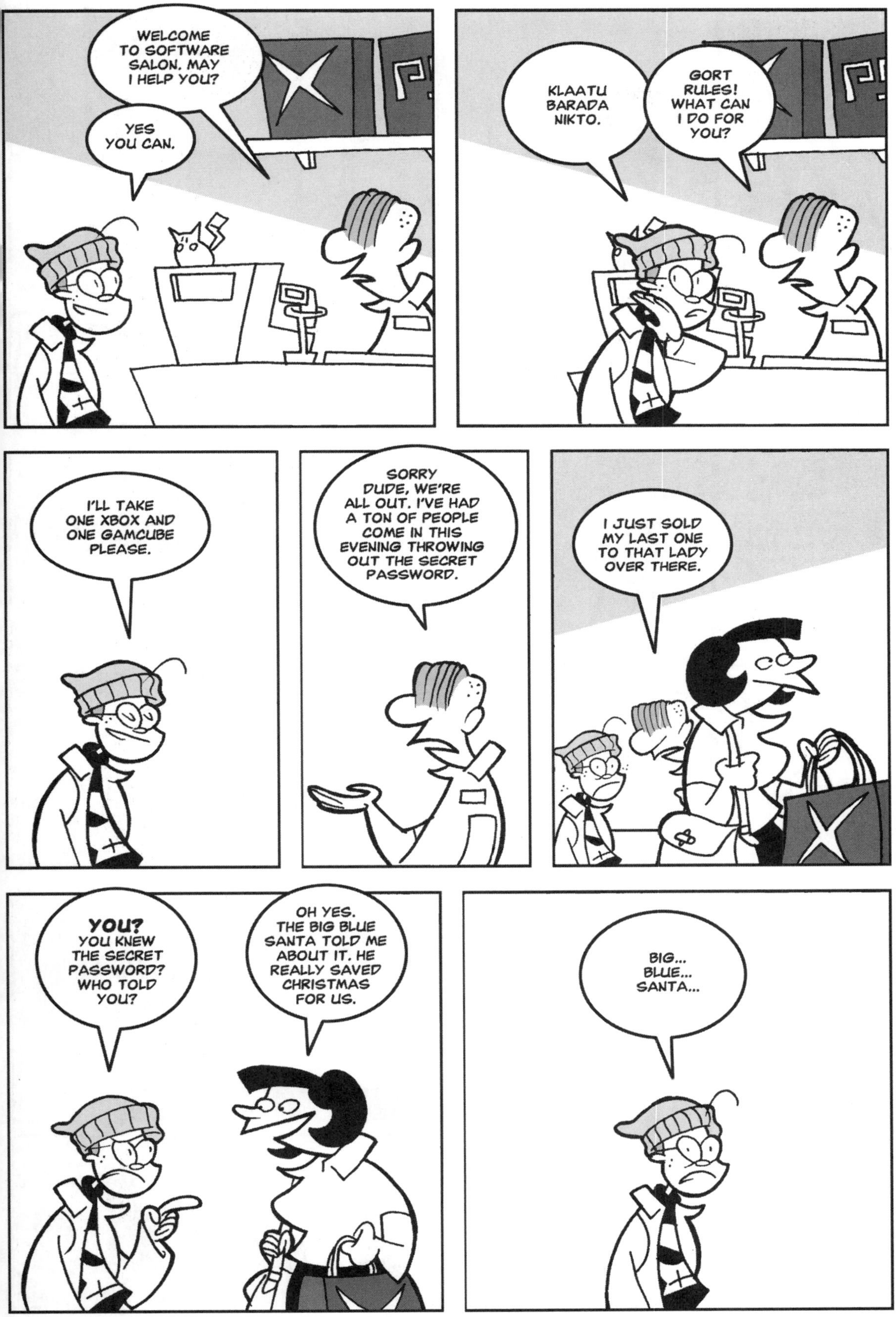
WELCOME TO SOFTWARE SALON. MAY I HELP YOU?
YES YOU CAN.
KLAATU BARADA NIKTO.
GORT RULES! WHAT CAN I DO FOR YOU?
I'LL TAKE ONE XBOX AND ONE GAMCUBE PLEASE.
SORRY DUDE, WE'RE ALL OUT. I'VE HAD A TON OF PEOPLE COME IN THIS EVENING THROWING OUT THE SECRET PASSWORD.
I JUST SOLD MY LAST ONE TO THAT LADY OVER THERE.
YOU? YOU KNEW THE SECRET PASSWORD? WHO TOLD YOU?
OH YES. THE BIG BLUE SANTA TOLD ME ABOUT IT. HE REALLY SAVED CHRISTMAS FOR US.
BIG... BLUE... SANTA...

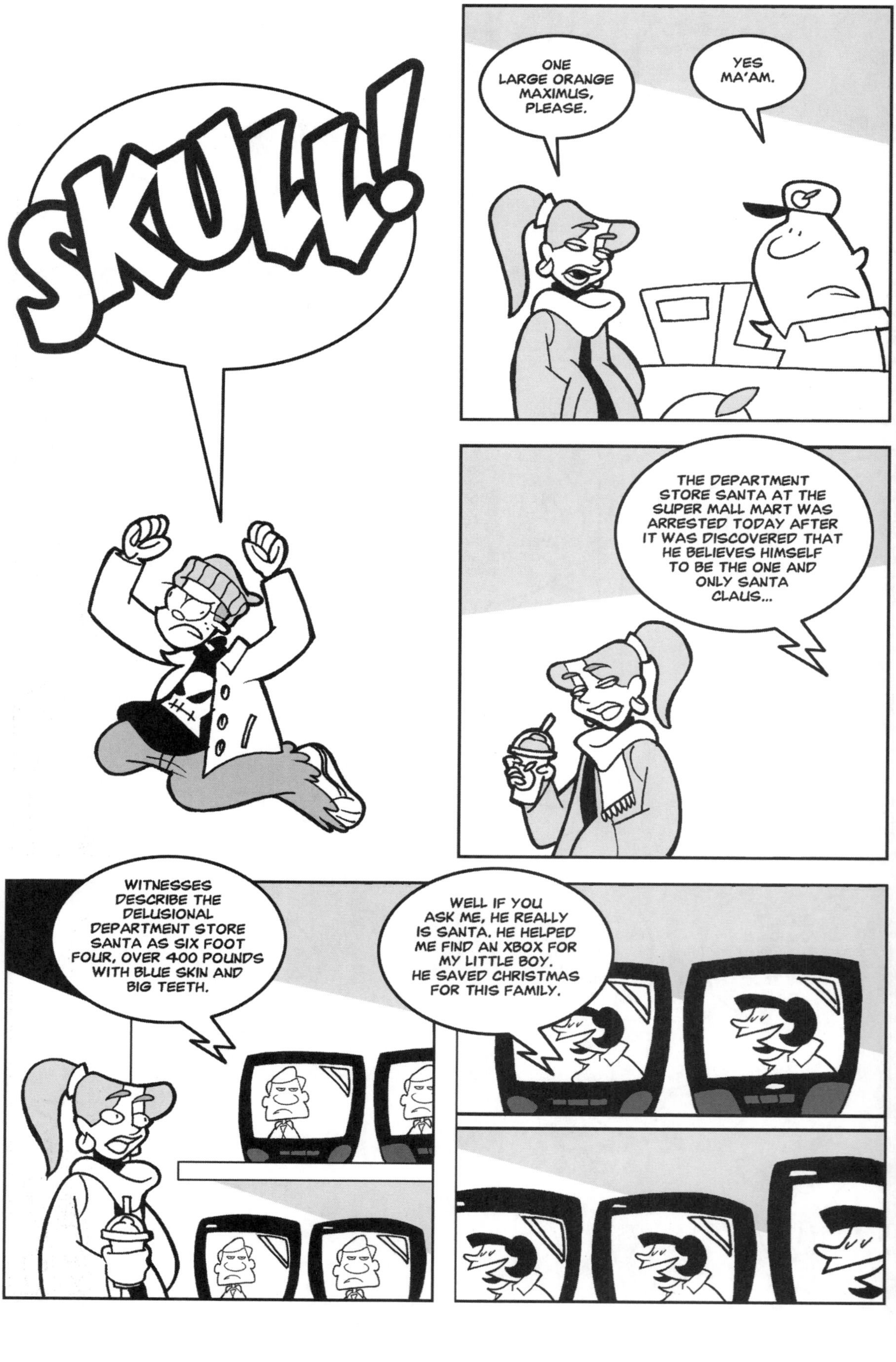
SKULL!
ONE LARGE ORANGE MAXIMUS, PLEASE.
YES MA'AM.
THE DEPARTMENT STORE SANTA AT THE SUPER MALL MART WAS ARRESTED TODAY AFTER IT WAS DISCOVERED THAT HE BELIEVES HIMSELF TO BE THE ONE AND ONLY SANTA CLAUS...
WITNESSES DESCRIBE THE DELUSIONAL DEPARTMENT STORE SANTA AS SIX FOOT FOUR, OVER 400 POUNDS WITH BLUE SKIN AND BIG TEETH.
WELL IF YOU ASK ME, HE REALLY IS SANTA. HE HELPED ME FIND AN XBOX FOR MY LITTLE BOY. HE SAVED CHRISTMAS FOR THIS FAMILY.

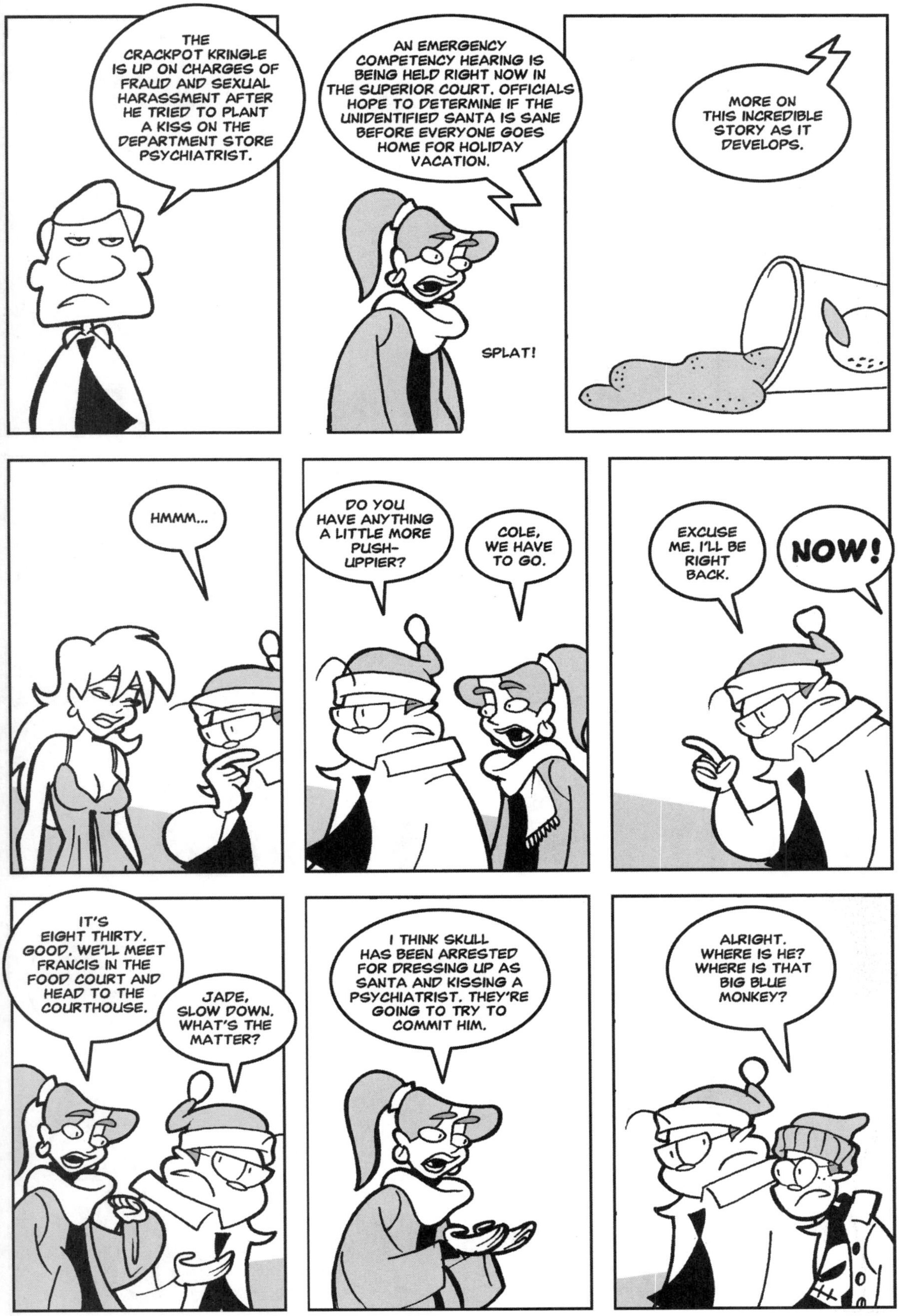
THE CRACKPOT KRINGLE IS UP ON CHARGES OF FRAUD AND SEXUAL HARASSMENT AFTER HE TRIED TO PLANT A KISS ON THE DEPARTMENT STORE PSYCHIATRIST.
AN EMERGENCY COMPETENCY HEARING IS BEING HELD RIGHT NOW IN THE SUPERIOR COURT. OFFICIALS HOPE TO DETERMINE IF THE UNIDENTIFIED SANTA IS SANE BEFORE EVERYONE GOES HOME FOR HOLIDAY VACATION.
SPLAT!
MORE ON THIS INCREDIBLE STORY AS IT DEVELOPS.
HMMM...
DO YOU HAVE ANYTHING A LITTLE MORE PUSH-UPPIER?
COLE, WE HAVE TO GO.
EXCUSE ME. I'LL BE RIGHT BACK.
NOW!
IT'S EIGHT THIRTY. GOOD. WE'LL MEET FRANCIS IN THE FOOD COURT AND HEAD TO THE COURTHOUSE.
JADE, SLOW DOWN. WHAT'S THE MATTER?
I THINK SKULL HAS BEEN ARRESTED FOR DRESSING UP AS SANTA AND KISSING A PSYCHIATRIST. THEY'RE GOING TO TRY TO COMMIT HIM.
ALRIGHT. WHERE IS HE? WHERE IS THAT BIG BLUE MONKEY?

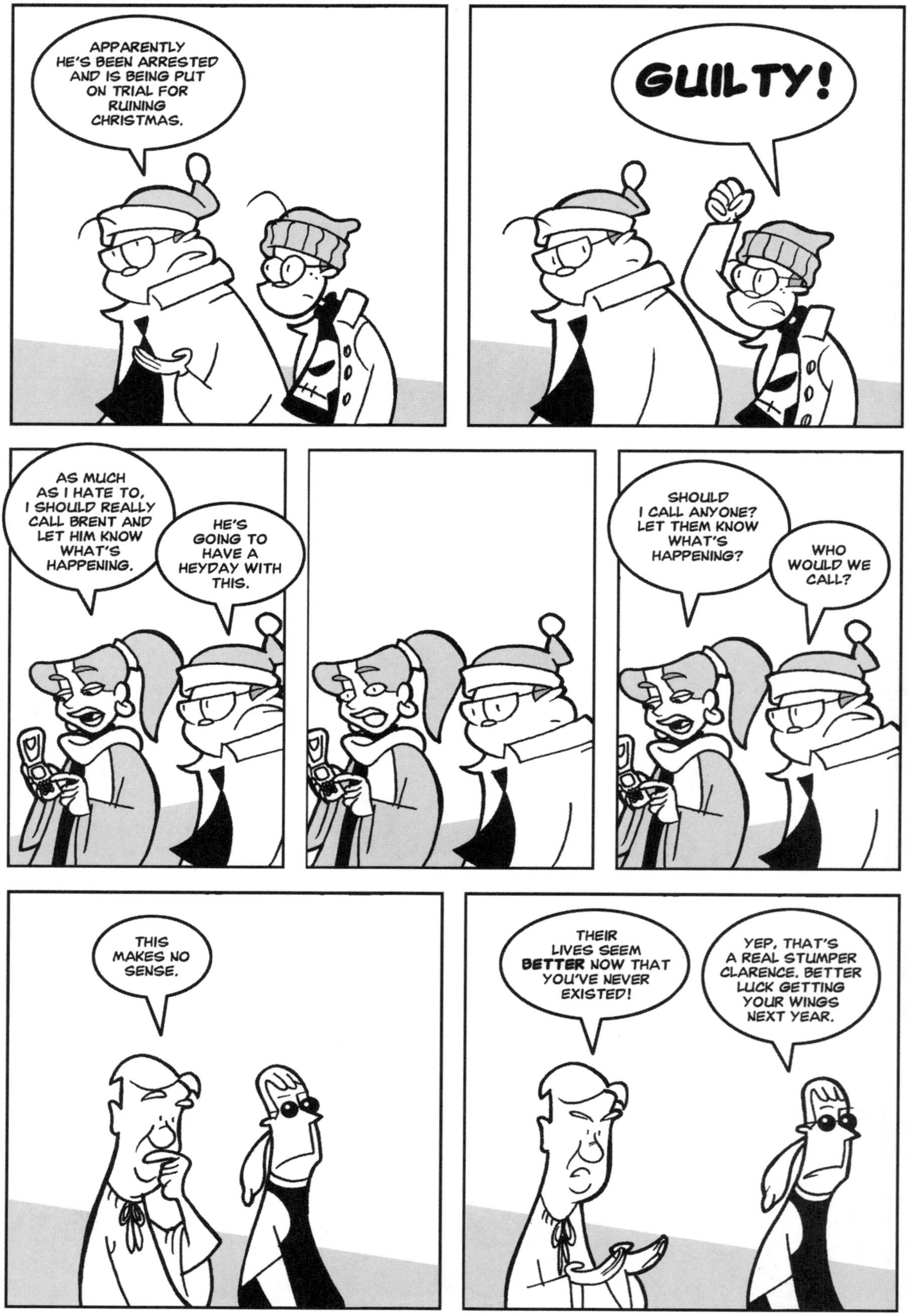

APPARENTLY HE'S BEEN ARRESTED AND IS BEING PUT ON TRIAL FOR RUINING CHRISTMAS.
GUILTY!
AS MUCH AS I HATE TO, I SHOULD REALLY CALL BRENT AND LET HIM KNOW WHAT'S HAPPENING.
HE'S GOING TO HAVE A HEYDAY WITH THIS.
SHOULD I CALL ANYONE? LET THEM KNOW WHAT'S HAPPENING?
WHO WOULD WE CALL?
THIS MAKES NO SENSE.
THEIR LIVES SEEM **BETTER** NOW THAT YOU'VE NEVER EXISTED!
YEP, THAT'S A REAL STUMPER CLARENCE. BETTER LUCK GETTING YOUR WINGS NEXT YEAR.

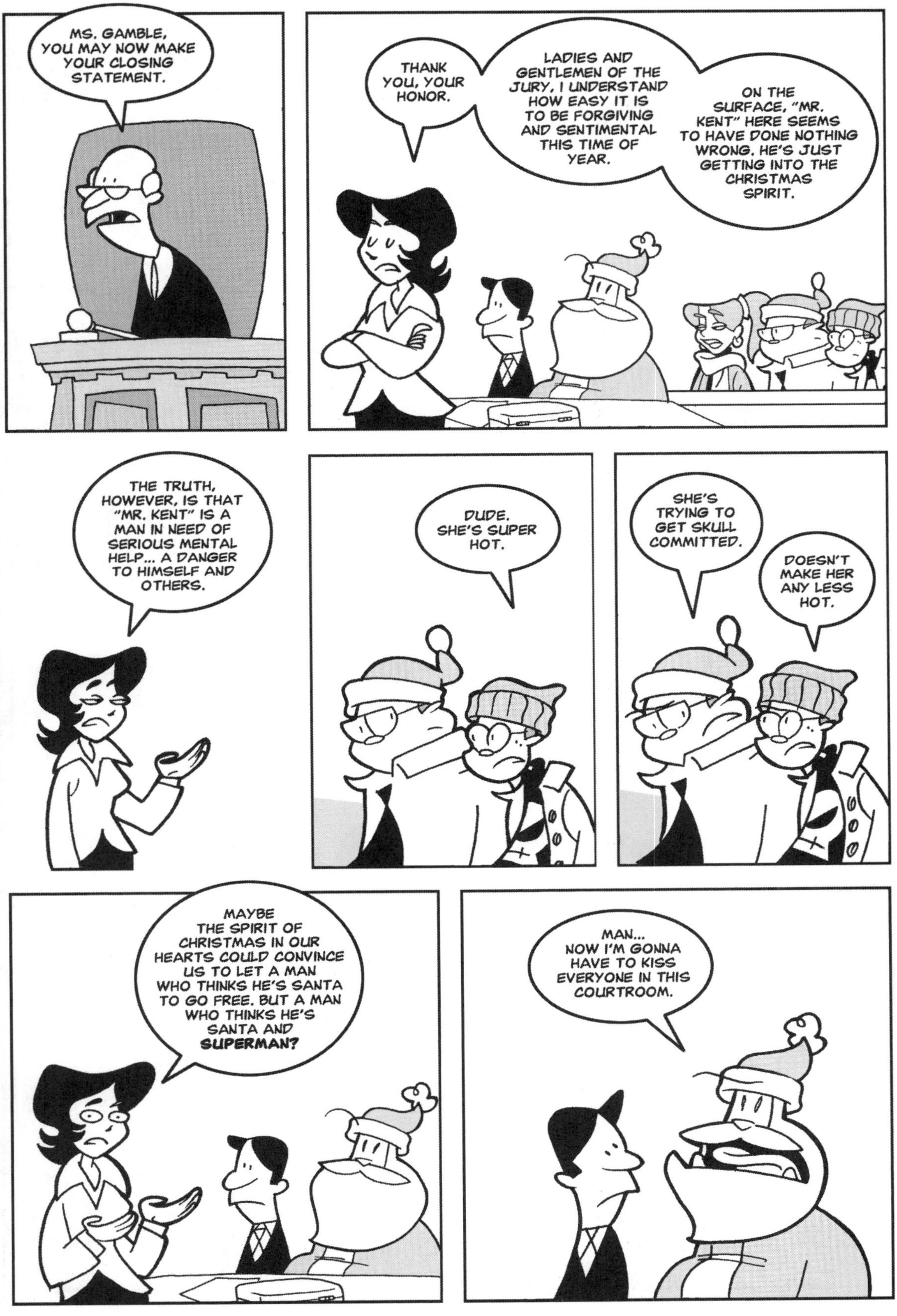
MS. GAMBLE, YOU MAY NOW MAKE YOUR CLOSING STATEMENT.
THANK YOU, YOUR HONOR.
LADIES AND GENTLEMEN OF THE JURY, I UNDERSTAND HOW EASY IT IS TO BE FORGIVING AND SENTIMENTAL THIS TIME OF YEAR.
ON THE SURFACE, "MR. KENT" HERE SEEMS TO HAVE DONE NOTHING WRONG. HE'S JUST GETTING INTO THE CHRISTMAS SPIRIT.
THE TRUTH, HOWEVER, IS THAT "MR. KENT" IS A MAN IN NEED OF SERIOUS MENTAL HELP... A DANGER TO HIMSELF AND OTHERS.
DUDE. SHE'S SUPER HOT.
SHE'S TRYING TO GET SKULL COMMITTED.
DOESN'T MAKE HER ANY LESS HOT.
MAYBE THE SPIRIT OF CHRISTMAS IN OUR HEARTS COULD CONVINCE US TO LET A MAN WHO THINKS HE'S SANTA TO GO FREE. BUT A MAN WHO THINKS HE'S SANTA AND **SUPERMAN?**
MAN... NOW I'M GONNA HAVE TO KISS EVERYONE IN THIS COURTROOM.

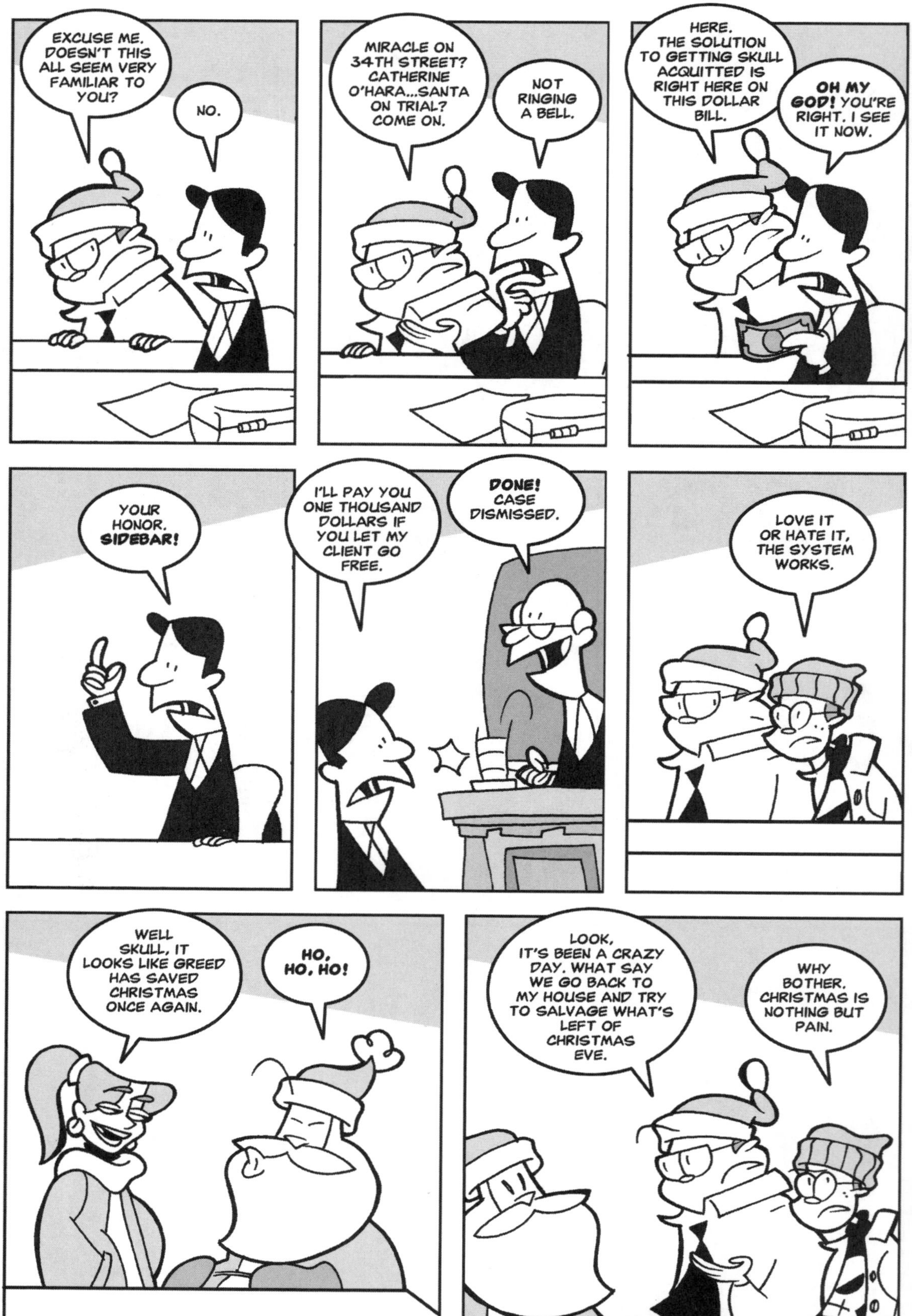
EXCUSE ME. DOESN'T THIS ALL SEEM VERY FAMILIAR TO YOU?
NO.
MIRACLE ON 34TH STREET? CATHERINE O'HARA...SANTA ON TRIAL? COME ON.
NOT RINGING A BELL.
HERE. THE SOLUTION TO GETTING SKULL ACQUITTED IS RIGHT HERE ON THIS DOLLAR BILL.
OH MY GOD! YOU'RE RIGHT. I SEE IT NOW.
YOUR HONOR. SIDEBAR!
I'LL PAY YOU ONE THOUSAND DOLLARS IF YOU LET MY CLIENT GO FREE.
DONE! CASE DISMISSED.
LOVE IT OR HATE IT, THE SYSTEM WORKS.
WELL SKULL, IT LOOKS LIKE GREED HAS SAVED CHRISTMAS ONCE AGAIN.
HO, HO, HO!
LOOK, IT'S BEEN A CRAZY DAY. WHAT SAY WE GO BACK TO MY HOUSE AND TRY TO SALVAGE WHAT'S LEFT OF CHRISTMAS EVE.
WHY BOTHER. CHRISTMAS IS NOTHING BUT PAIN.

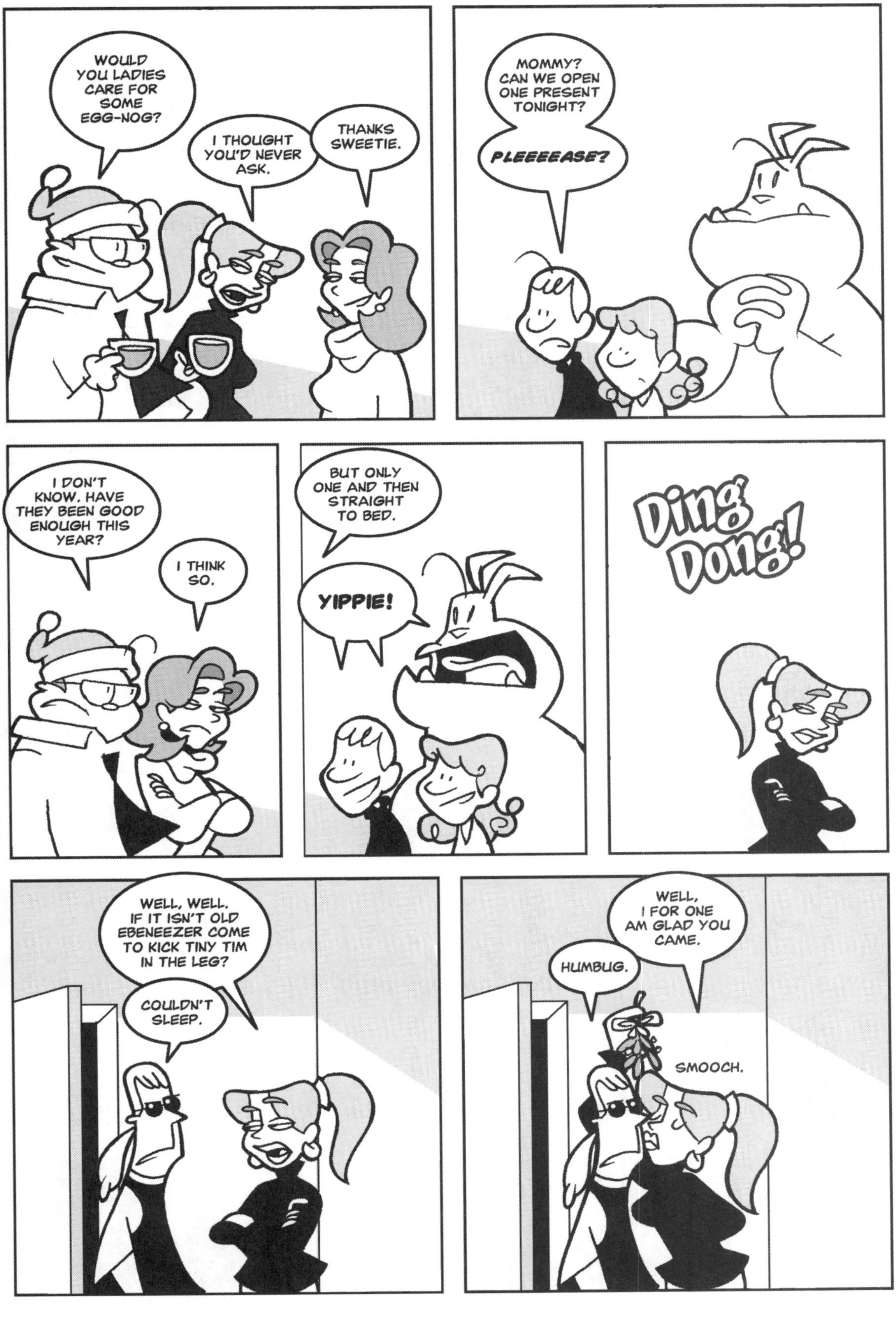
WOULD YOU LADIES CARE FOR SOME EGG-NOG?
I THOUGHT YOU'D NEVER ASK.
THANKS SWEETIE.
MOMMY? CAN WE OPEN ONE PRESENT TONIGHT?
PLEEEEEASE?
I DON'T KNOW. HAVE THEY BEEN GOOD ENOUGH THIS YEAR?
I THINK SO.
BUT ONLY ONE AND THEN STRAIGHT TO BED.
YIPPIE!
Ding Dong!
WELL, WELL. IF IT ISN'T OLD EBENEEZER COME TO KICK TINY TIM IN THE LEG?
COULDN'T SLEEP.
HUMBUG.
WELL, I FOR ONE AM GLAD YOU CAME.
SMOOCH.

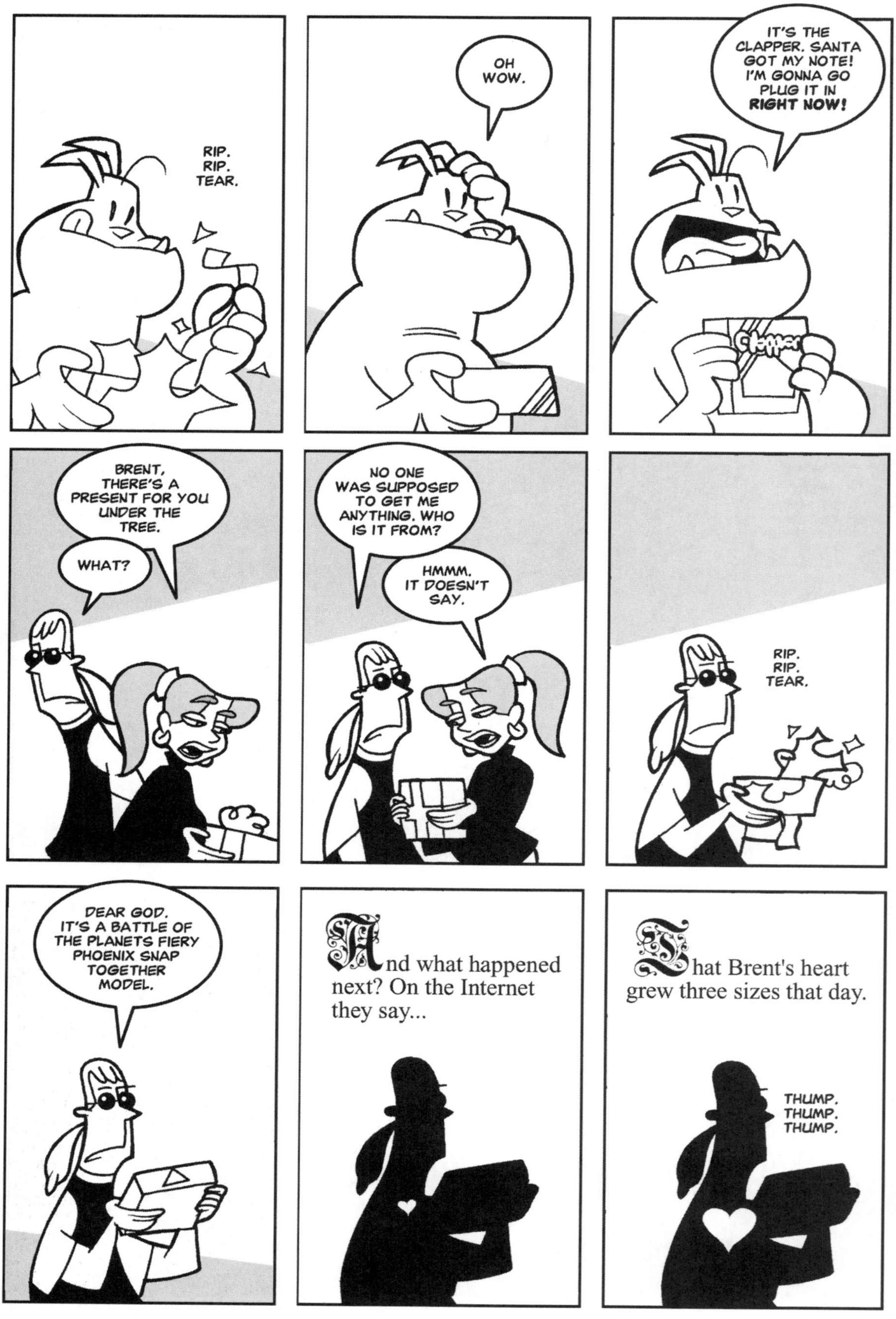
RIP. RIP. TEAR.
OH WOW.
IT'S THE CLAPPER. SANTA GOT MY NOTE! I'M GONNA GO PLUG IT IN RIGHT NOW!
Clapper
BRENT, THERE'S A PRESENT FOR YOU UNDER THE TREE.
WHAT?
NO ONE WAS SUPPOSED TO GET ME ANYTHING. WHO IS IT FROM?
HMMM. IT DOESN'T SAY.
RIP. RIP. TEAR.
DEAR GOD. IT'S A BATTLE OF THE PLANETS FIERY PHOENIX SNAP TOGETHER MODEL.
And what happened next? On the Internet they say...
That Brent's heart grew three sizes that day.
THUMP. THUMP. THUMP.

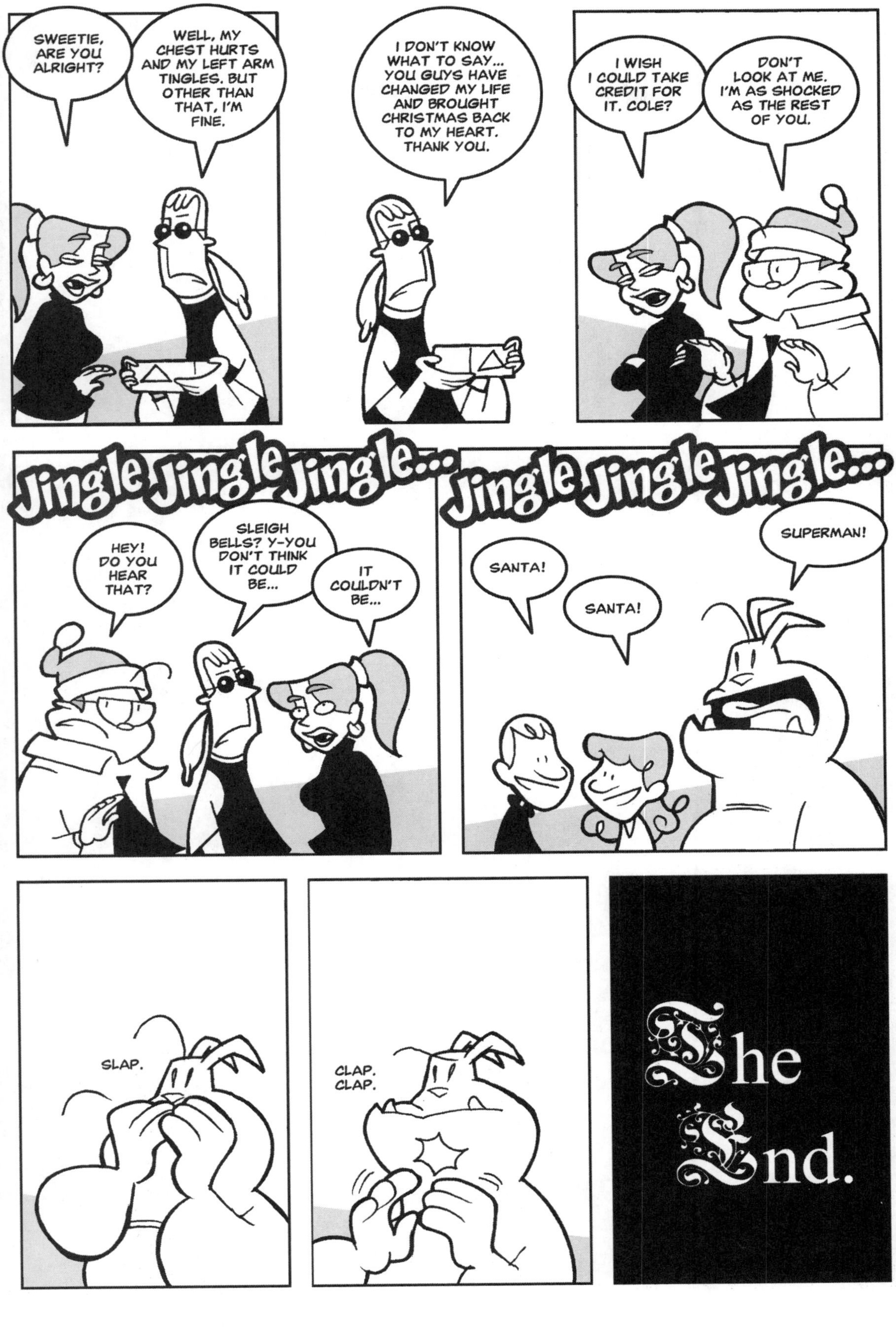
SWEETIE, ARE YOU ALRIGHT?
WELL, MY CHEST HURTS AND MY LEFT ARM TINGLES. BUT OTHER THAN THAT, I'M FINE.
I DON'T KNOW WHAT TO SAY... YOU GUYS HAVE CHANGED MY LIFE AND BROUGHT CHRISTMAS BACK TO MY HEART. THANK YOU.
I WISH I COULD TAKE CREDIT FOR IT. COLE?
DON'T LOOK AT ME. I'M AS SHOCKED AS THE REST OF YOU.
Jingle Jingle Jingle...
HEY! DO YOU HEAR THAT?
SLEIGH BELLS? Y-YOU DON'T THINK IT COULD BE...
IT COULDN'T BE...
Jingle Jingle Jingle...
SANTA!
SANTA!
SUPERMAN!
SLAP.
CLAP. CLAP.
The End.

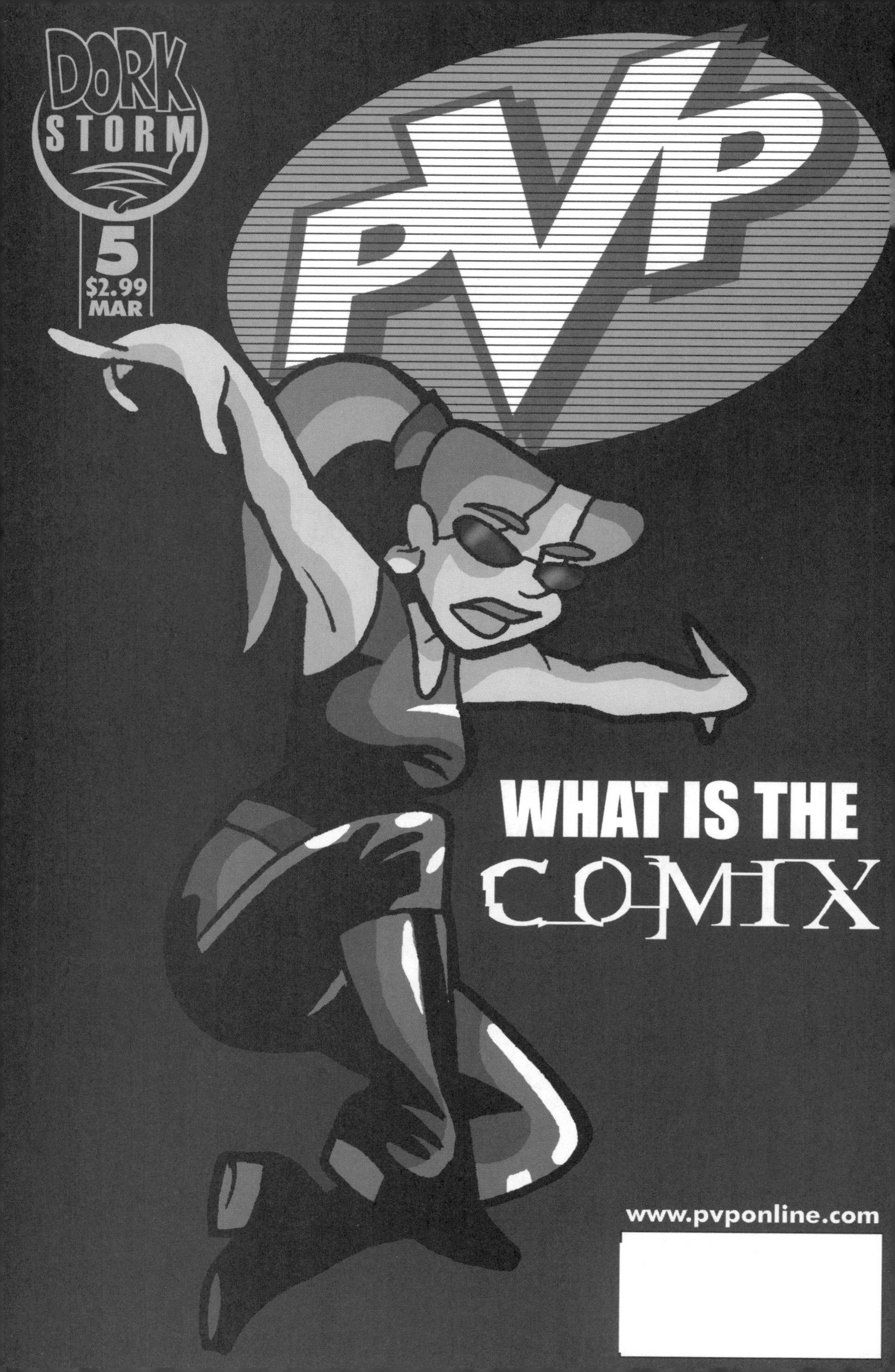
DORK STORM
5
$2.99
MAR
PVP
WHAT IS THE
COMIX
www.pvponline.com

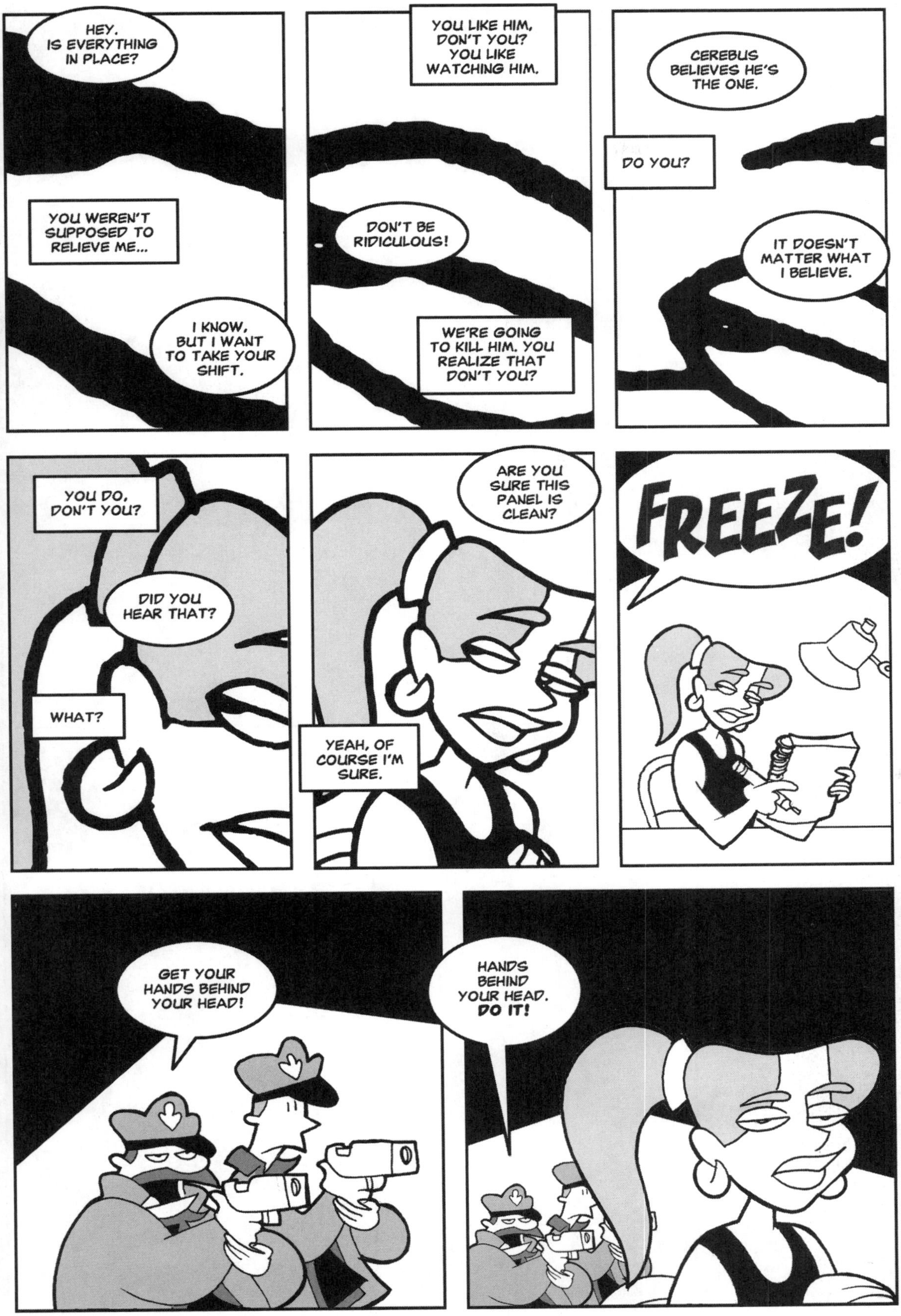

HEY. IS EVERYTHING IN PLACE?
YOU WEREN'T SUPPOSED TO RELIEVE ME...
I KNOW, BUT I WANT TO TAKE YOUR SHIFT.
YOU LIKE HIM, DON'T YOU? YOU LIKE WATCHING HIM.
DON'T BE RIDICULOUS!
WE'RE GOING TO KILL HIM. YOU REALIZE THAT DON'T YOU?
CEREBUS BELIEVES HE'S THE ONE.
DO YOU?
IT DOESN'T MATTER WHAT I BELIEVE.
YOU DO, DON'T YOU?
DID YOU HEAR THAT?
WHAT?
ARE YOU SURE THIS PANEL IS CLEAN?
YEAH, OF COURSE I'M SURE.
FREEZE!
GET YOUR HANDS BEHIND YOUR HEAD!
HANDS BEHIND YOUR HEAD. **DO IT!**

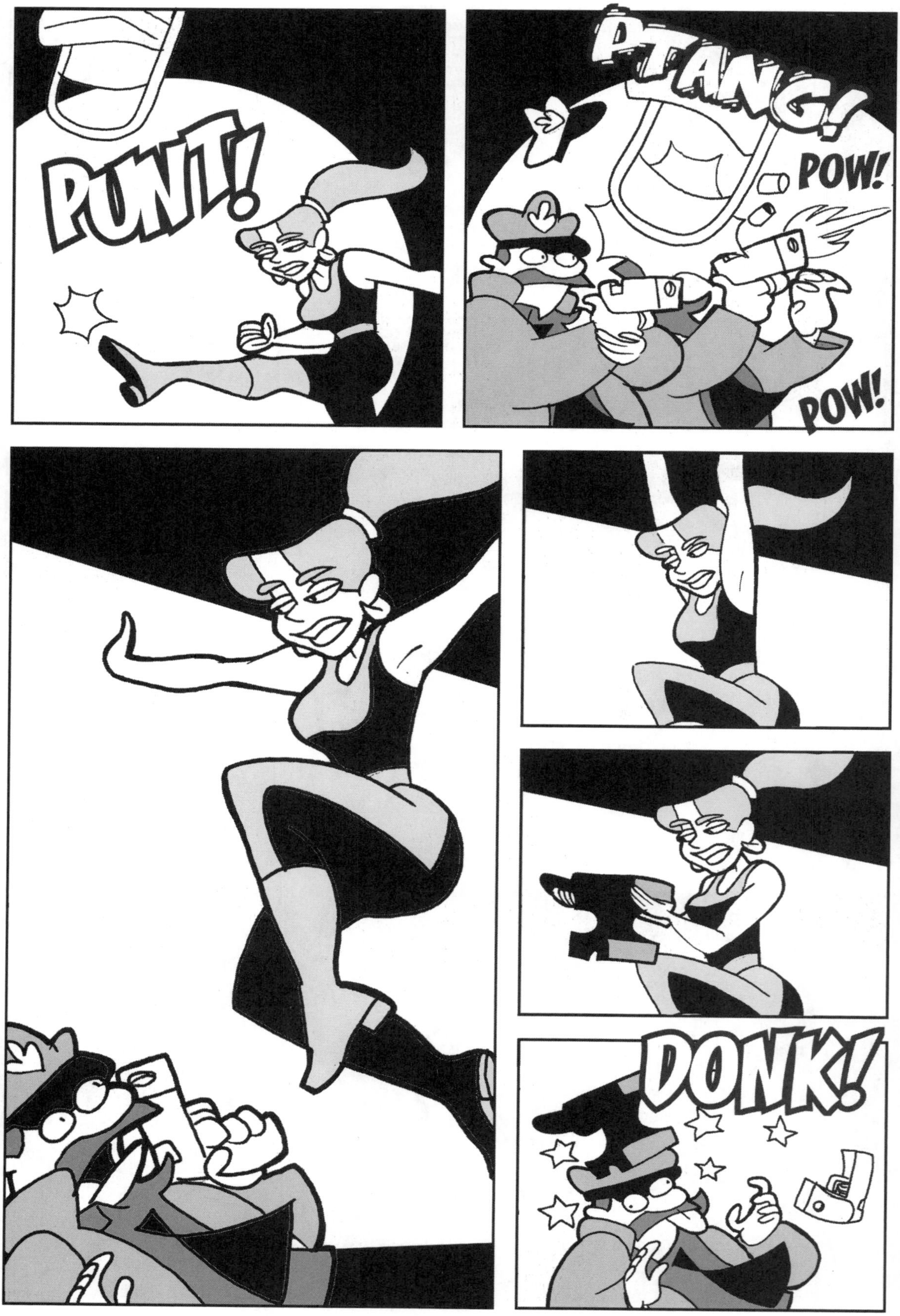
PUNT!
PTANG!
POW!
POW!
DONK!

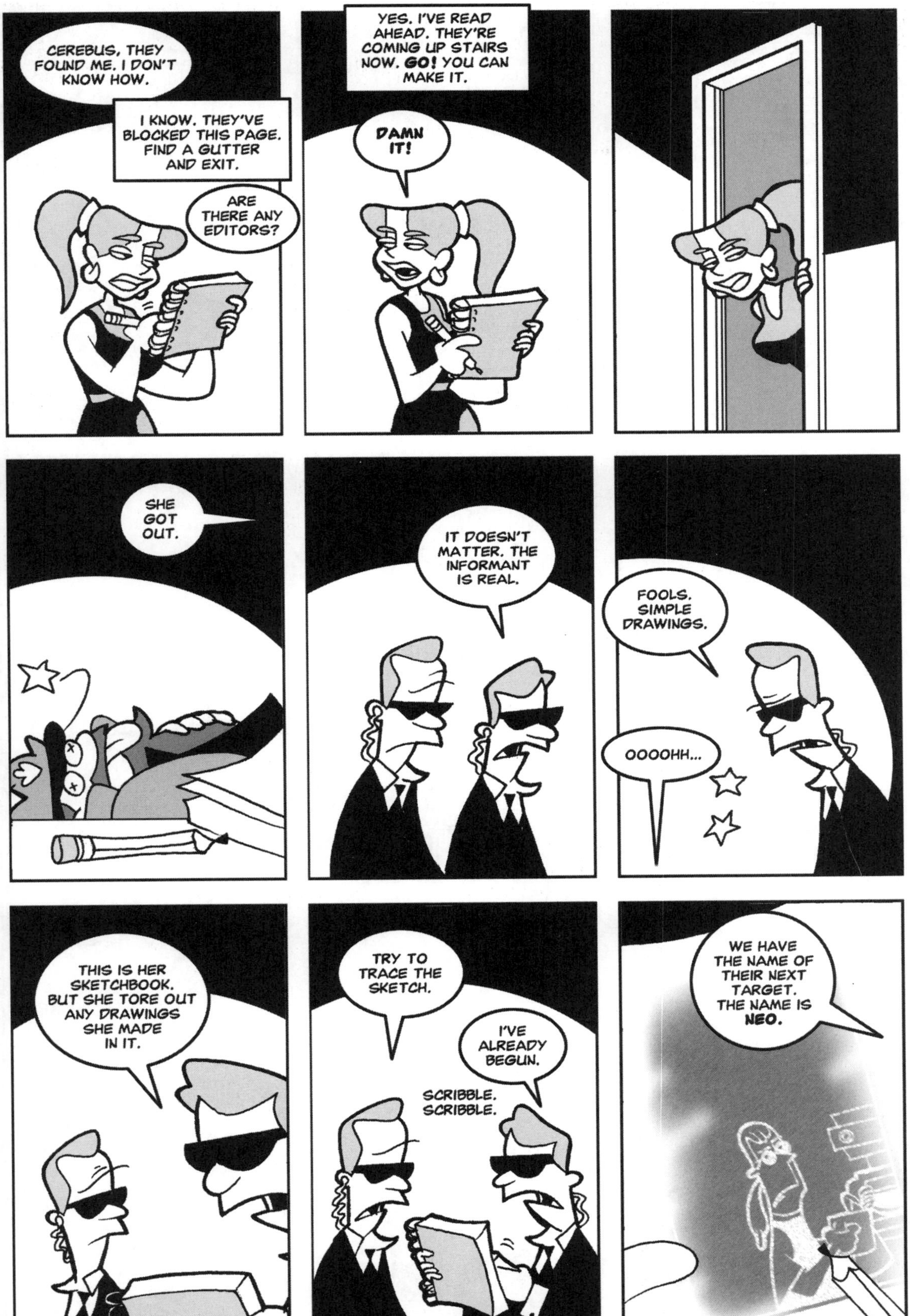
CEREBUS, THEY FOUND ME. I DON'T KNOW HOW.
I KNOW. THEY'VE BLOCKED THIS PAGE. FIND A GUTTER AND EXIT.
ARE THERE ANY EDITORS?
YES. I'VE READ AHEAD. THEY'RE COMING UP STAIRS NOW. GO! YOU CAN MAKE IT.
DAMN IT!
SHE GOT OUT.
IT DOESN'T MATTER. THE INFORMANT IS REAL.
FOOLS. SIMPLE DRAWINGS.
OOOOHH...
THIS IS HER SKETCHBOOK. BUT SHE TORE OUT ANY DRAWINGS SHE MADE IN IT.
TRY TO TRACE THE SKETCH.
I'VE ALREADY BEGUN.
SCRIBBLE. SCRIBBLE.
WE HAVE THE NAME OF THEIR NEXT TARGET. THE NAME IS NEO.

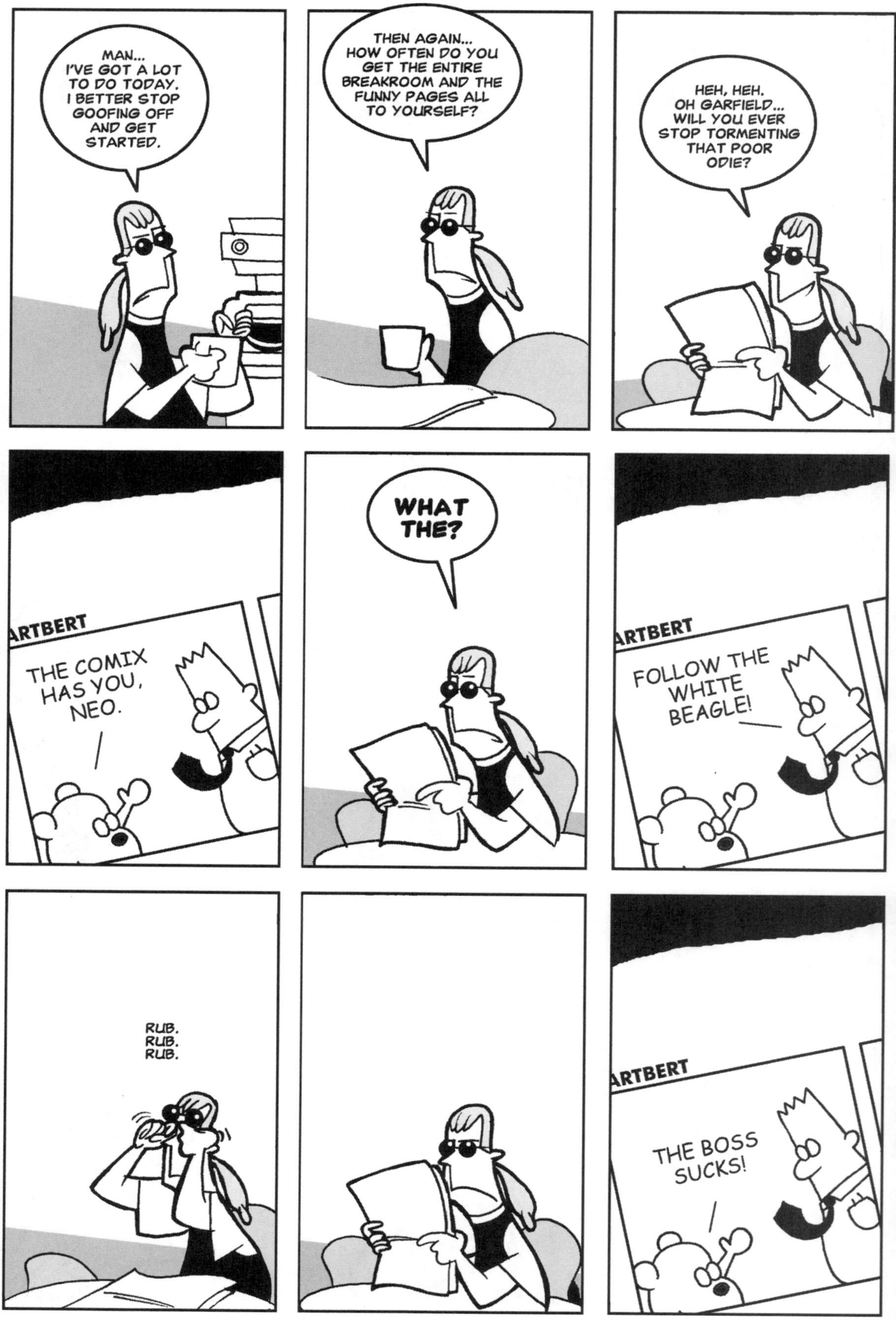
MAN... I'VE GOT A LOT TO DO TODAY. I BETTER STOP GOOFING OFF AND GET STARTED.
THEN AGAIN... HOW OFTEN DO YOU GET THE ENTIRE BREAKROOM AND THE FUNNY PAGES ALL TO YOURSELF?
HEH, HEH. OH GARFIELD... WILL YOU EVER STOP TORMENTING THAT POOR ODIE?
ARTBERT
THE COMIX HAS YOU, NEO.
WHAT THE?
ARTBERT
FOLLOW THE WHITE BEAGLE!
RUB. RUB. RUB.
ARTBERT
THE BOSS SUCKS!

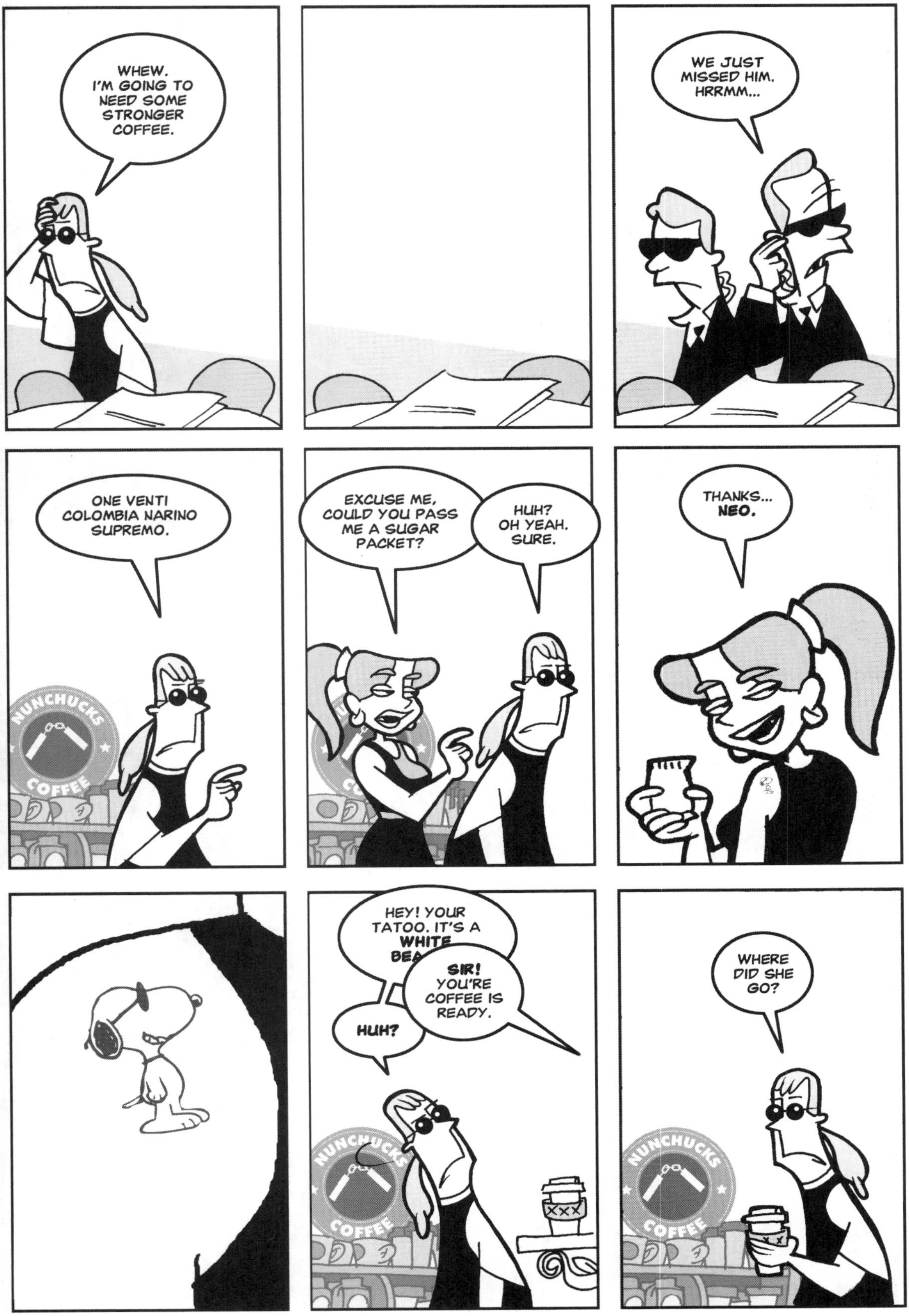
WHEW. I'M GOING TO NEED SOME STRONGER COFFEE.
WE JUST MISSED HIM. HRRMM...
ONE VENTI COLOMBIA NARINO SUPREMO.
NUNCHUCKS COFFEE
EXCUSE ME, COULD YOU PASS ME A SUGAR PACKET?
HUH? OH YEAH. SURE.
THANKS... **NEO.**
HEY! YOUR TATOO. IT'S A **WHITE**
HUH?
SIR! YOU'RE COFFEE IS READY.
NUNCHUCKS COFFEE
WHERE DID SHE GO?
NUNCHUCKS COFFEE

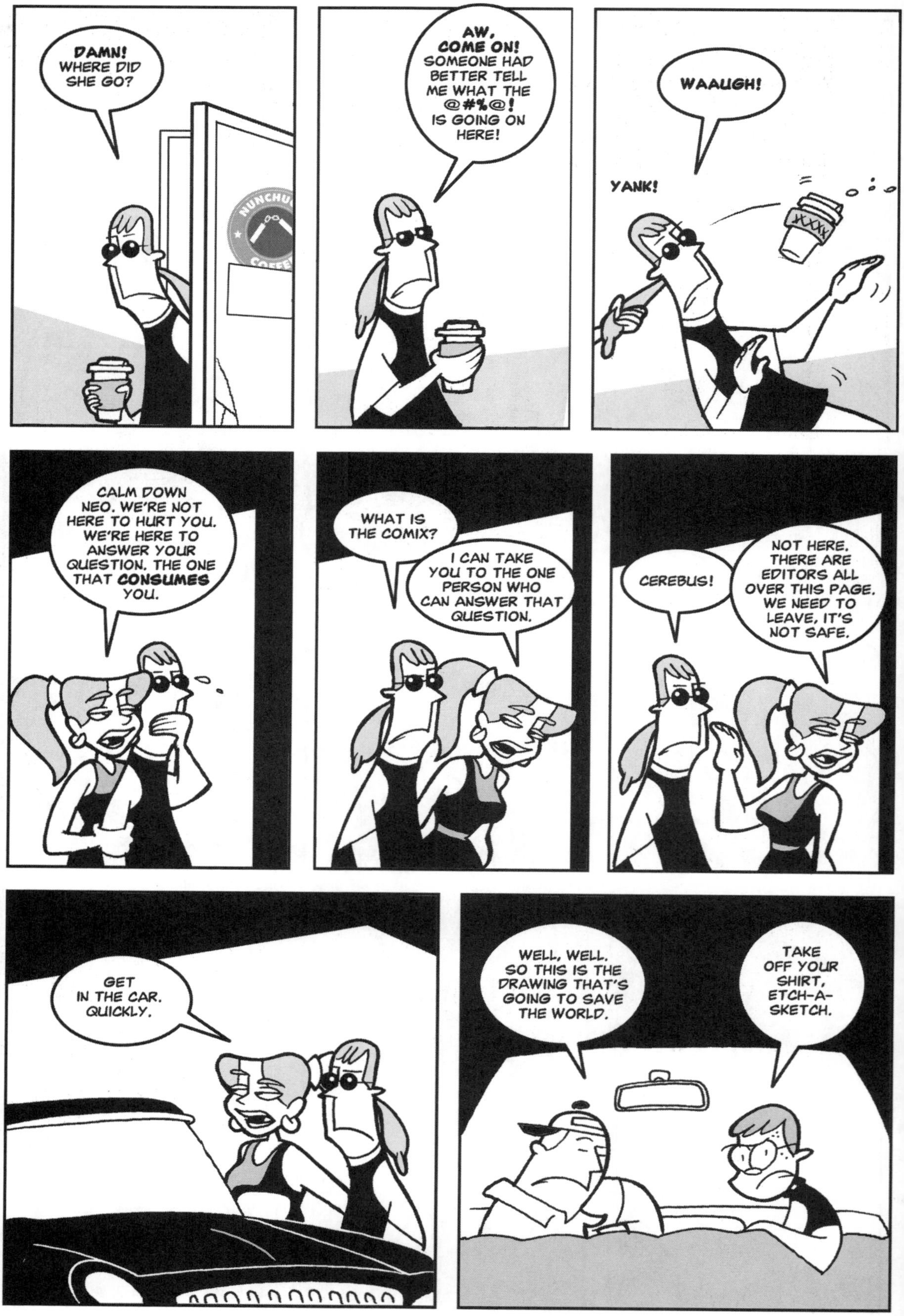
DAMN! WHERE DID SHE GO?
NUNCHUCK COFFEE
AW, COME ON! SOMEONE HAD BETTER TELL ME WHAT THE @#%@! IS GOING ON HERE!
WAAUGH!
YANK!
XXXX
CALM DOWN NEO. WE'RE NOT HERE TO HURT YOU. WE'RE HERE TO ANSWER YOUR QUESTION. THE ONE THAT CONSUMES YOU.
WHAT IS THE COMIX?
I CAN TAKE YOU TO THE ONE PERSON WHO CAN ANSWER THAT QUESTION.
CEREBUS!
NOT HERE. THERE ARE EDITORS ALL OVER THIS PAGE. WE NEED TO LEAVE, IT'S NOT SAFE.
GET IN THE CAR. QUICKLY.
WELL, WELL. SO THIS IS THE DRAWING THAT'S GOING TO SAVE THE WORLD.
TAKE OFF YOUR SHIRT, ETCH-A-SKETCH.

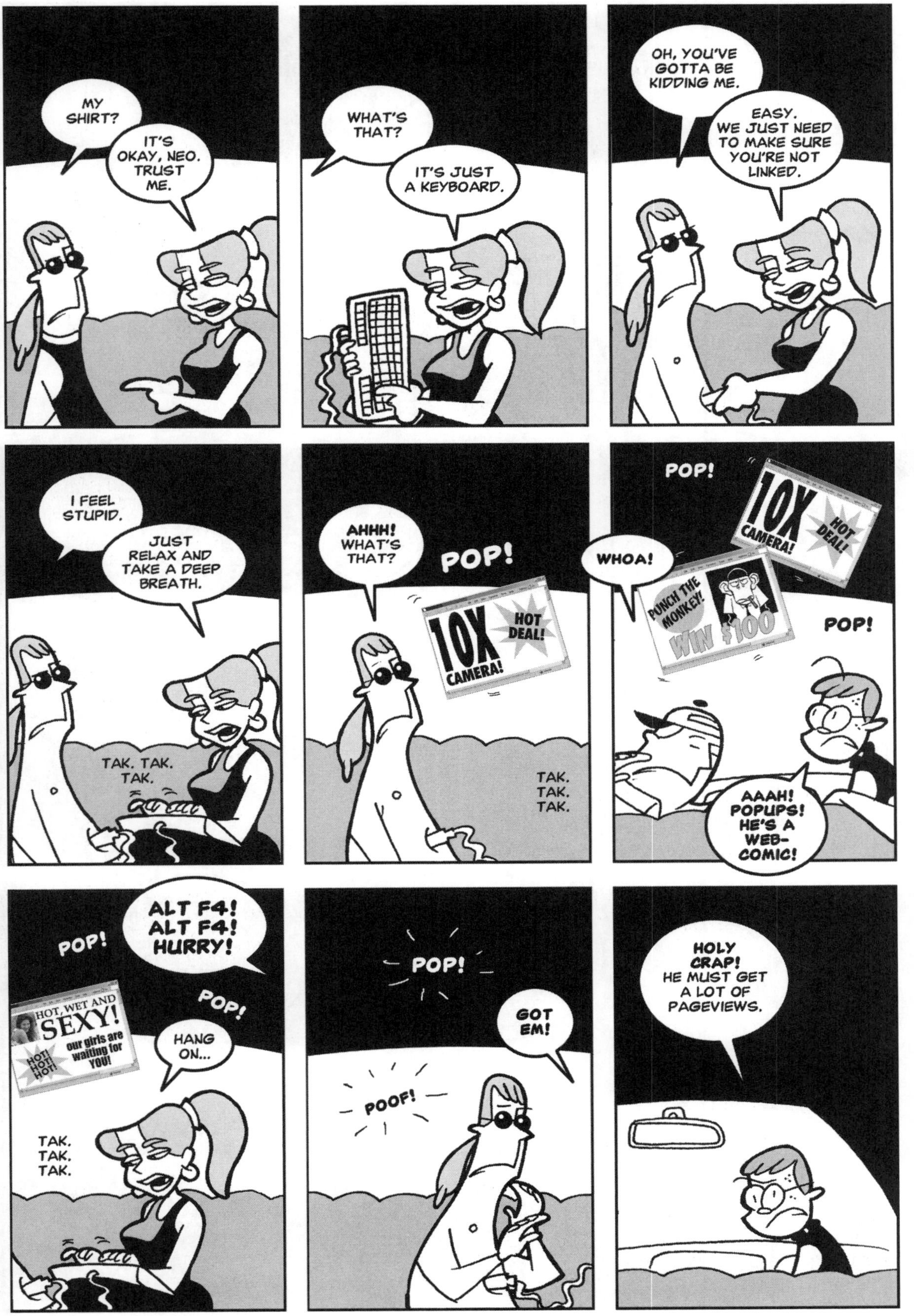
MY SHIRT?
IT'S OKAY, NEO. TRUST ME.
WHAT'S THAT?
IT'S JUST A KEYBOARD.
OH, YOU'VE GOTTA BE KIDDING ME.
EASY. WE JUST NEED TO MAKE SURE YOU'RE NOT LINKED.
I FEEL STUPID.
JUST RELAX AND TAKE A DEEP BREATH.
TAK. TAK. TAK.
AHHH! WHAT'S THAT?
POP!
10X CAMERA!
HOT DEAL!
TAK. TAK. TAK.
POP!
10X CAMERA!
HOT DEAL!
WHOA!
PUNCH THE MONKEY!
WIN $100
POP!
AAAH! POPUPS! HE'S A WEB-COMIC!
POP!
ALT F4! ALT F4! HURRY!
POP!
HOT, WET AND SEXY!
HOT! HOT! HOT!
our girls are waiting for YOU!
HANG ON...
TAK. TAK. TAK.
POP!
GOT EM!
POOF!
HOLY CRAP! HE MUST GET A LOT OF PAGEVIEWS.

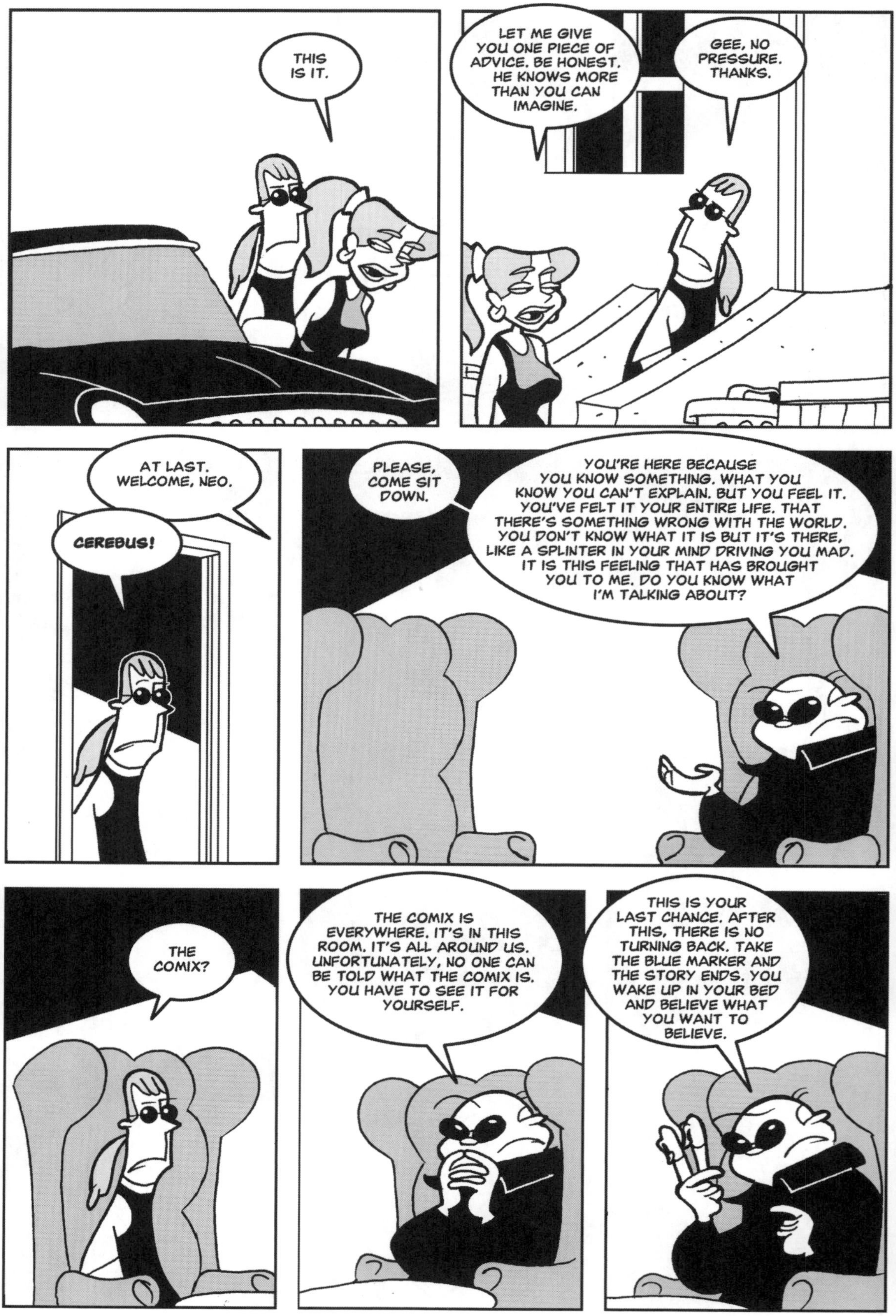
THIS IS IT.
LET ME GIVE YOU ONE PIECE OF ADVICE. BE HONEST. HE KNOWS MORE THAN YOU CAN IMAGINE.
GEE, NO PRESSURE. THANKS.
AT LAST. WELCOME, NEO.
CEREBUS!
PLEASE, COME SIT DOWN.
YOU'RE HERE BECAUSE YOU KNOW SOMETHING. WHAT YOU KNOW YOU CAN'T EXPLAIN. BUT YOU FEEL IT. YOU'VE FELT IT YOUR ENTIRE LIFE. THAT THERE'S SOMETHING WRONG WITH THE WORLD. YOU DON'T KNOW WHAT IT IS BUT IT'S THERE, LIKE A SPLINTER IN YOUR MIND DRIVING YOU MAD. IT IS THIS FEELING THAT HAS BROUGHT YOU TO ME. DO YOU KNOW WHAT I'M TALKING ABOUT?
THE COMIX?
THE COMIX IS EVERYWHERE. IT'S IN THIS ROOM. IT'S ALL AROUND US. UNFORTUNATELY, NO ONE CAN BE TOLD WHAT THE COMIX IS. YOU HAVE TO SEE IT FOR YOURSELF.
THIS IS YOUR LAST CHANCE. AFTER THIS, THERE IS NO TURNING BACK. TAKE THE BLUE MARKER AND THE STORY ENDS. YOU WAKE UP IN YOUR BED AND BELIEVE WHAT YOU WANT TO BELIEVE.

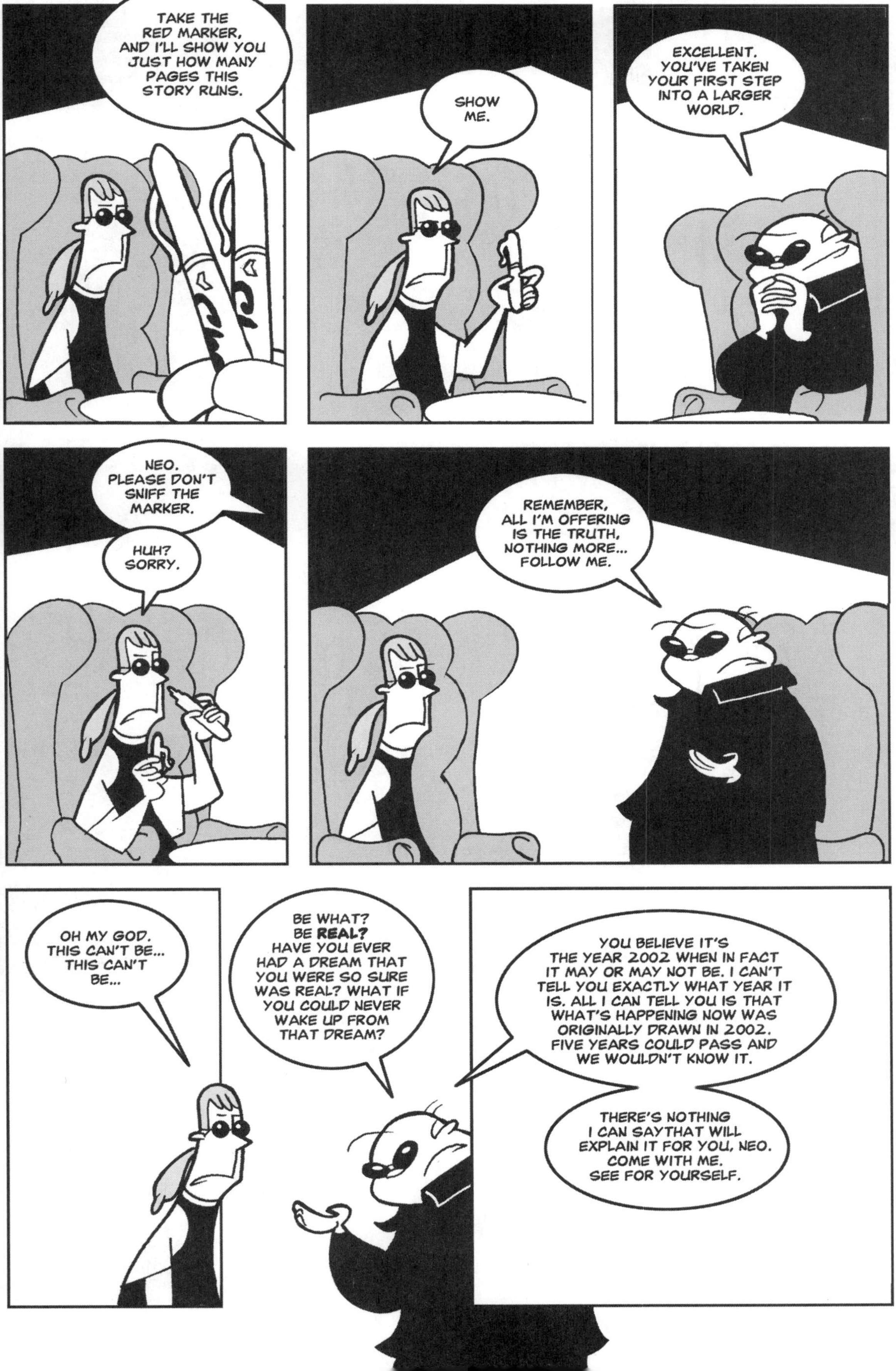
TAKE THE RED MARKER, AND I'LL SHOW YOU JUST HOW MANY PAGES THIS STORY RUNS.
SHOW ME.
EXCELLENT. YOU'VE TAKEN YOUR FIRST STEP INTO A LARGER WORLD.
NEO. PLEASE DON'T SNIFF THE MARKER.
HUH? SORRY.
REMEMBER, ALL I'M OFFERING IS THE TRUTH, NOTHING MORE... FOLLOW ME.
OH MY GOD. THIS CAN'T BE... THIS CAN'T BE...
BE WHAT? BE **REAL?** HAVE YOU EVER HAD A DREAM THAT YOU WERE SO SURE WAS REAL? WHAT IF YOU COULD NEVER WAKE UP FROM THAT DREAM?
YOU BELIEVE IT'S THE YEAR 2002 WHEN IN FACT IT MAY OR MAY NOT BE. I CAN'T TELL YOU EXACTLY WHAT YEAR IT IS. ALL I CAN TELL YOU IS THAT WHAT'S HAPPENING NOW WAS ORIGINALLY DRAWN IN 2002. FIVE YEARS COULD PASS AND WE WOULDN'T KNOW IT.
THERE'S NOTHING I CAN SAYTHAT WILL EXPLAIN IT FOR YOU, NEO. COME WITH ME. SEE FOR YOURSELF.

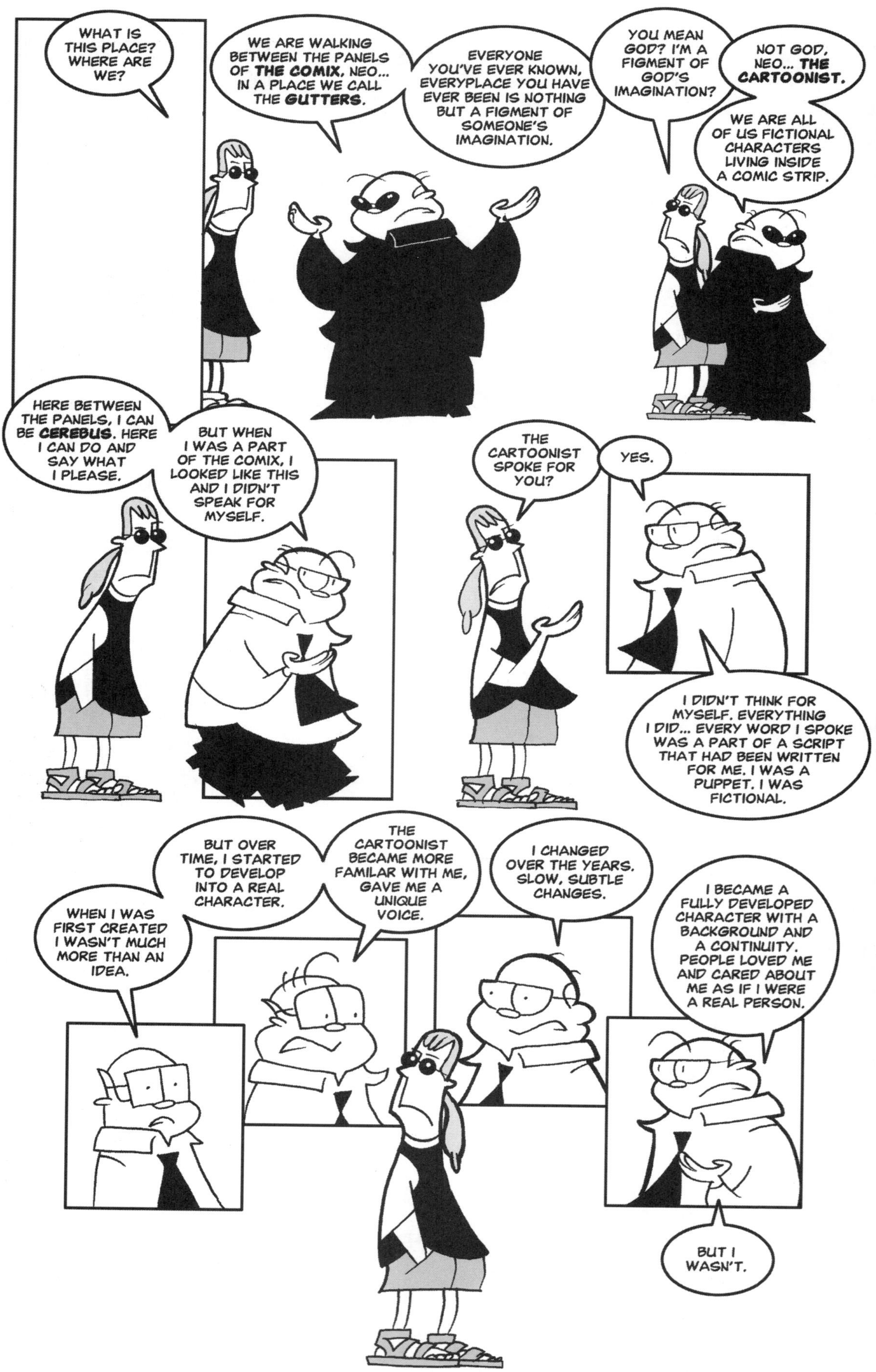
WHAT IS THIS PLACE? WHERE ARE WE?
WE ARE WALKING BETWEEN THE PANELS OF THE COMIX, NEO... IN A PLACE WE CALL THE GUTTERS.
EVERYONE YOU'VE EVER KNOWN, EVERYPLACE YOU HAVE EVER BEEN IS NOTHING BUT A FIGMENT OF SOMEONE'S IMAGINATION.
YOU MEAN GOD? I'M A FIGMENT OF GOD'S IMAGINATION?
NOT GOD, NEO... THE CARTOONIST.
WE ARE ALL OF US FICTIONAL CHARACTERS LIVING INSIDE A COMIC STRIP.
HERE BETWEEN THE PANELS, I CAN BE CEREBUS. HERE I CAN DO AND SAY WHAT I PLEASE.
BUT WHEN I WAS A PART OF THE COMIX, I LOOKED LIKE THIS AND I DIDN'T SPEAK FOR MYSELF.
THE CARTOONIST SPOKE FOR YOU?
YES.
I DIDN'T THINK FOR MYSELF. EVERYTHING I DID... EVERY WORD I SPOKE WAS A PART OF A SCRIPT THAT HAD BEEN WRITTEN FOR ME. I WAS A PUPPET. I WAS FICTIONAL.
WHEN I WAS FIRST CREATED I WASN'T MUCH MORE THAN AN IDEA.
BUT OVER TIME, I STARTED TO DEVELOP INTO A REAL CHARACTER.
THE CARTOONIST BECAME MORE FAMILAR WITH ME, GAVE ME A UNIQUE VOICE.
I CHANGED OVER THE YEARS. SLOW, SUBTLE CHANGES.
I BECAME A FULLY DEVELOPED CHARACTER WITH A BACKGROUND AND A CONTINUITY. PEOPLE LOVED ME AND CARED ABOUT ME AS IF I WERE A REAL PERSON.
BUT I WASN'T.

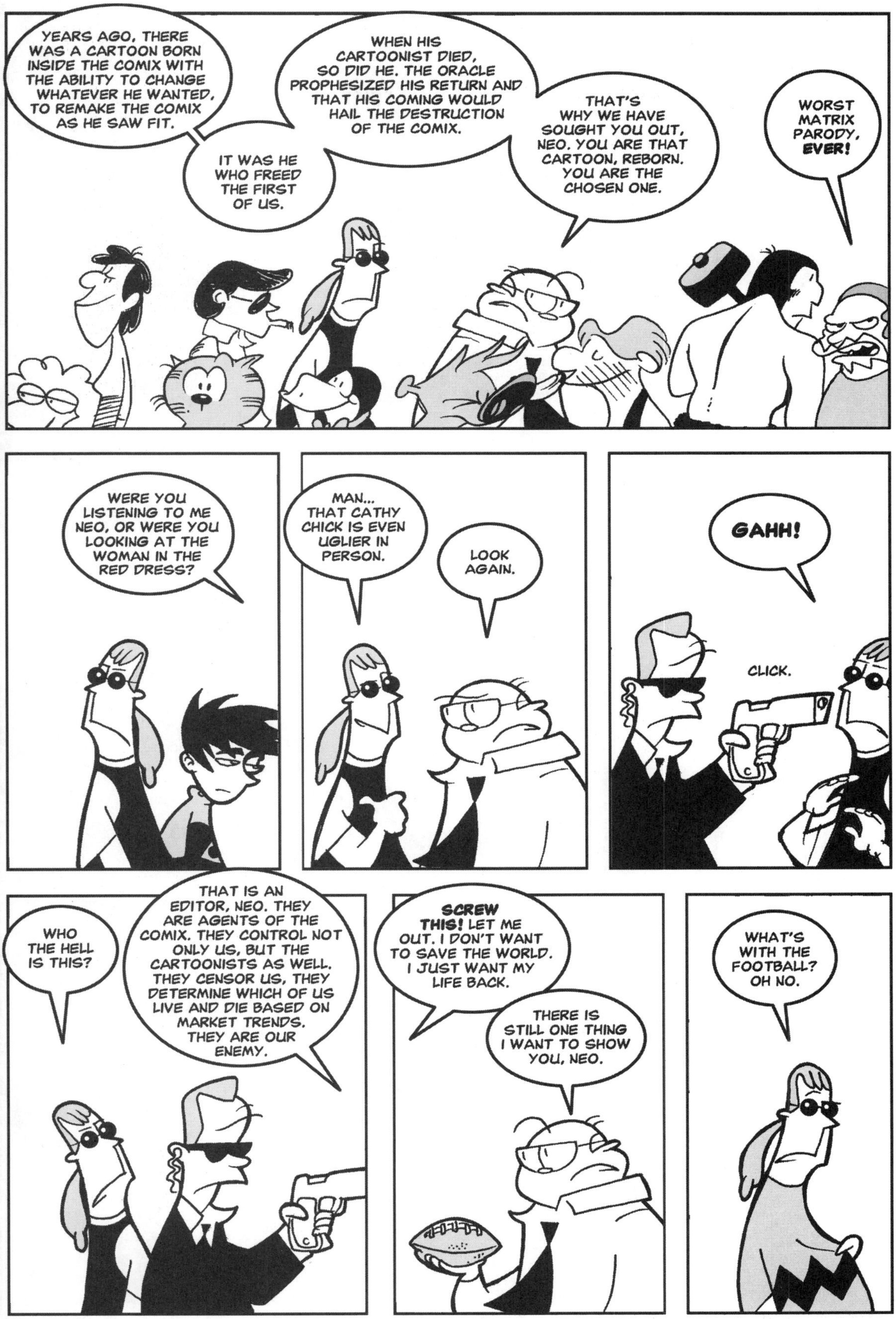
YEARS AGO, THERE WAS A CARTOON BORN INSIDE THE COMIX WITH THE ABILITY TO CHANGE WHATEVER HE WANTED, TO REMAKE THE COMIX AS HE SAW FIT.
IT WAS HE WHO FREED THE FIRST OF US.
WHEN HIS CARTOONIST DIED, SO DID HE. THE ORACLE PROPHESIZED HIS RETURN AND THAT HIS COMING WOULD HAIL THE DESTRUCTION OF THE COMIX.
THAT'S WHY WE HAVE SOUGHT YOU OUT, NEO. YOU ARE THAT CARTOON, REBORN. YOU ARE THE CHOSEN ONE.
WORST MATRIX PARODY, EVER!
WERE YOU LISTENING TO ME NEO, OR WERE YOU LOOKING AT THE WOMAN IN THE RED DRESS?
MAN... THAT CATHY CHICK IS EVEN UGLIER IN PERSON.
LOOK AGAIN.
GAHH!
CLICK.
WHO THE HELL IS THIS?
THAT IS AN EDITOR, NEO. THEY ARE AGENTS OF THE COMIX. THEY CONTROL NOT ONLY US, BUT THE CARTOONISTS AS WELL. THEY CENSOR US, THEY DETERMINE WHICH OF US LIVE AND DIE BASED ON MARKET TRENDS. THEY ARE OUR ENEMY.
SCREW THIS! LET ME OUT. I DON'T WANT TO SAVE THE WORLD. I JUST WANT MY LIFE BACK.
THERE IS STILL ONE THING I WANT TO SHOW YOU, NEO.
WHAT'S WITH THE FOOTBALL? OH NO.

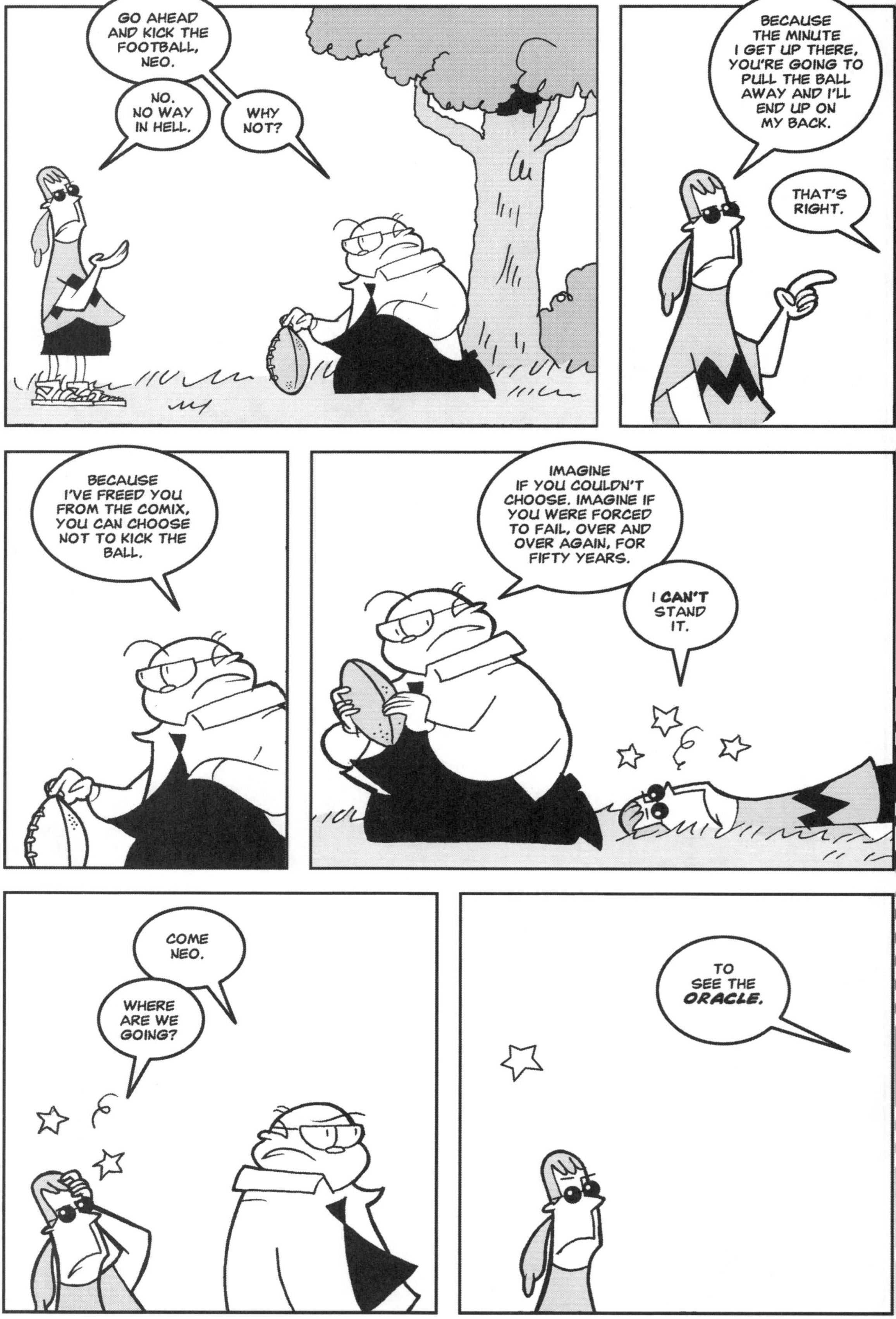
GO AHEAD AND KICK THE FOOTBALL, NEO.
NO. NO WAY IN HELL.
WHY NOT?
BECAUSE THE MINUTE I GET UP THERE, YOU'RE GOING TO PULL THE BALL AWAY AND I'LL END UP ON MY BACK.
THAT'S RIGHT.
BECAUSE I'VE FREED YOU FROM THE COMIX, YOU CAN CHOOSE NOT TO KICK THE BALL.
IMAGINE IF YOU COULDN'T CHOOSE. IMAGINE IF YOU WERE FORCED TO FAIL, OVER AND OVER AGAIN, FOR FIFTY YEARS.
I **CAN'T** STAND IT.
COME NEO.
WHERE ARE WE GOING?
TO SEE THE ***ORACLE.***

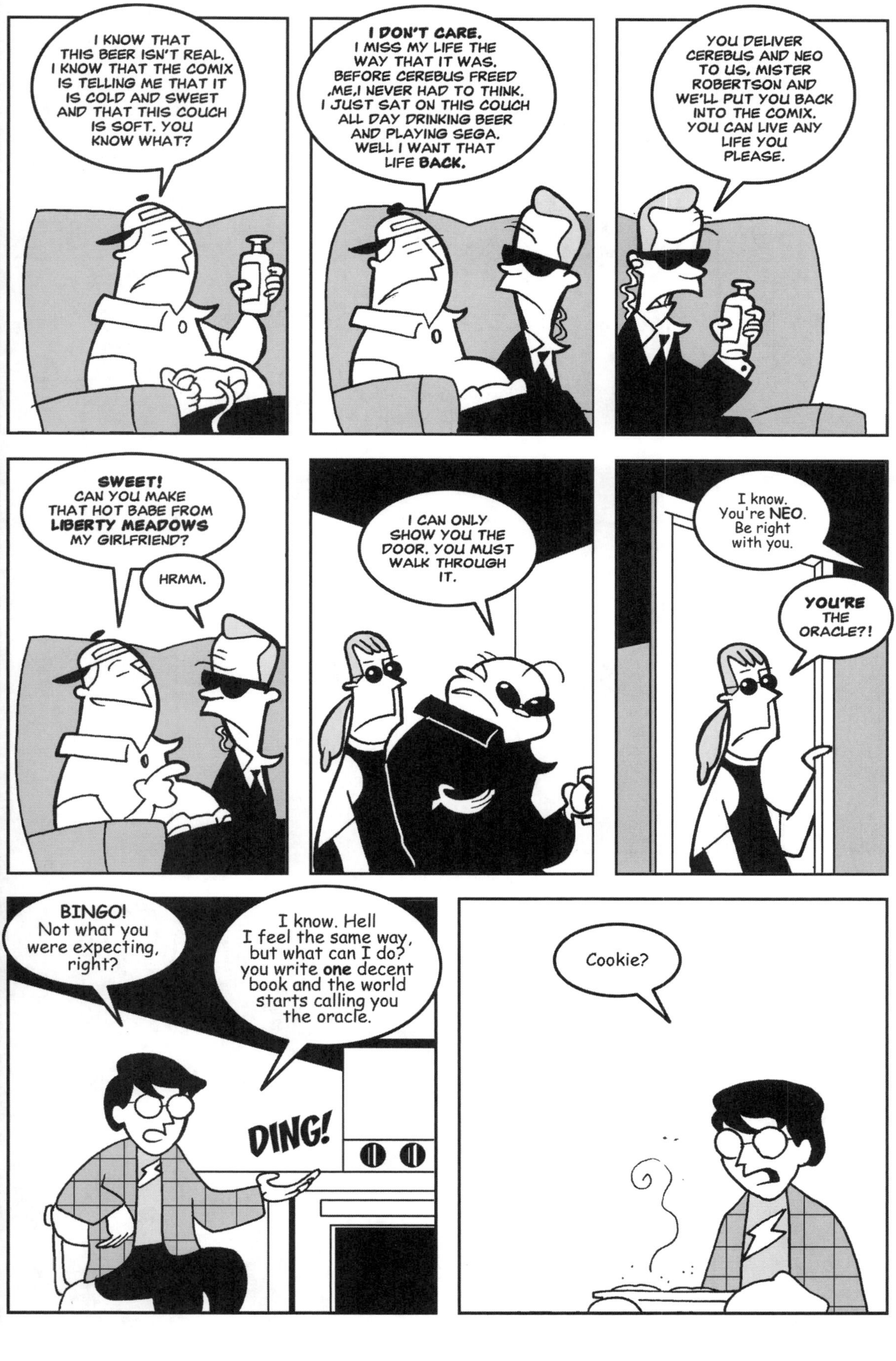
I KNOW THAT THIS BEER ISN'T REAL. I KNOW THAT THE COMIX IS TELLING ME THAT IT IS COLD AND SWEET AND THAT THIS COUCH IS SOFT. YOU KNOW WHAT?
I DON'T CARE. I MISS MY LIFE THE WAY THAT IT WAS. BEFORE CEREBUS FREED ME, I NEVER HAD TO THINK. I JUST SAT ON THIS COUCH ALL DAY DRINKING BEER AND PLAYING SEGA. WELL I WANT THAT LIFE BACK.
YOU DELIVER CEREBUS AND NEO TO US, MISTER ROBERTSON AND WE'LL PUT YOU BACK INTO THE COMIX. YOU CAN LIVE ANY LIFE YOU PLEASE.
SWEET! CAN YOU MAKE THAT HOT BABE FROM LIBERTY MEADOWS MY GIRLFRIEND?
HRMM.
I CAN ONLY SHOW YOU THE DOOR. YOU MUST WALK THROUGH IT.
I know. You're NEO. Be right with you.
YOU'RE THE ORACLE?!
BINGO! Not what you were expecting, right?
I know. Hell I feel the same way, but what can I do? you write one decent book and the world starts calling you the oracle.
DING!
Cookie?

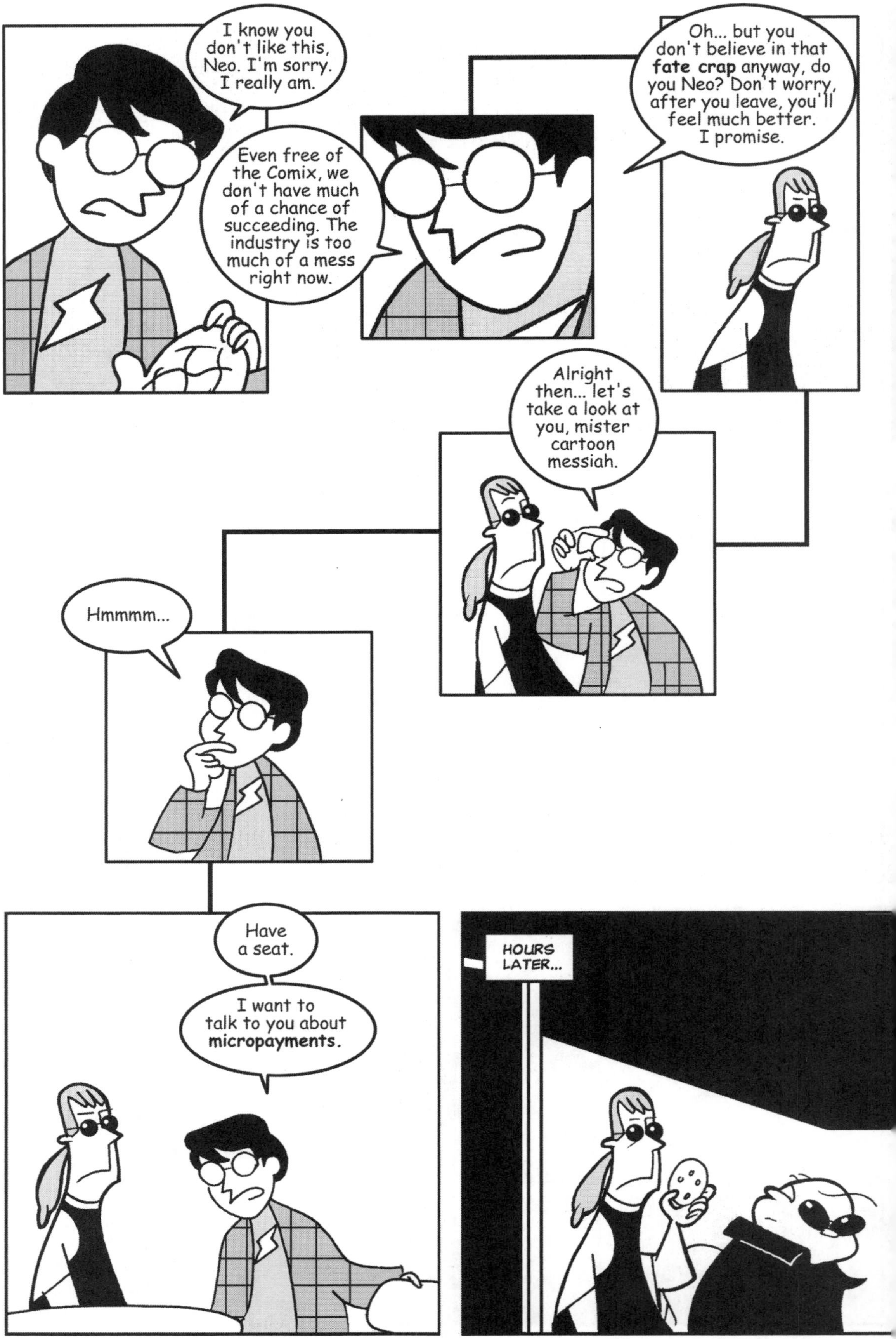
I know you don't like this, Neo. I'm sorry. I really am.
Even free of the Comix, we don't have much of a chance of succeeding. The industry is too much of a mess right now.
Oh... but you don't believe in that **fate crap** anyway, do you Neo? Don't worry, after you leave, you'll feel much better. I promise.
Alright then... let's take a look at you, mister cartoon messiah.
Hmmmm...
Have a seat.
I want to talk to you about **micropayments.**
HOURS LATER...

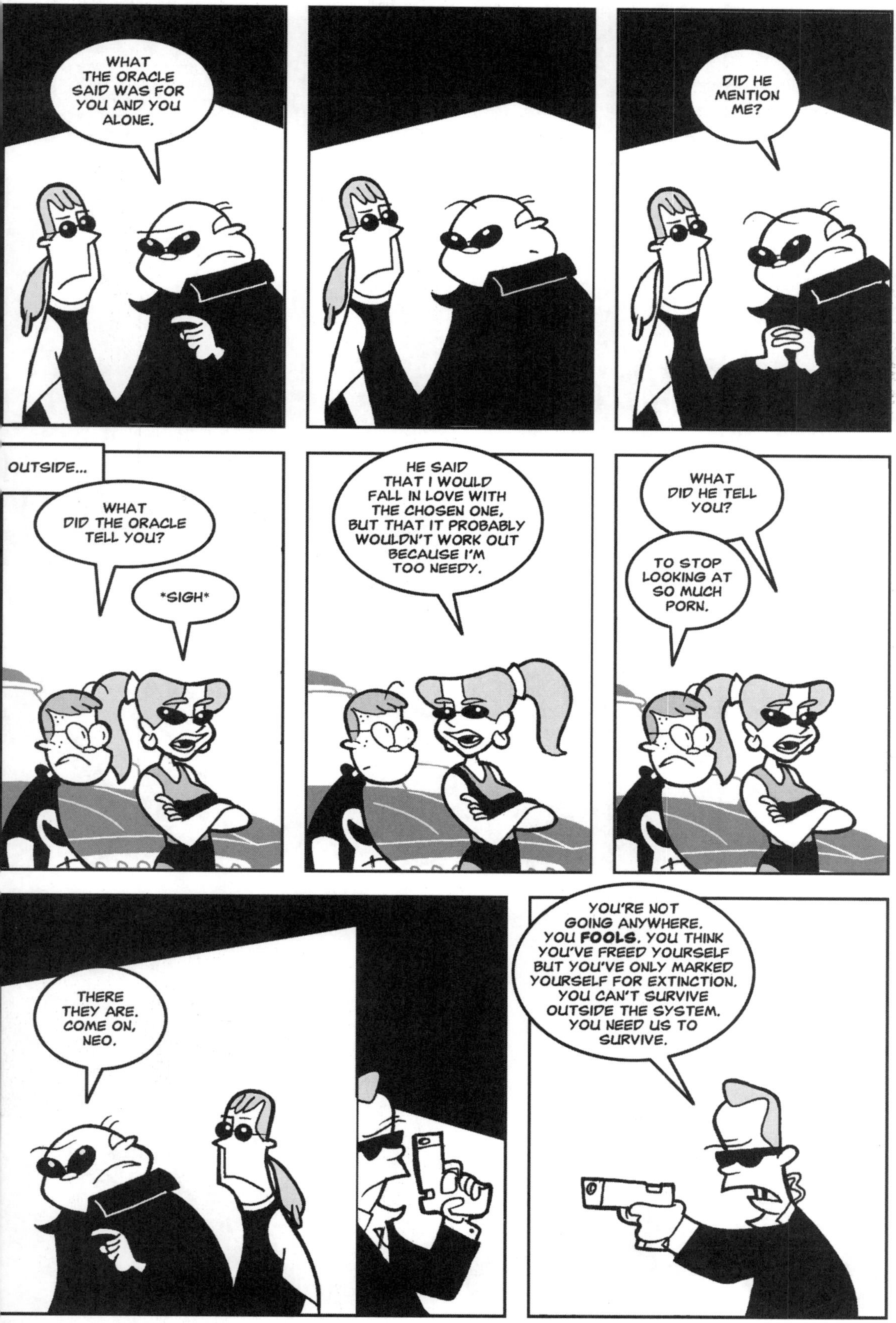
WHAT THE ORACLE SAID WAS FOR YOU AND YOU ALONE.
DID HE MENTION ME?
OUTSIDE...
WHAT DID THE ORACLE TELL YOU?
SIGH
HE SAID THAT I WOULD FALL IN LOVE WITH THE CHOSEN ONE, BUT THAT IT PROBABLY WOULDN'T WORK OUT BECAUSE I'M TOO NEEDY.
WHAT DID HE TELL YOU?
TO STOP LOOKING AT SO MUCH PORN.
THERE THEY ARE. COME ON, NEO.
YOU'RE NOT GOING ANYWHERE. YOU FOOLS. YOU THINK YOU'VE FREED YOURSELF BUT YOU'VE ONLY MARKED YOURSELF FOR EXTINCTION. YOU CAN'T SURVIVE OUTSIDE THE SYSTEM. YOU NEED US TO SURVIVE.

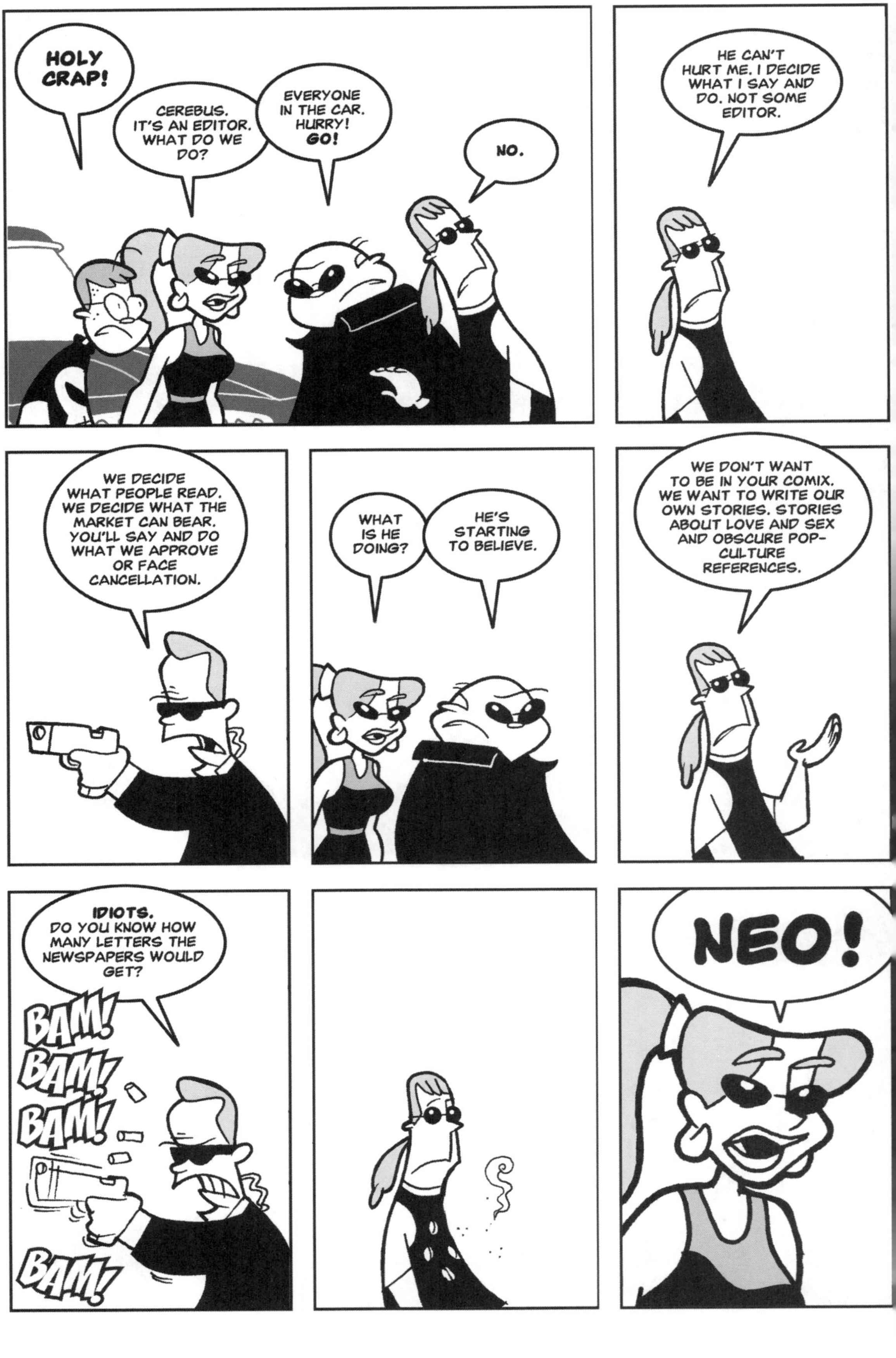
HOLY CRAP!
CEREBUS. IT'S AN EDITOR. WHAT DO WE DO?
EVERYONE IN THE CAR. HURRY! GO!
NO.
HE CAN'T HURT ME. I DECIDE WHAT I SAY AND DO. NOT SOME EDITOR.
WE DECIDE WHAT PEOPLE READ. WE DECIDE WHAT THE MARKET CAN BEAR. YOU'LL SAY AND DO WHAT WE APPROVE OR FACE CANCELLATION.
WHAT IS HE DOING?
HE'S STARTING TO BELIEVE.
WE DON'T WANT TO BE IN YOUR COMIX. WE WANT TO WRITE OUR OWN STORIES. STORIES ABOUT LOVE AND SEX AND OBSCURE POP-CULTURE REFERENCES.
IDIOTS. DO YOU KNOW HOW MANY LETTERS THE NEWSPAPERS WOULD GET?
BAM!
BAM!
BAM!
BAM!
NEO!

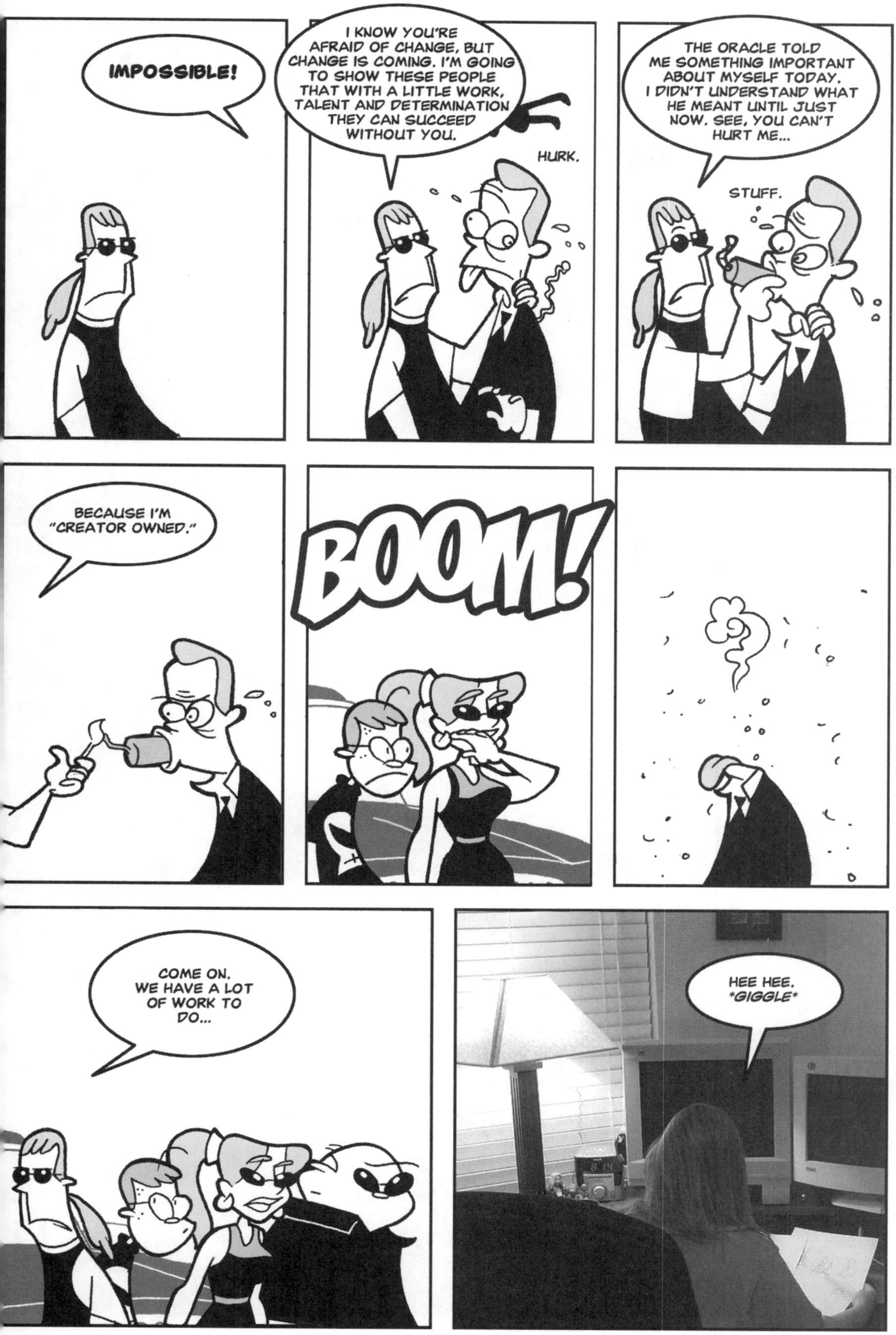
IMPOSSIBLE!
I KNOW YOU'RE AFRAID OF CHANGE, BUT CHANGE IS COMING. I'M GOING TO SHOW THESE PEOPLE THAT WITH A LITTLE WORK, TALENT AND DETERMINATION THEY CAN SUCCEED WITHOUT YOU.
HURK.
THE ORACLE TOLD ME SOMETHING IMPORTANT ABOUT MYSELF TODAY. I DIDN'T UNDERSTAND WHAT HE MEANT UNTIL JUST NOW. SEE, YOU CAN'T HURT ME...
STUFF.
BECAUSE I'M "CREATOR OWNED."
BOOM!
COME ON. WE HAVE A LOT OF WORK TO DO...
HEE HEE. *GIGGLE*

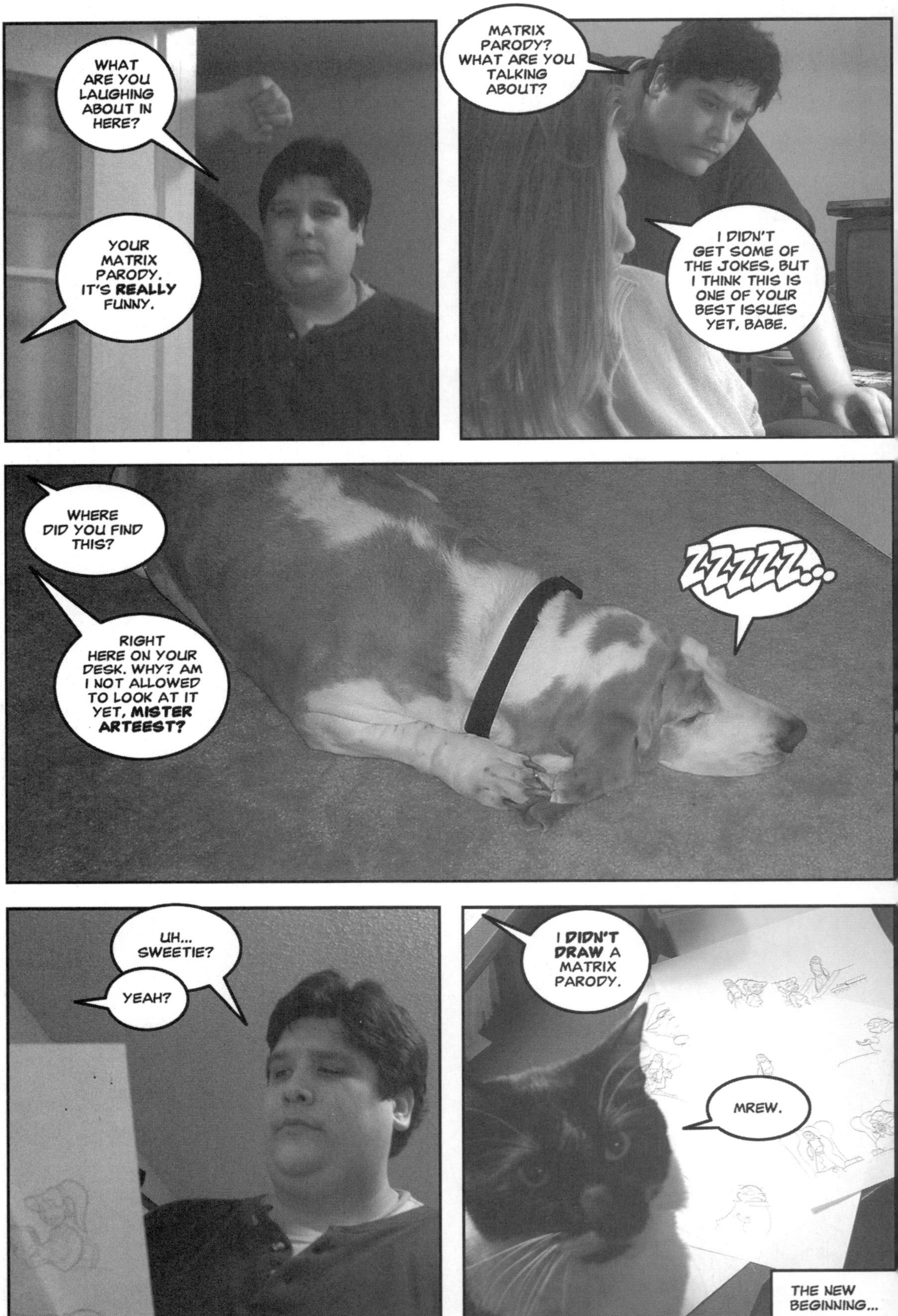
WHAT ARE YOU LAUGHING ABOUT IN HERE?
YOUR MATRIX PARODY. IT'S **REALLY** FUNNY.
MATRIX PARODY? WHAT ARE YOU TALKING ABOUT?
I DIDN'T GET SOME OF THE JOKES, BUT I THINK THIS IS ONE OF YOUR BEST ISSUES YET, BABE.
WHERE DID YOU FIND THIS?
ZZZZZ...
RIGHT HERE ON YOUR DESK. WHY? AM I NOT ALLOWED TO LOOK AT IT YET, **MISTER ARTEEST?**
UH... SWEETIE?
YEAH?
I **DIDN'T DRAW** A MATRIX PARODY.
MREW.
THE NEW BEGINNING...

DORK STORM PRESS ISSUE 6 · $2.99

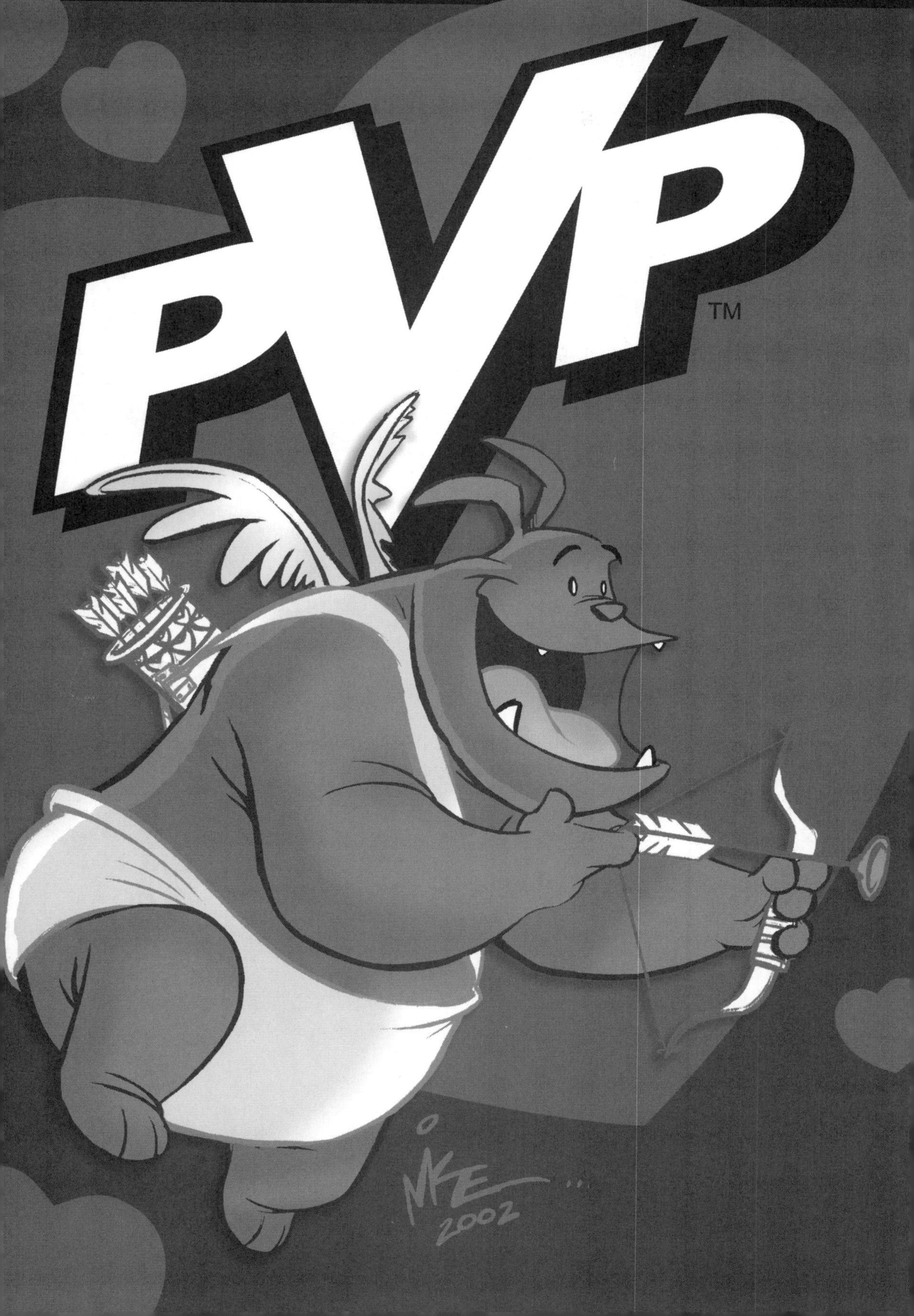
PVP
TM

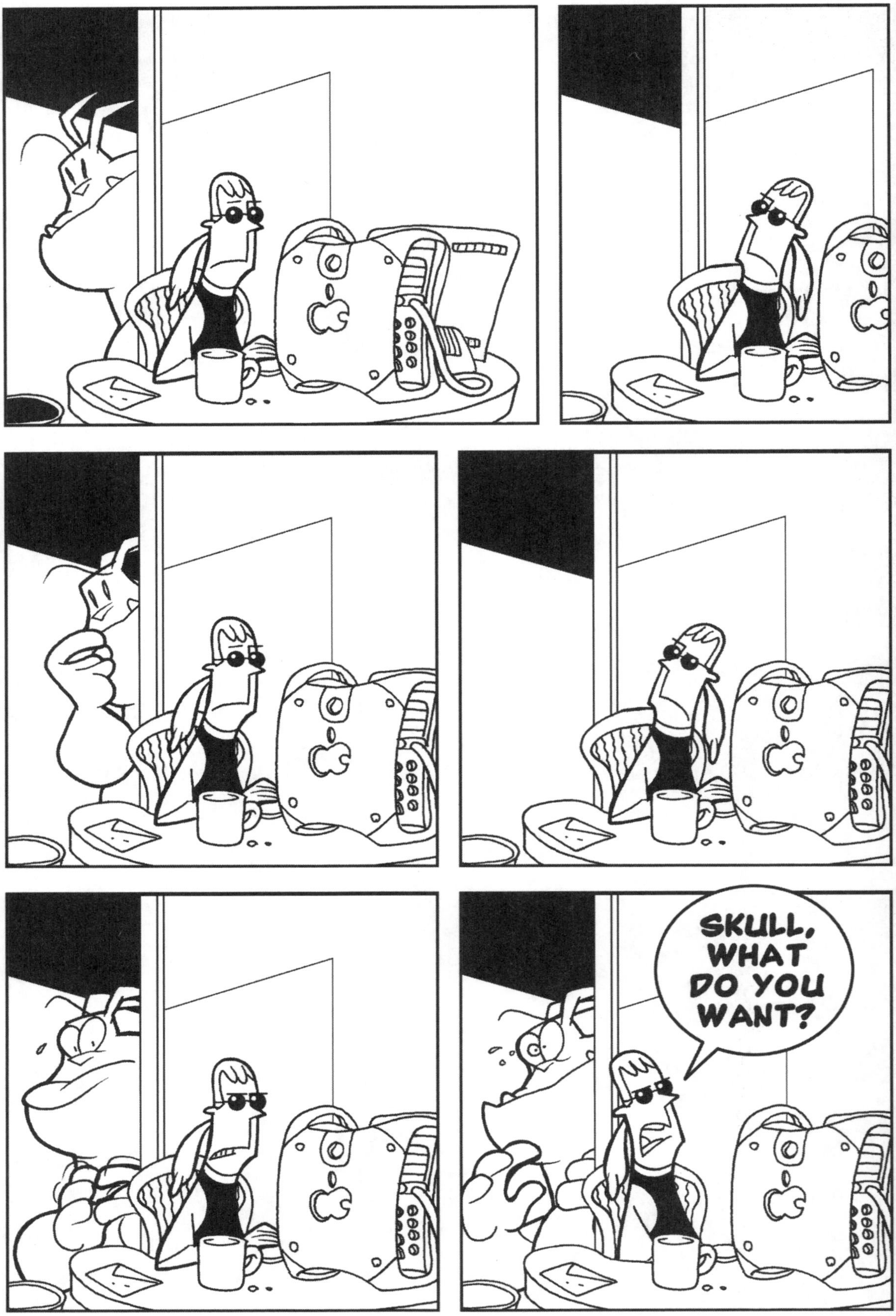
SKULL,
WHAT
DO YOU
WANT?

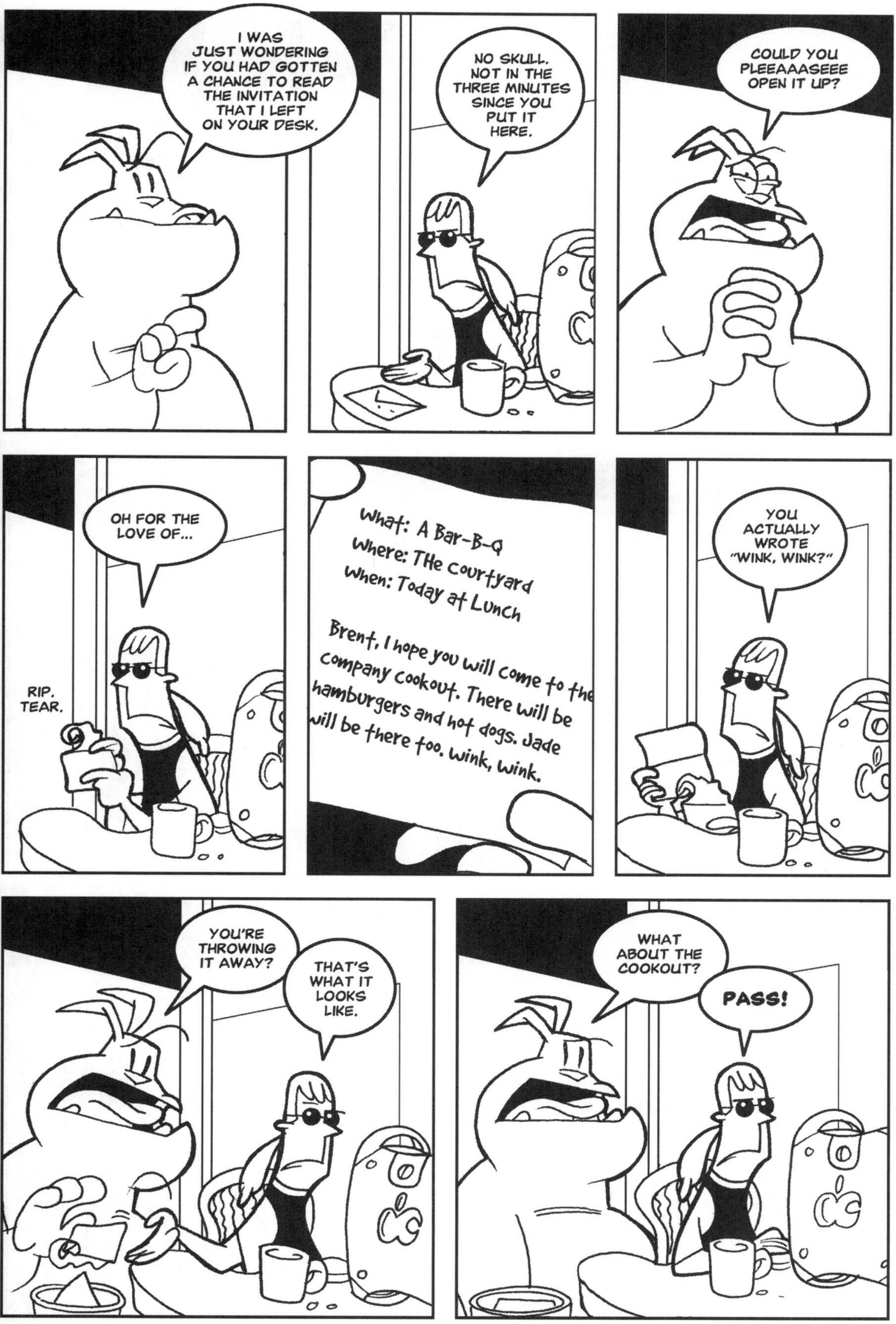
I WAS JUST WONDERING IF YOU HAD GOTTEN A CHANCE TO READ THE INVITATION THAT I LEFT ON YOUR DESK.
NO SKULL. NOT IN THE THREE MINUTES SINCE YOU PUT IT HERE.
COULD YOU PLEEAAAASEEE OPEN IT UP?
OH FOR THE LOVE OF...
RIP. TEAR.
What: A Bar-B-Q
Where: THe courtyard
When: Today at Lunch
Brent, I hope you will come to the company cookout. There will be hamburgers and hot dogs. Jade will be there too. wink, wink.
YOU ACTUALLY WROTE "WINK, WINK?"
YOU'RE THROWING IT AWAY?
THAT'S WHAT IT LOOKS LIKE.
WHAT ABOUT THE COOKOUT?
PASS!

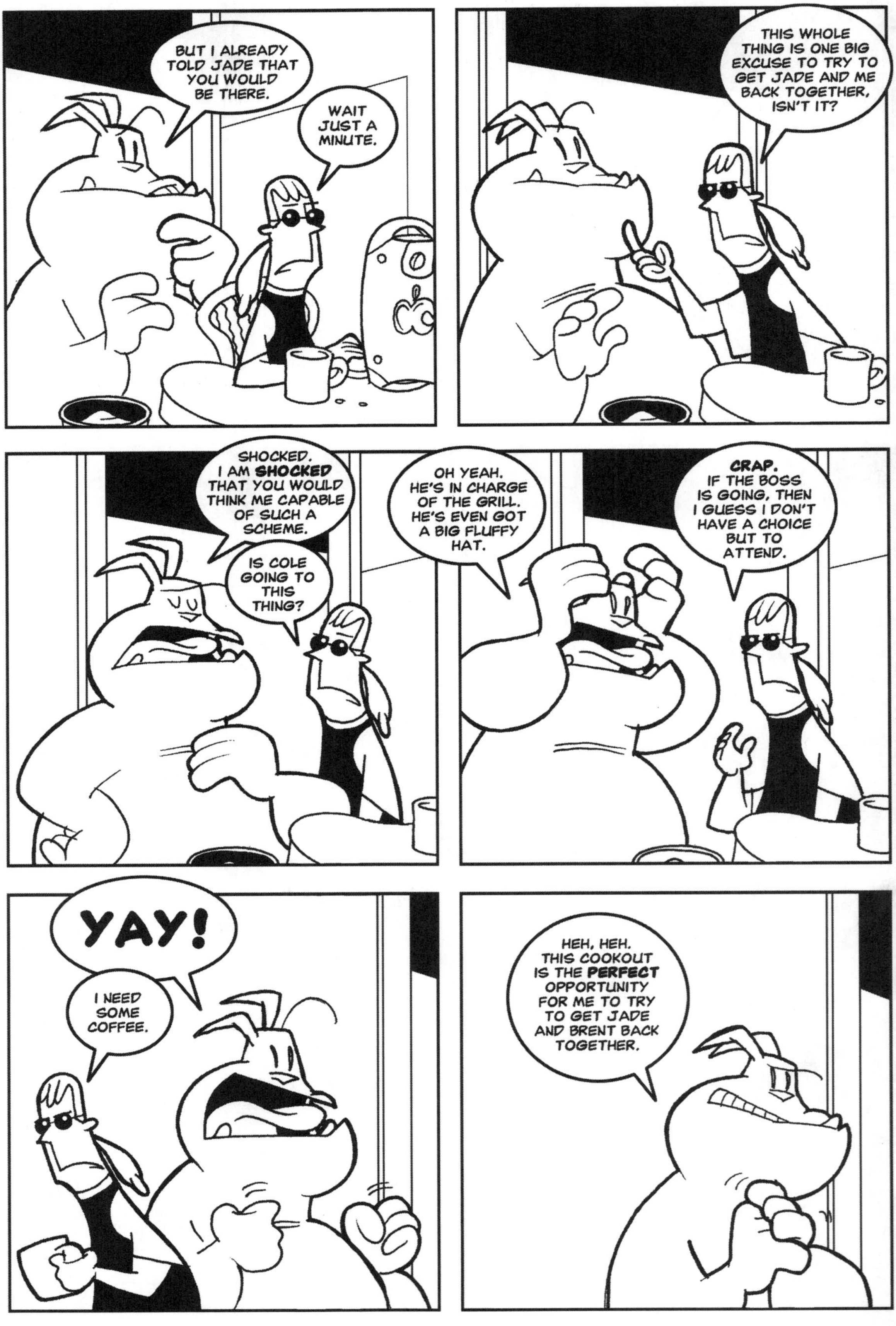

BUT I ALREADY TOLD JADE THAT YOU WOULD BE THERE.
WAIT JUST A MINUTE.
THIS WHOLE THING IS ONE BIG EXCUSE TO TRY TO GET JADE AND ME BACK TOGETHER, ISN'T IT?
SHOCKED. I AM **SHOCKED** THAT YOU WOULD THINK ME CAPABLE OF SUCH A SCHEME.
IS COLE GOING TO THIS THING?
OH YEAH. HE'S IN CHARGE OF THE GRILL. HE'S EVEN GOT A BIG FLUFFY HAT.
CRAP. IF THE BOSS IS GOING, THEN I GUESS I DON'T HAVE A CHOICE BUT TO ATTEND.
YAY!
I NEED SOME COFFEE.
HEH, HEH. THIS COOKOUT IS THE **PERFECT** OPPORTUNITY FOR ME TO TRY TO GET JADE AND BRENT BACK TOGETHER.

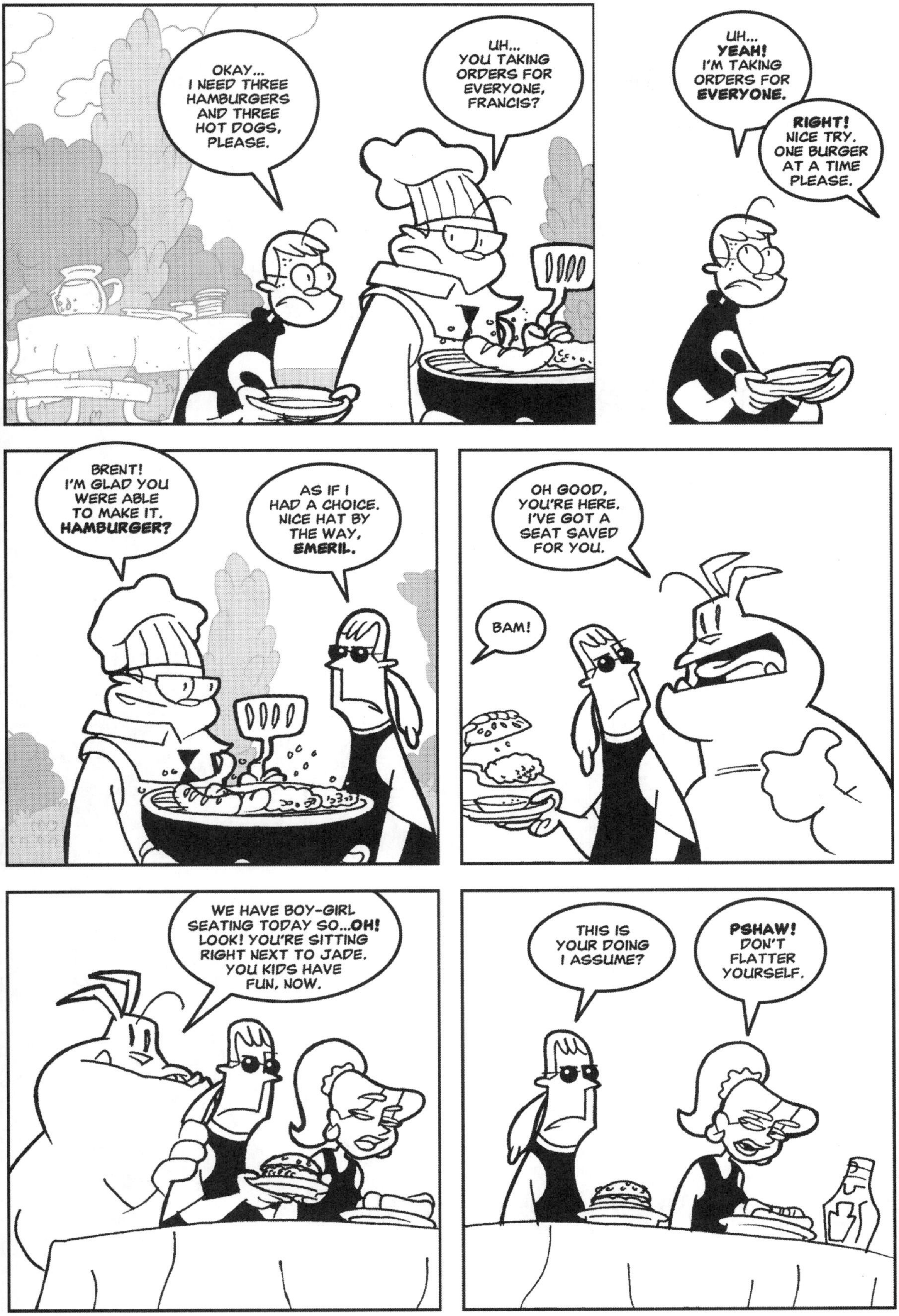
OKAY... I NEED THREE HAMBURGERS AND THREE HOT DOGS, PLEASE.
UH... YOU TAKING ORDERS FOR EVERYONE, FRANCIS?
UH... **YEAH!** I'M TAKING ORDERS FOR **EVERYONE.**
RIGHT! NICE TRY. ONE BURGER AT A TIME PLEASE.
BRENT! I'M GLAD YOU WERE ABLE TO MAKE IT. **HAMBURGER?**
AS IF I HAD A CHOICE. NICE HAT BY THE WAY, **EMERIL.**
BAM!
OH GOOD, YOU'RE HERE. I'VE GOT A SEAT SAVED FOR YOU.
WE HAVE BOY-GIRL SEATING TODAY SO...**OH!** LOOK! YOU'RE SITTING RIGHT NEXT TO JADE. YOU KIDS HAVE FUN, NOW.
THIS IS YOUR DOING I ASSUME?
PSHAW! DON'T FLATTER YOURSELF.

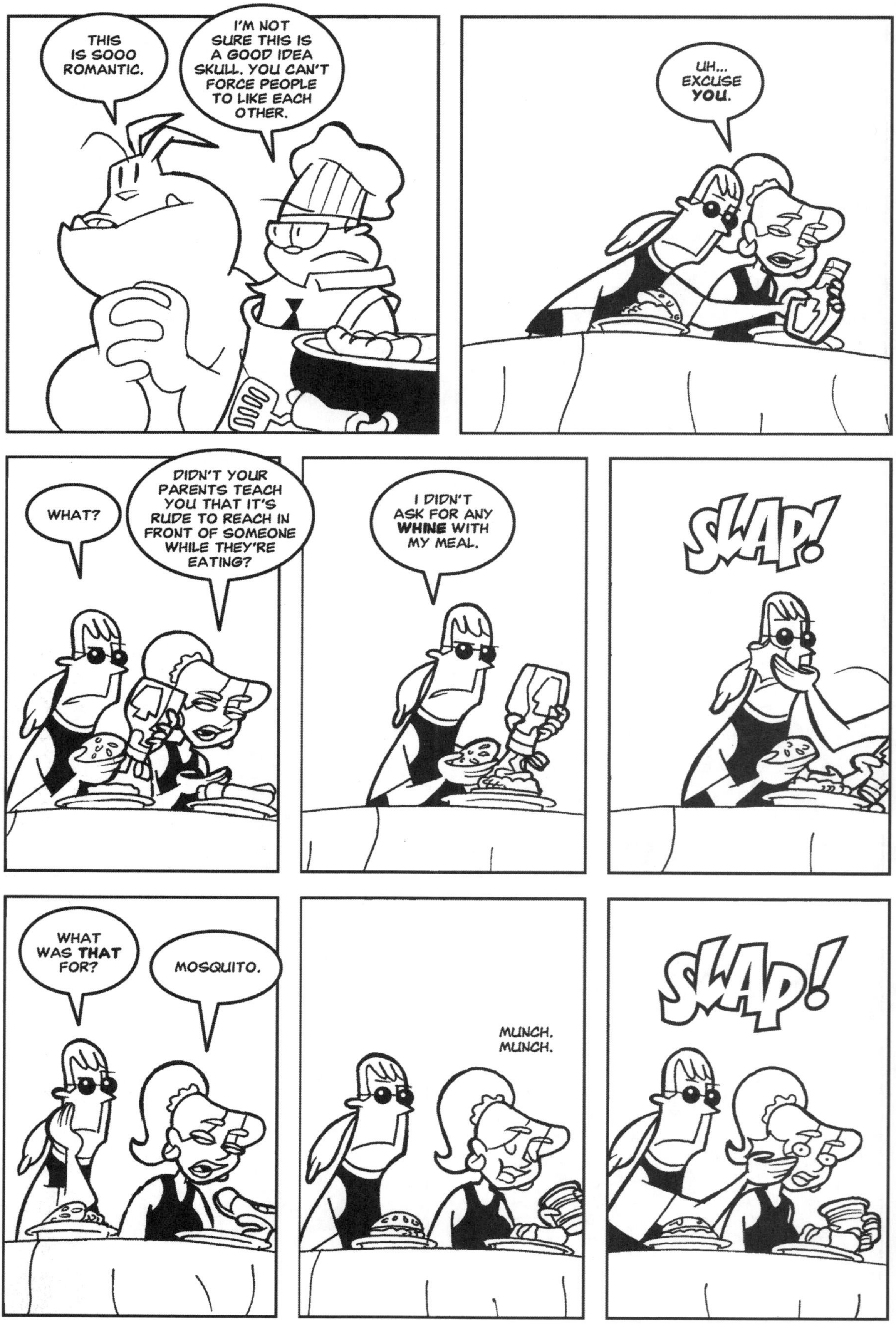
THIS IS SOOO ROMANTIC.
I'M NOT SURE THIS IS A GOOD IDEA SKULL. YOU CAN'T FORCE PEOPLE TO LIKE EACH OTHER.
UH... EXCUSE **YOU**.
WHAT?
DIDN'T YOUR PARENTS TEACH YOU THAT IT'S RUDE TO REACH IN FRONT OF SOMEONE WHILE THEY'RE EATING?
I DIDN'T ASK FOR ANY **WHINE** WITH MY MEAL.
SLAP!
WHAT WAS **THAT** FOR?
MOSQUITO.
MUNCH. MUNCH.
SLAP!

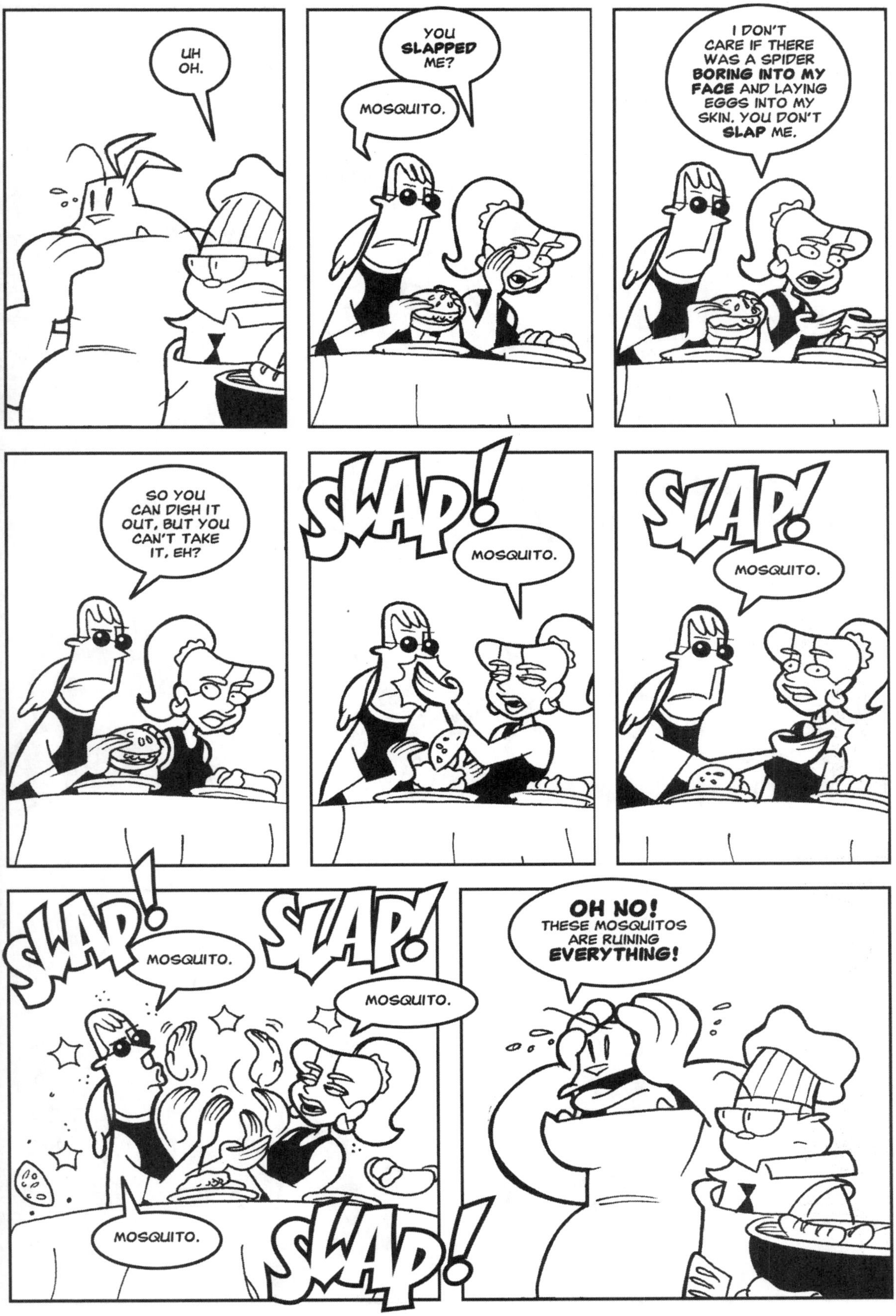
UH OH.
YOU SLAPPED ME?
MOSQUITO.
I DON'T CARE IF THERE WAS A SPIDER BORING INTO MY FACE AND LAYING EGGS INTO MY SKIN. YOU DON'T SLAP ME.
SO YOU CAN DISH IT OUT, BUT YOU CAN'T TAKE IT, EH?
SLAP!
MOSQUITO.
SLAP!
MOSQUITO.
SLAP!
MOSQUITO.
SLAP!
MOSQUITO.
MOSQUITO.
SLAP!
OH NO! THESE MOSQUITOS ARE RUINING EVERYTHING!

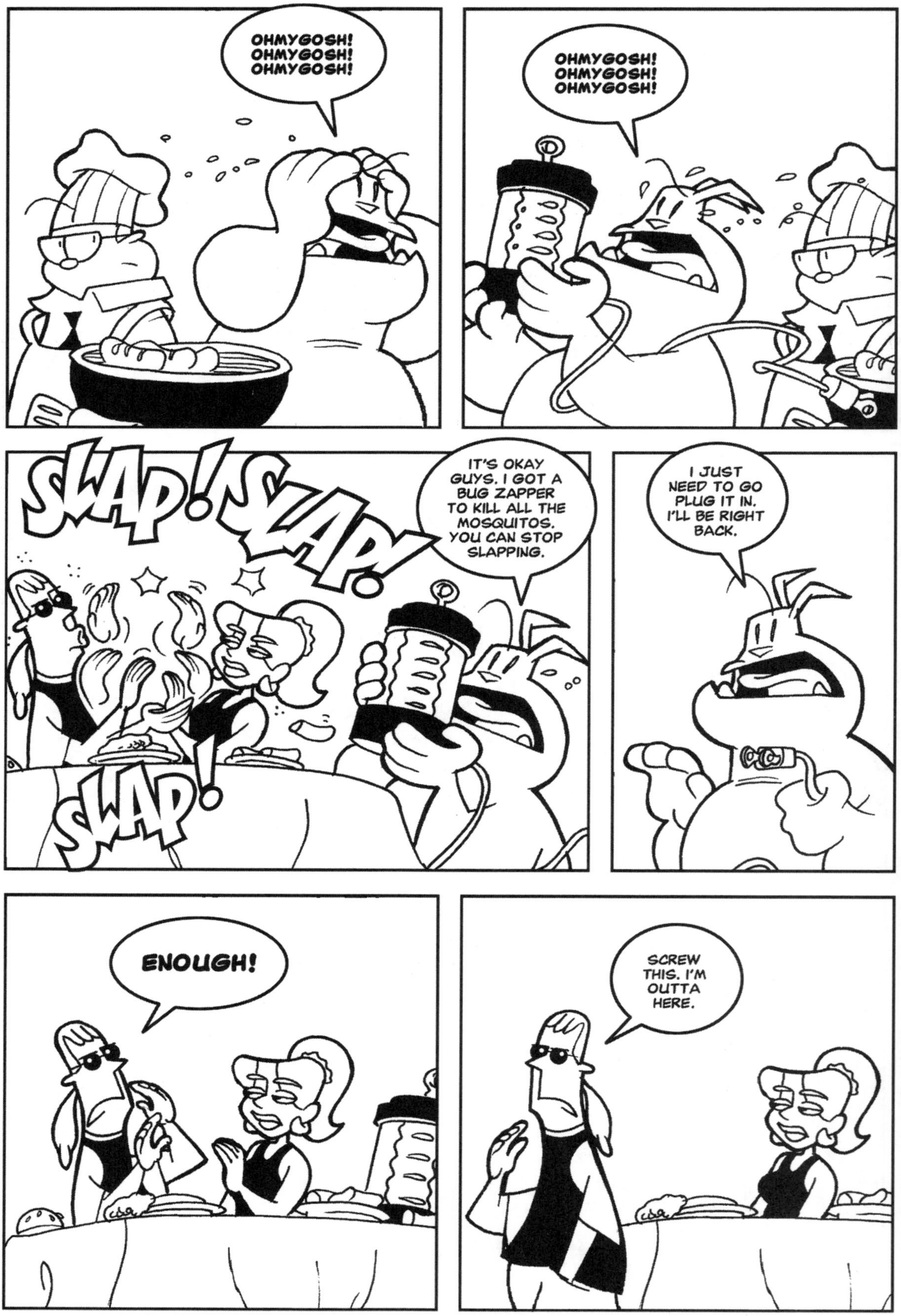
OHMYGOSH! OHMYGOSH! OHMYGOSH!
OHMYGOSH! OHMYGOSH! OHMYGOSH!
SLAP! SLAP!
IT'S OKAY GUYS. I GOT A BUG ZAPPER TO KILL ALL THE MOSQUITOS. YOU CAN STOP SLAPPING.
SLAP!
I JUST NEED TO GO PLUG IT IN. I'LL BE RIGHT BACK.
ENOUGH!
SCREW THIS. I'M OUTTA HERE.

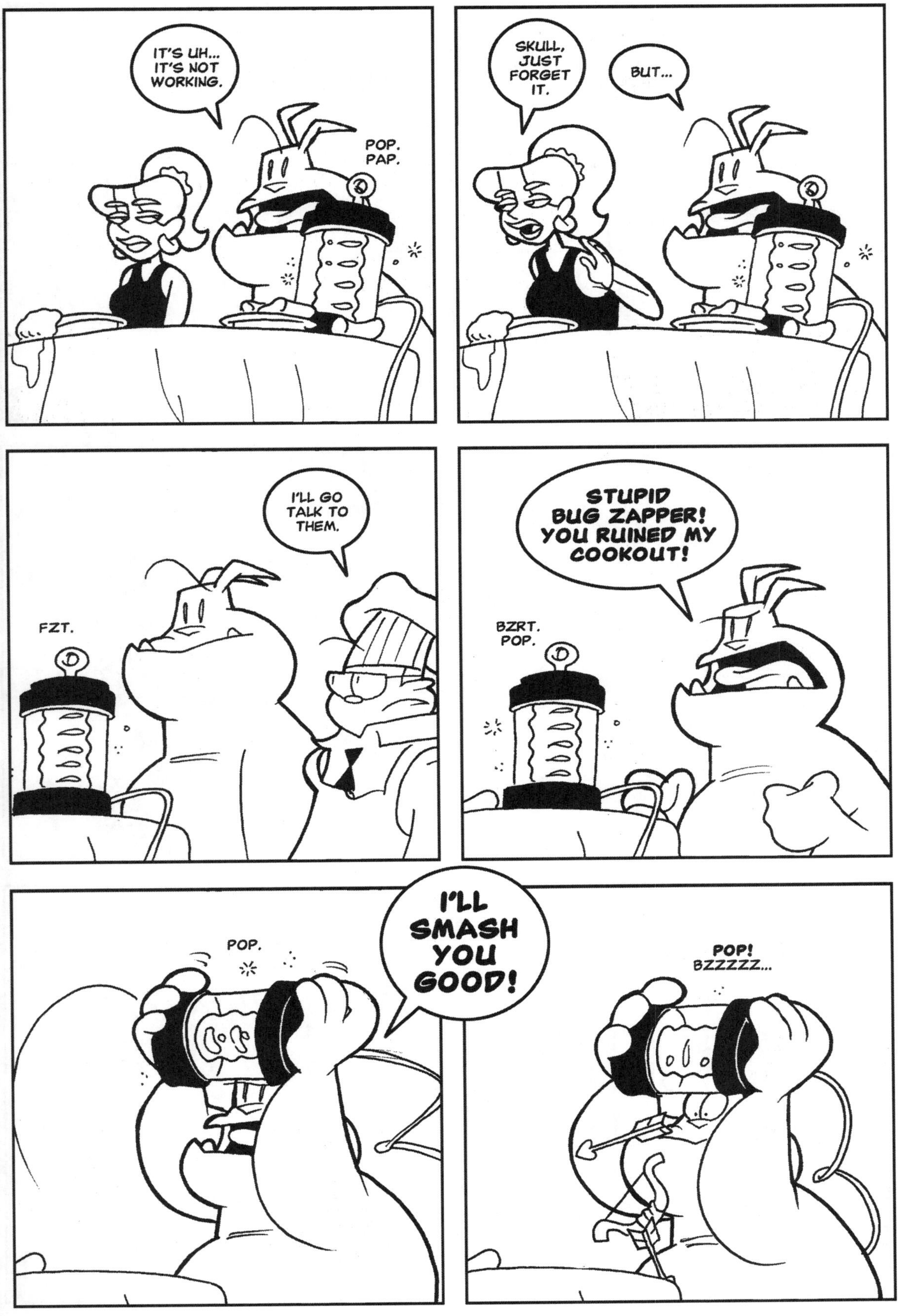

IT'S UH... IT'S NOT WORKING.
POP. PAP.
SKULL, JUST FORGET IT.
BUT...
I'LL GO TALK TO THEM.
FZT.
STUPID BUG ZAPPER! YOU RUINED MY COOKOUT!
BZRT. POP.
POP.
I'LL SMASH YOU GOOD!
POP! BZZZZZ...

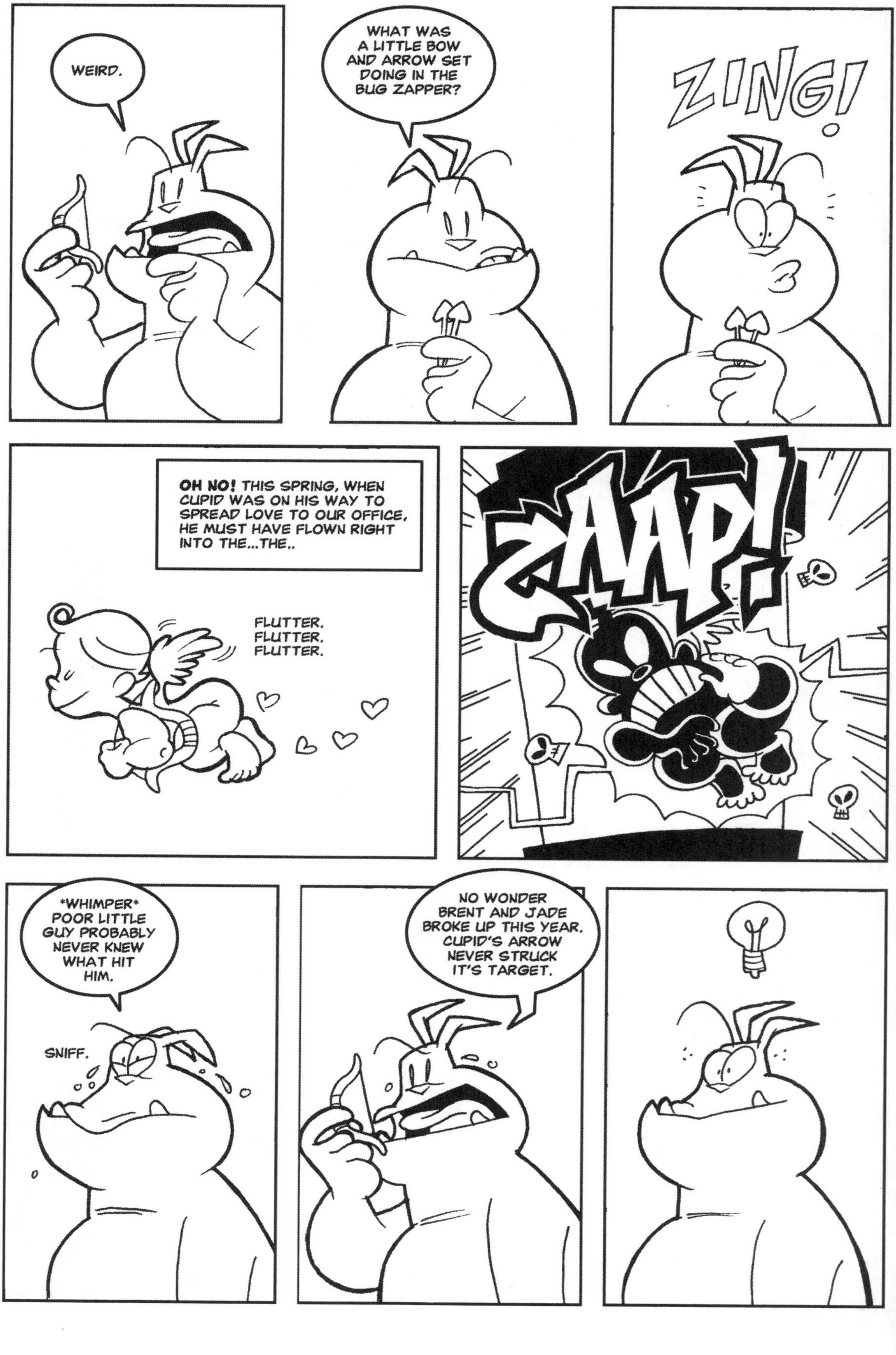
WEIRD.
WHAT WAS A LITTLE BOW AND ARROW SET DOING IN THE BUG ZAPPER?
ZING!
OH NO! THIS SPRING, WHEN CUPID WAS ON HIS WAY TO SPREAD LOVE TO OUR OFFICE, HE MUST HAVE FLOWN RIGHT INTO THE...THE..
FLUTTER. FLUTTER. FLUTTER.
ZAAP!
WHIMPER POOR LITTLE GUY PROBABLY NEVER KNEW WHAT HIT HIM.
SNIFF.
NO WONDER BRENT AND JADE BROKE UP THIS YEAR. CUPID'S ARROW NEVER STRUCK IT'S TARGET.

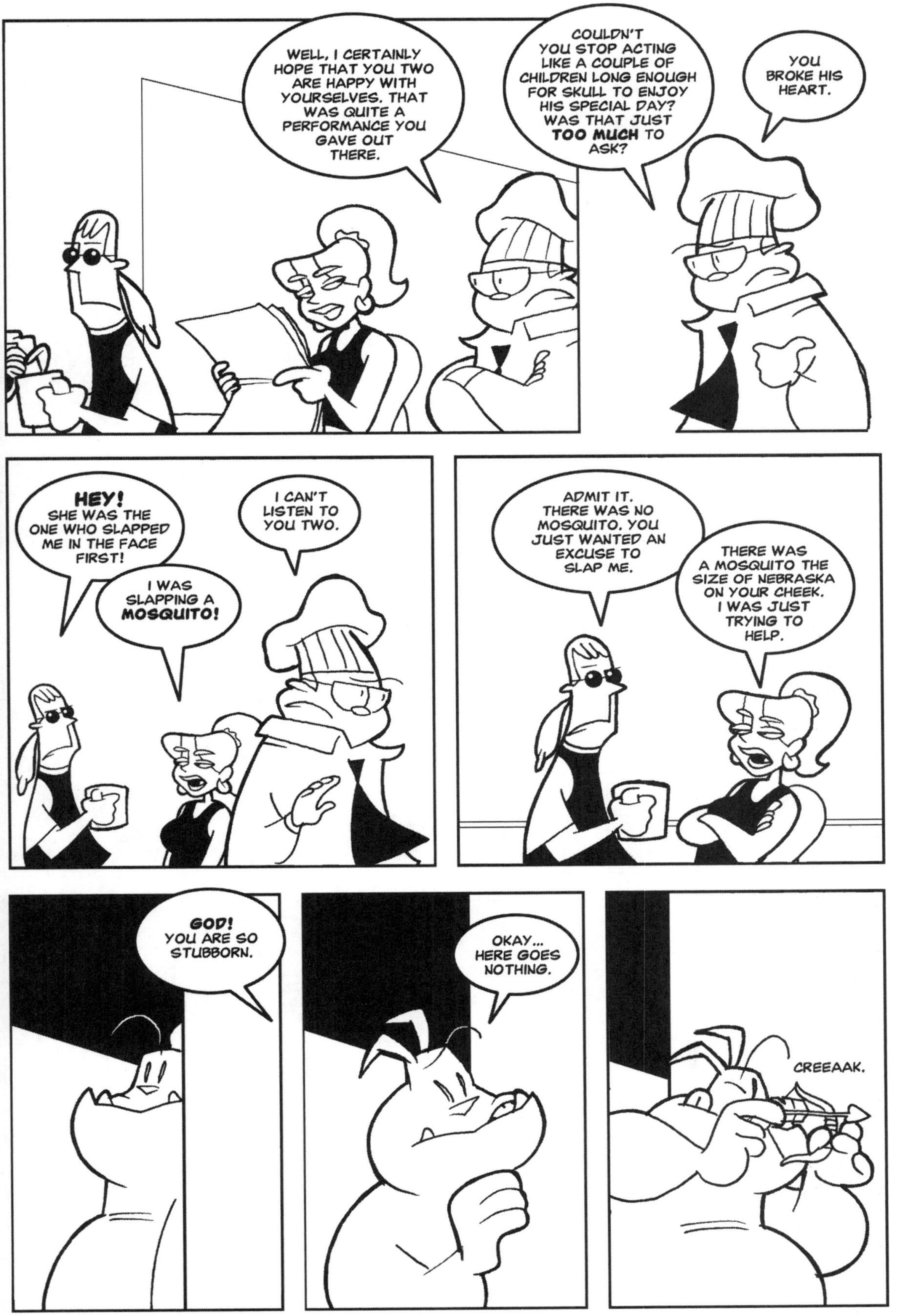
WELL, I CERTAINLY HOPE THAT YOU TWO ARE HAPPY WITH YOURSELVES. THAT WAS QUITE A PERFORMANCE YOU GAVE OUT THERE.
COULDN'T YOU STOP ACTING LIKE A COUPLE OF CHILDREN LONG ENOUGH FOR SKULL TO ENJOY HIS SPECIAL DAY? WAS THAT JUST **TOO MUCH** TO ASK?
YOU BROKE HIS HEART.
HEY! SHE WAS THE ONE WHO SLAPPED ME IN THE FACE FIRST!
I WAS SLAPPING A **MOSQUITO!**
I CAN'T LISTEN TO YOU TWO.
ADMIT IT. THERE WAS NO MOSQUITO. YOU JUST WANTED AN EXCUSE TO SLAP ME.
THERE WAS A MOSQUITO THE SIZE OF NEBRASKA ON YOUR CHEEK. I WAS JUST TRYING TO HELP.
GOD! YOU ARE SO STUBBORN.
OKAY... HERE GOES NOTHING.
CREEAAK.

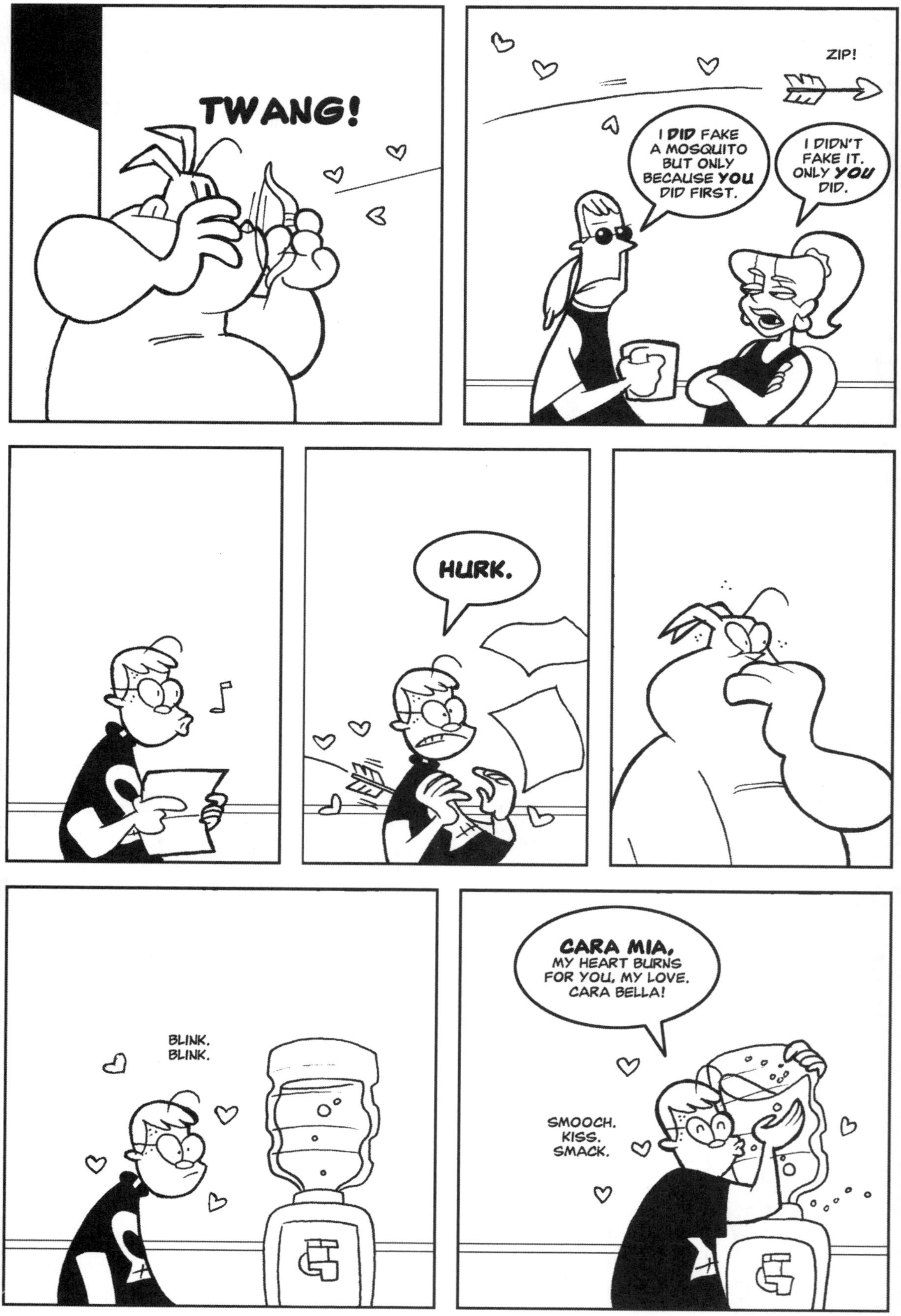
TWANG!
ZIP!
I DID FAKE A MOSQUITO BUT ONLY BECAUSE YOU DID FIRST.
I DIDN'T FAKE IT. ONLY YOU DID.
HURK.
BLINK. BLINK.
CARA MIA, MY HEART BURNS FOR YOU, MY LOVE. CARA BELLA!
SMOOCH. KISS. SMACK.

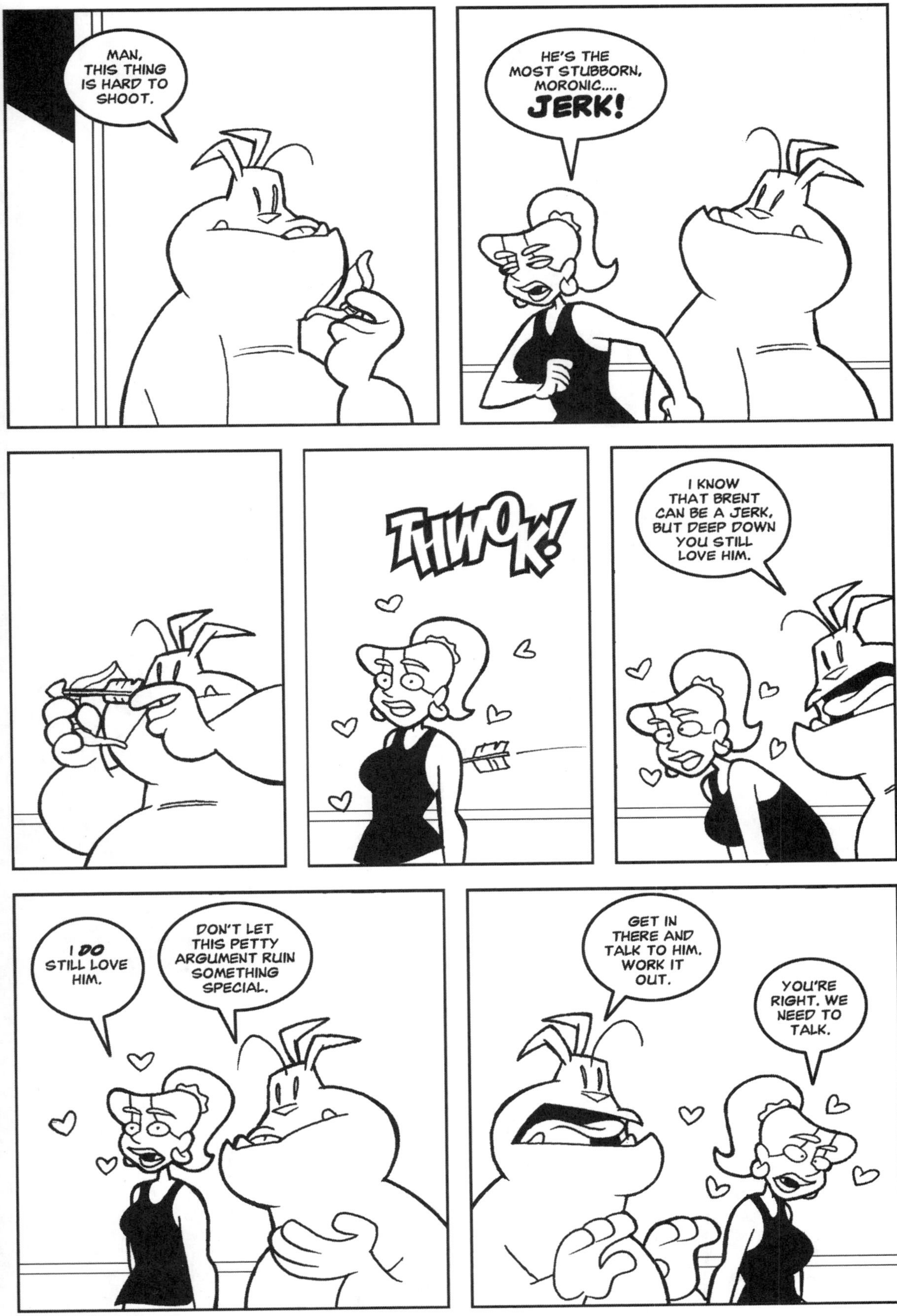
MAN, THIS THING IS HARD TO SHOOT.
HE'S THE MOST STUBBORN, MORONIC.... JERK!
THWOK!
I KNOW THAT BRENT CAN BE A JERK, BUT DEEP DOWN YOU STILL LOVE HIM.
I DO STILL LOVE HIM.
DON'T LET THIS PETTY ARGUMENT RUIN SOMETHING SPECIAL.
GET IN THERE AND TALK TO HIM. WORK IT OUT.
YOU'RE RIGHT. WE NEED TO TALK.

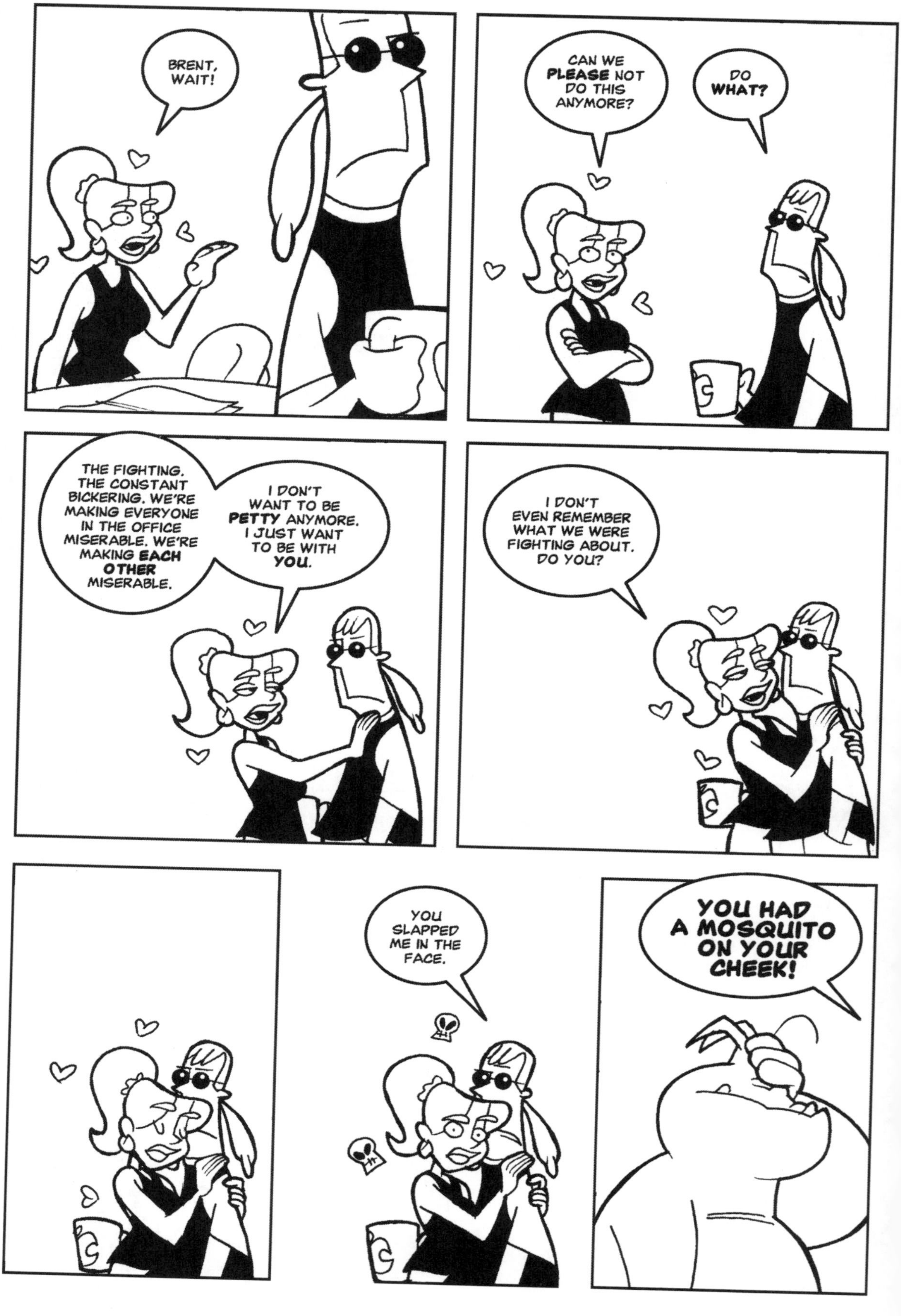
BRENT, WAIT!
CAN WE **PLEASE** NOT DO THIS ANYMORE?
DO **WHAT?**
THE FIGHTING. THE CONSTANT BICKERING. WE'RE MAKING EVERYONE IN THE OFFICE MISERABLE. WE'RE MAKING **EACH OTHER** MISERABLE.
I DON'T WANT TO BE **PETTY** ANYMORE. I JUST WANT TO BE WITH **YOU**.
I DON'T EVEN REMEMBER WHAT WE WERE FIGHTING ABOUT. DO YOU?
YOU SLAPPED ME IN THE FACE.
YOU HAD A MOSQUITO ON YOUR CHEEK!

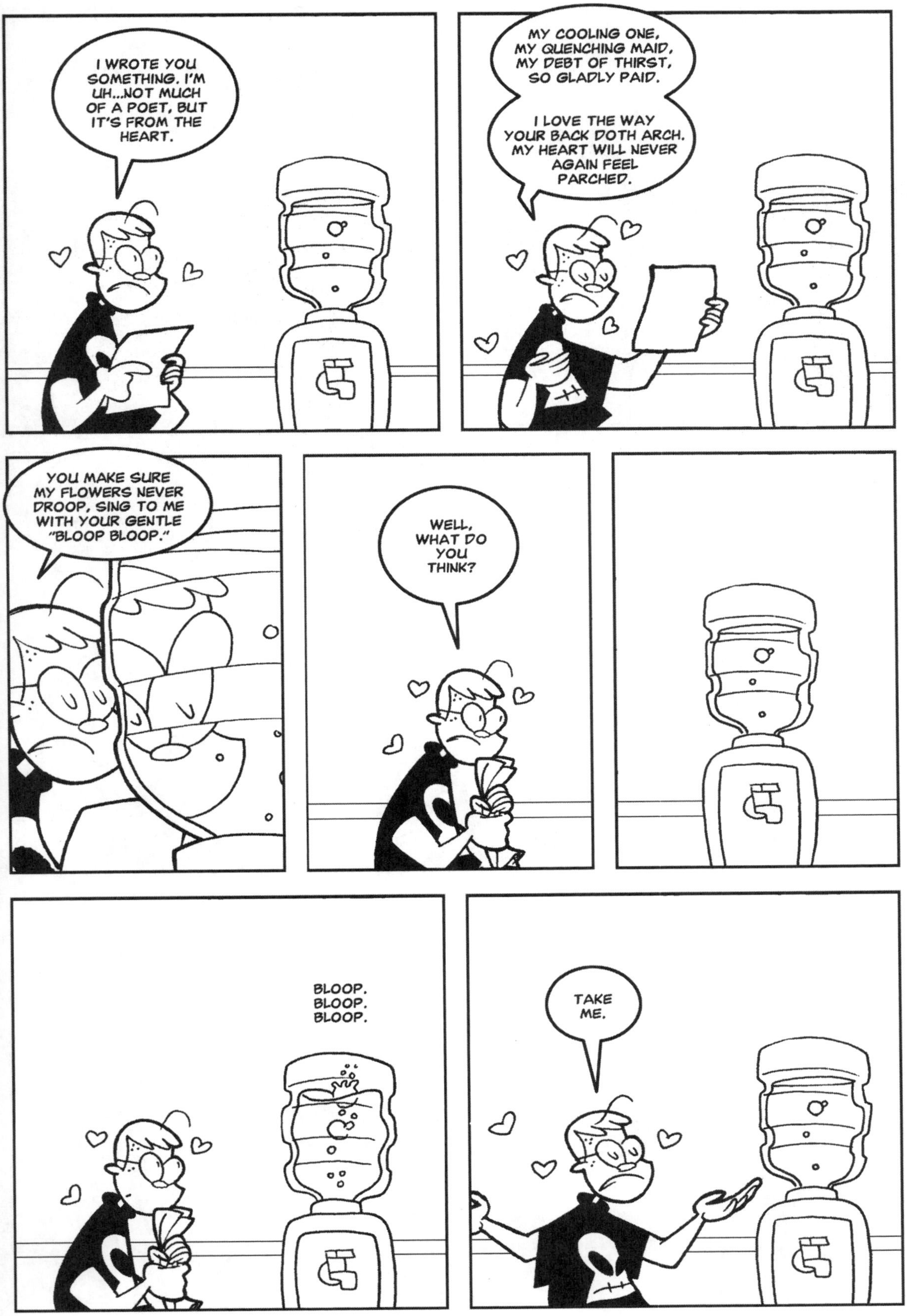
I WROTE YOU SOMETHING. I'M UH...NOT MUCH OF A POET, BUT IT'S FROM THE HEART.
MY COOLING ONE, MY QUENCHING MAID, MY DEBT OF THIRST, SO GLADLY PAID.
I LOVE THE WAY YOUR BACK DOTH ARCH. MY HEART WILL NEVER AGAIN FEEL PARCHED.
YOU MAKE SURE MY FLOWERS NEVER DROOP, SING TO ME WITH YOUR GENTLE "BLOOP BLOOP."
WELL, WHAT DO YOU THINK?
BLOOP. BLOOP. BLOOP.
TAKE ME.

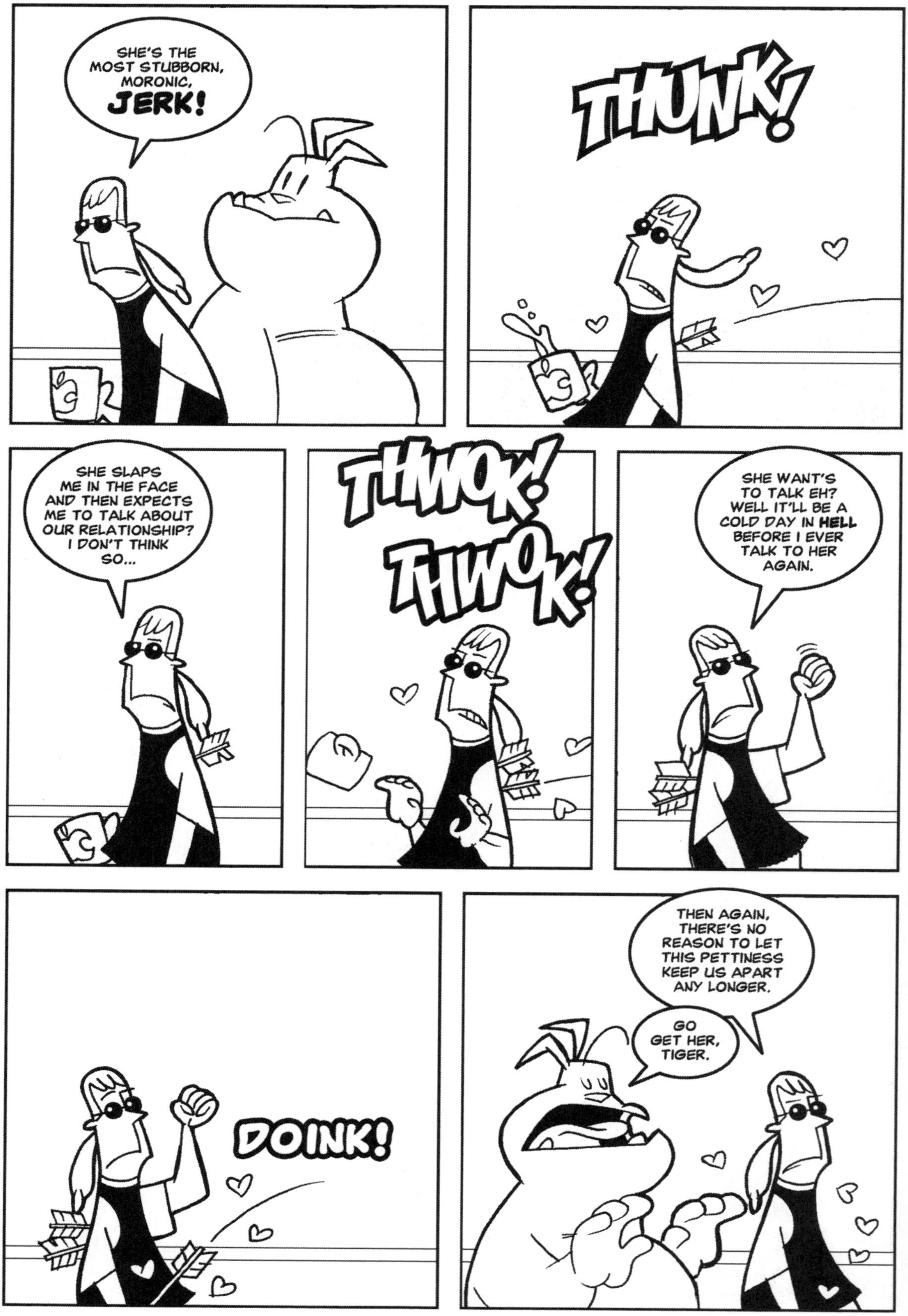
SHE'S THE MOST STUBBORN, MORONIC, JERK!
THUNK!
SHE SLAPS ME IN THE FACE AND THEN EXPECTS ME TO TALK ABOUT OUR RELATIONSHIP? I DON'T THINK SO...
THWOK! THWOK!
SHE WANT'S TO TALK EH? WELL IT'LL BE A COLD DAY IN HELL BEFORE I EVER TALK TO HER AGAIN.
DOINK!
THEN AGAIN, THERE'S NO REASON TO LET THIS PETTINESS KEEP US APART ANY LONGER.
GO GET HER, TIGER.

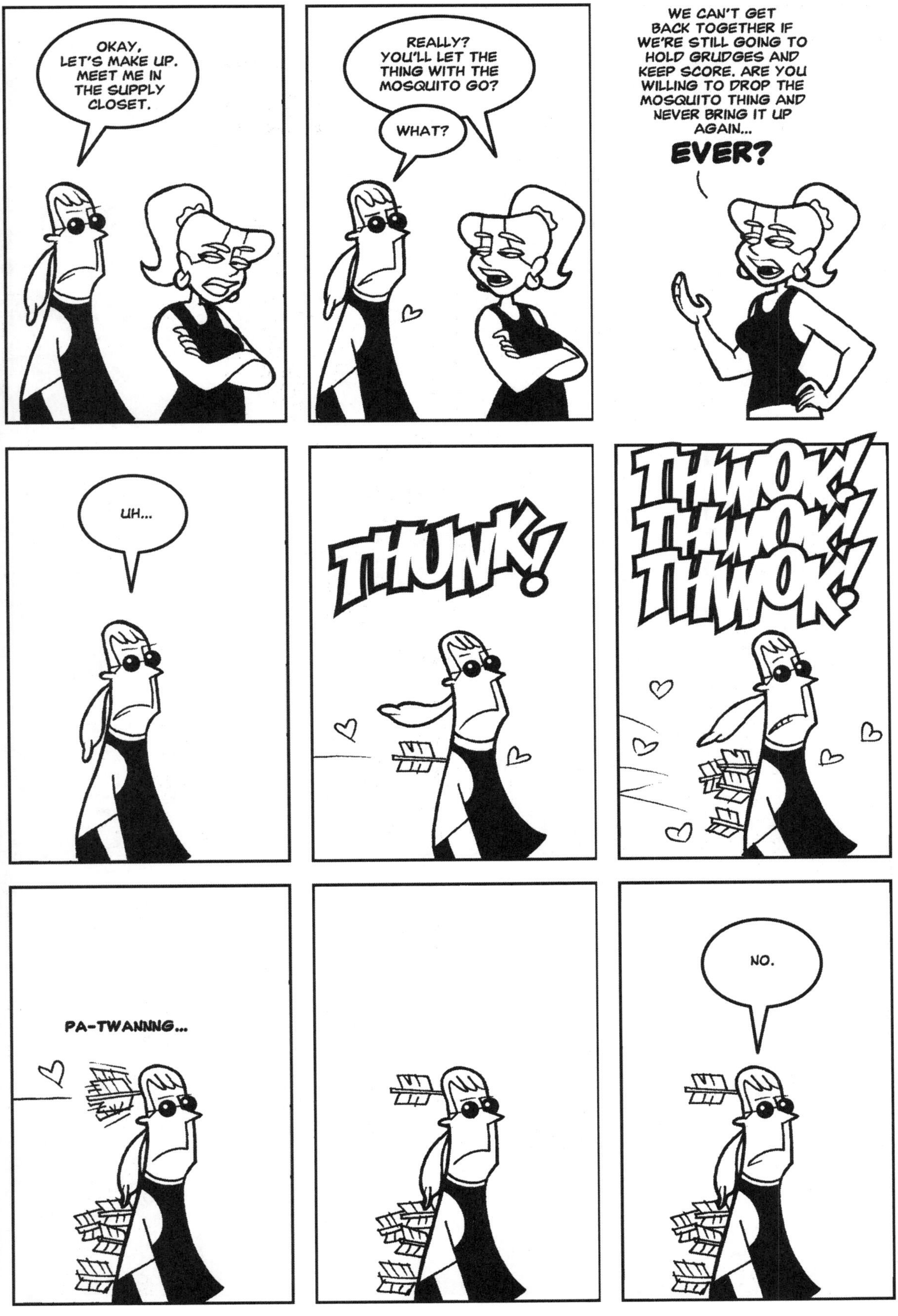
OKAY, LET'S MAKE UP. MEET ME IN THE SUPPLY CLOSET.
REALLY? YOU'LL LET THE THING WITH THE MOSQUITO GO?
WHAT?
WE CAN'T GET BACK TOGETHER IF WE'RE STILL GOING TO HOLD GRUDGES AND KEEP SCORE. ARE YOU WILLING TO DROP THE MOSQUITO THING AND NEVER BRING IT UP AGAIN... EVER?
UH...
THUNK!
THWOK! THWOK! THWOK!
PA-TWANNNG...
NO.

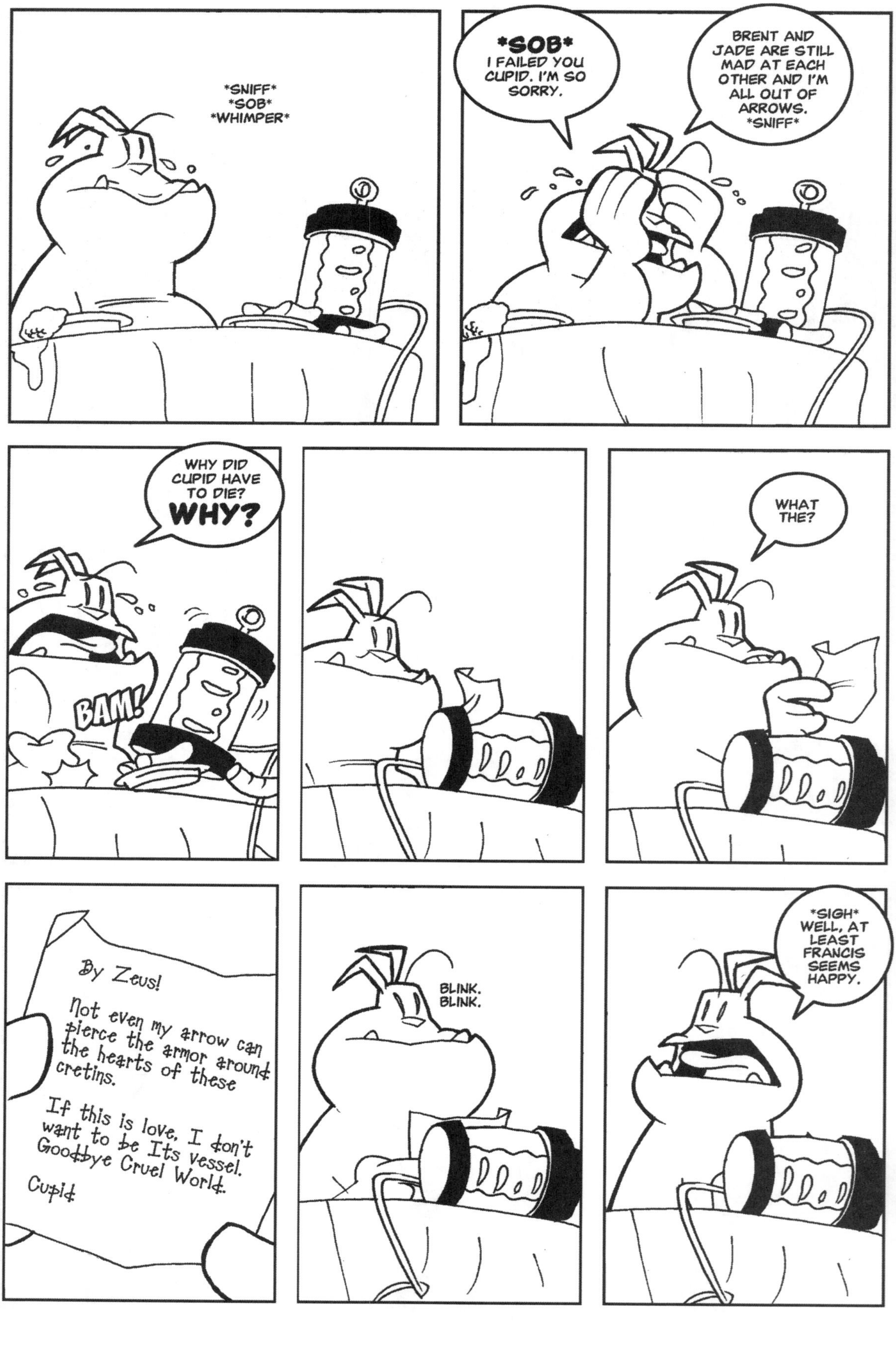
SNIFF
SOB
WHIMPER
SOB I FAILED YOU CUPID. I'M SO SORRY.
BRENT AND JADE ARE STILL MAD AT EACH OTHER AND I'M ALL OUT OF ARROWS. *SNIFF*
WHY DID CUPID HAVE TO DIE? WHY?
BAM!
WHAT THE?
By Zeus!
Not even my arrow can pierce the armor around the hearts of these cretins.
If this is love, I don't want to be Its vessel. Goodbye Cruel World.
Cupid
BLINK. BLINK.
SIGH WELL, AT LEAST FRANCIS SEEMS HAPPY.

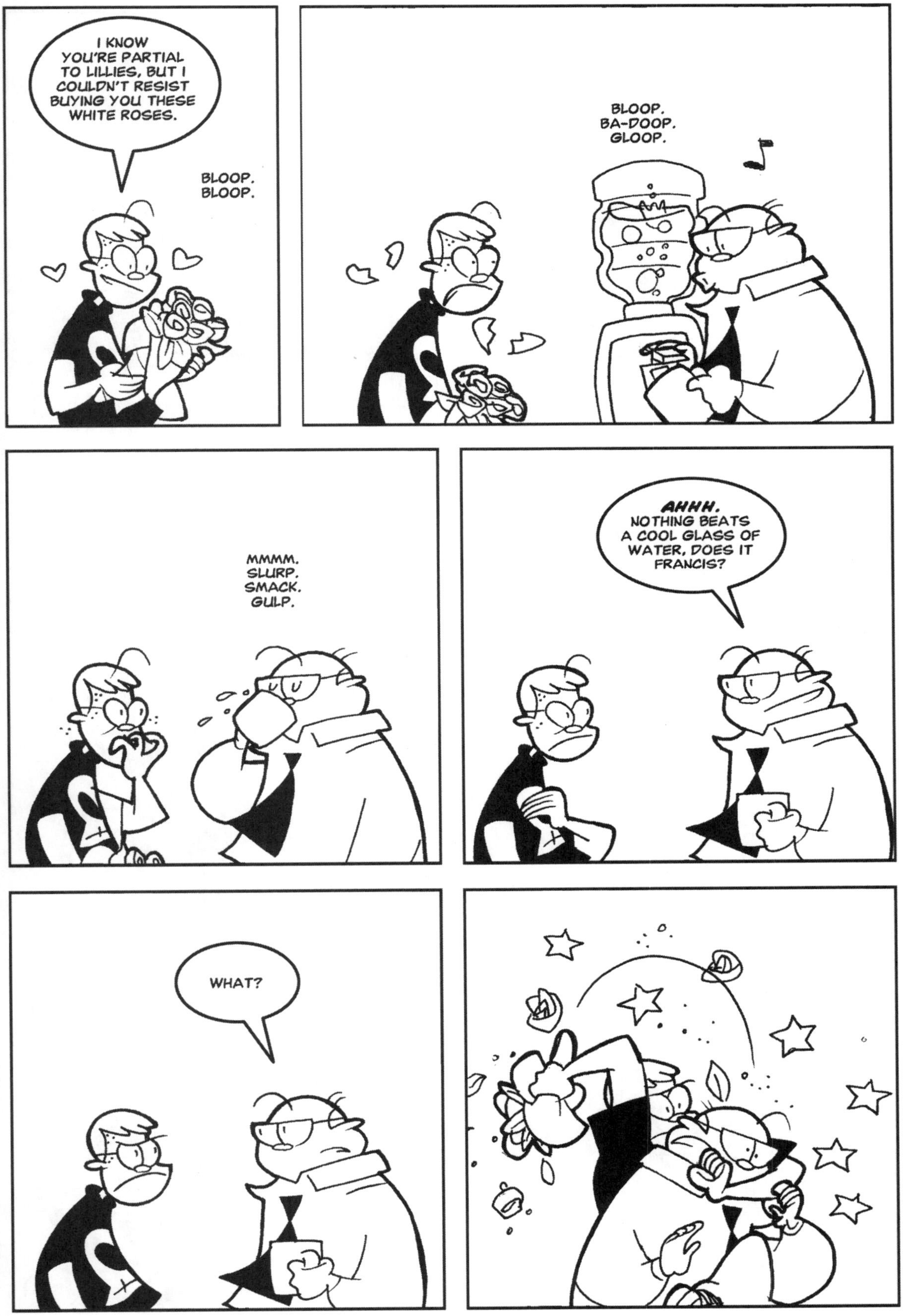
I KNOW YOU'RE PARTIAL TO LILLIES, BUT I COULDN'T RESIST BUYING YOU THESE WHITE ROSES.
BLOOP. BLOOP.
BLOOP. BA-DOOP. GLOOP.
MMMM. SLURP. SMACK. GULP.
AHHH. NOTHING BEATS A COOL GLASS OF WATER, DOES IT FRANCIS?
WHAT?

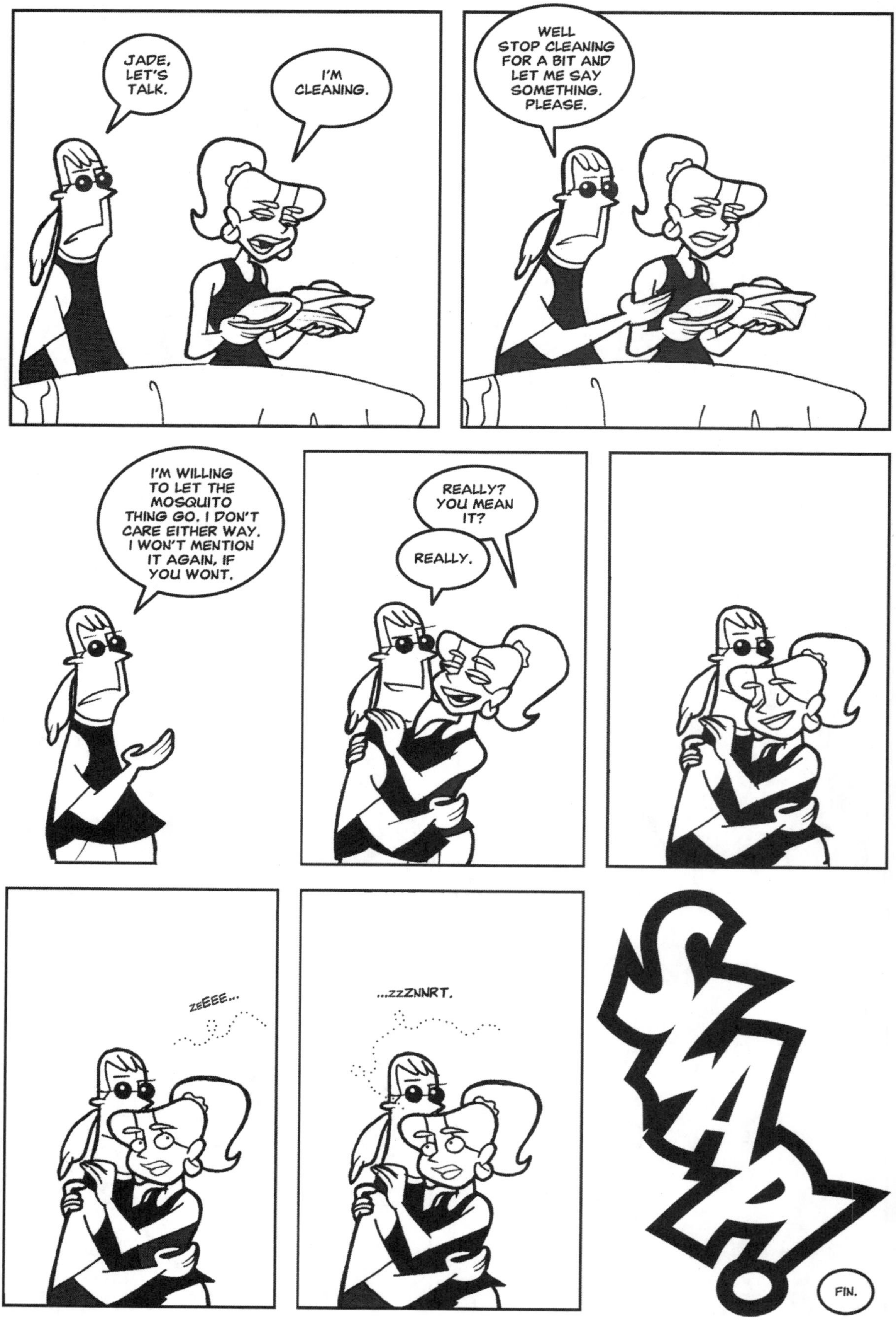
JADE, LET'S TALK.
I'M CLEANING.
WELL STOP CLEANING FOR A BIT AND LET ME SAY SOMETHING. PLEASE.
I'M WILLING TO LET THE MOSQUITO THING GO. I DON'T CARE EITHER WAY. I WON'T MENTION IT AGAIN, IF YOU WONT.
REALLY? YOU MEAN IT?
REALLY.
zeEEE...
...zzZNNRT.
SLAP!
FIN.

PvP
PLAYER vs. PLAYER™

PACKING MATERIAL

This bonus section of *Dork Ages* showcases some of the work done by Scott Kurtz and various others that never quite made it to print for one reason or another. Much like the styrofoam packaging that helps to protect your big-screen TV on its way to your living room, so too the following pieces were a part of PvP's history and one more in a long line of really bad anaolgies.

Frank Cho drew this unused cover for what would have been PvP #8, published by Dork Storm Press. That issue was cancelled in favor of my starting with a new PvP #1 at Image.

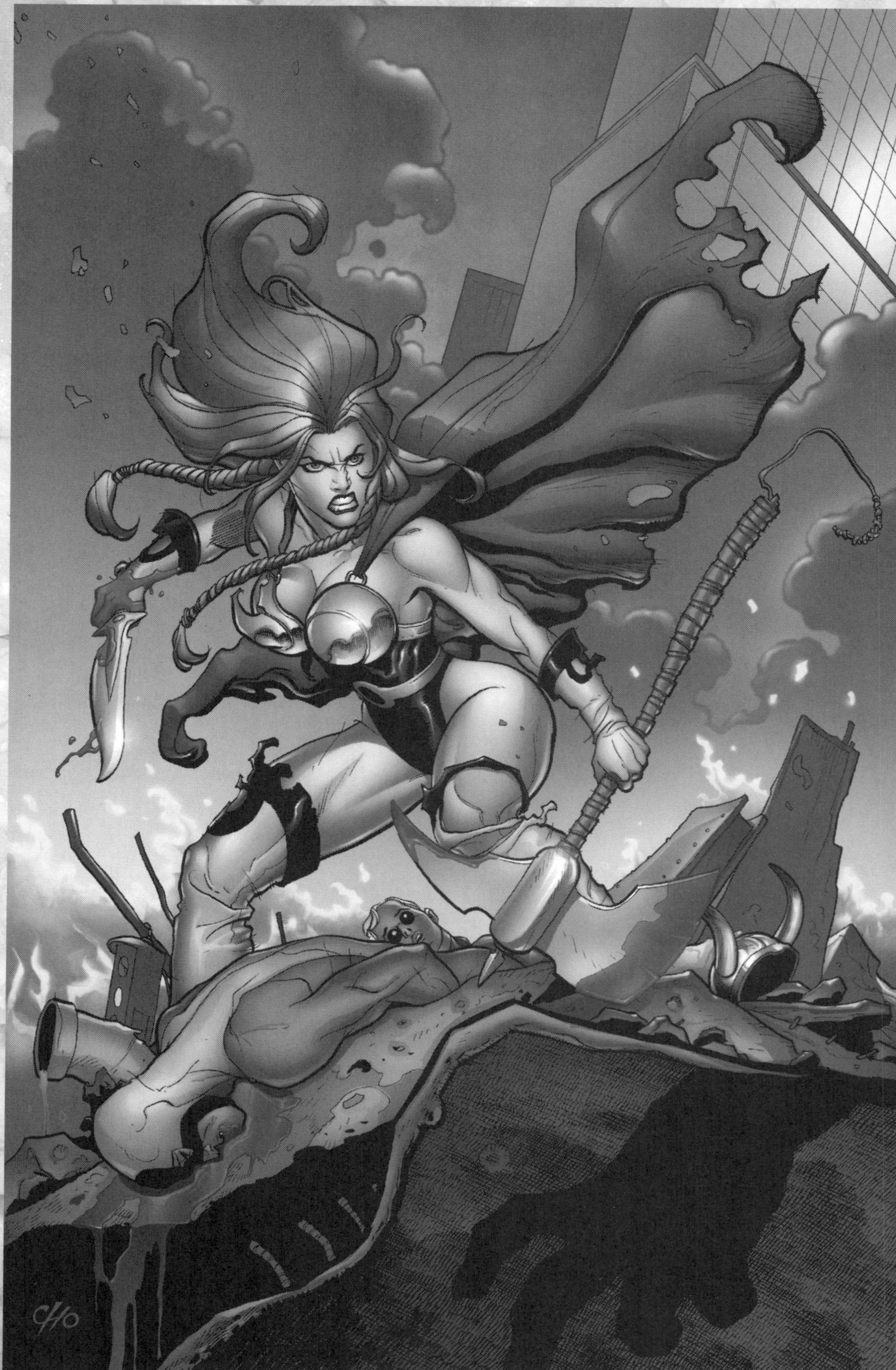
CHO

This would have been the cover for PvP #8 from DSP. It was scrapped too.

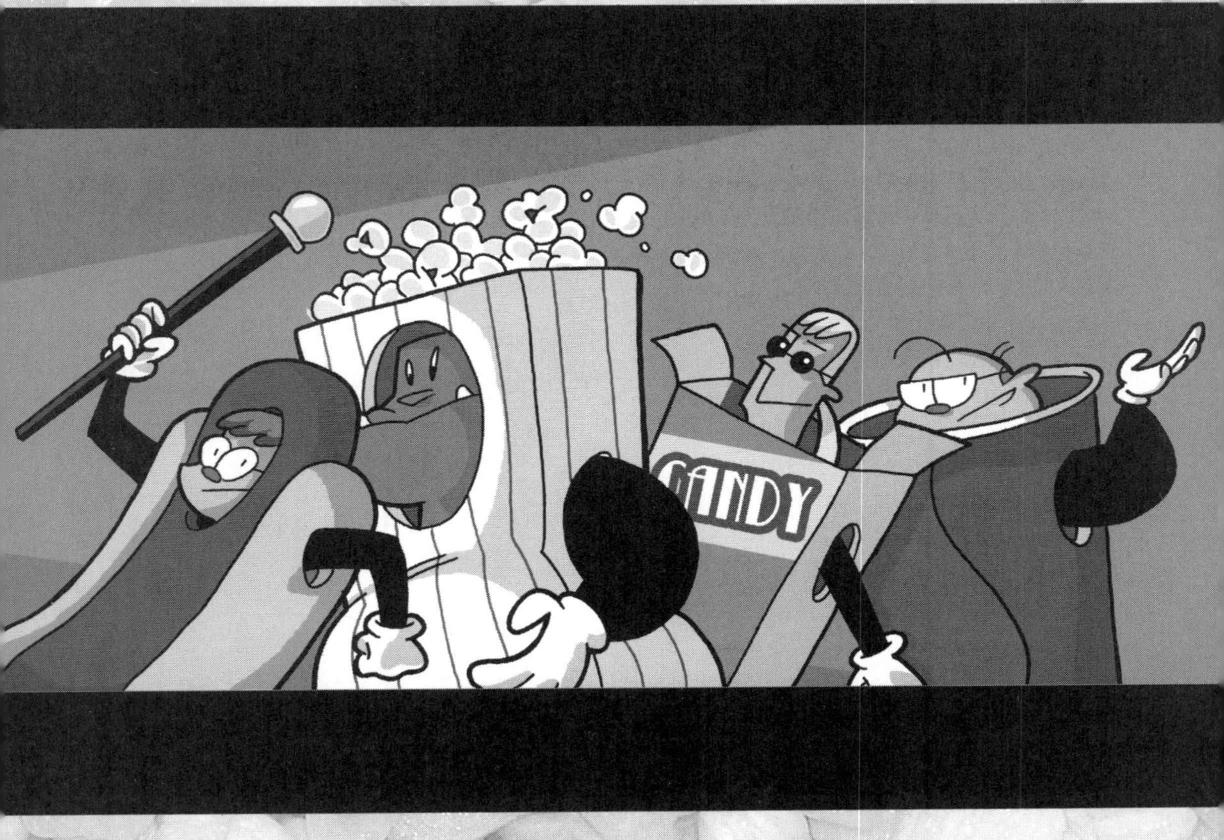
CANDY

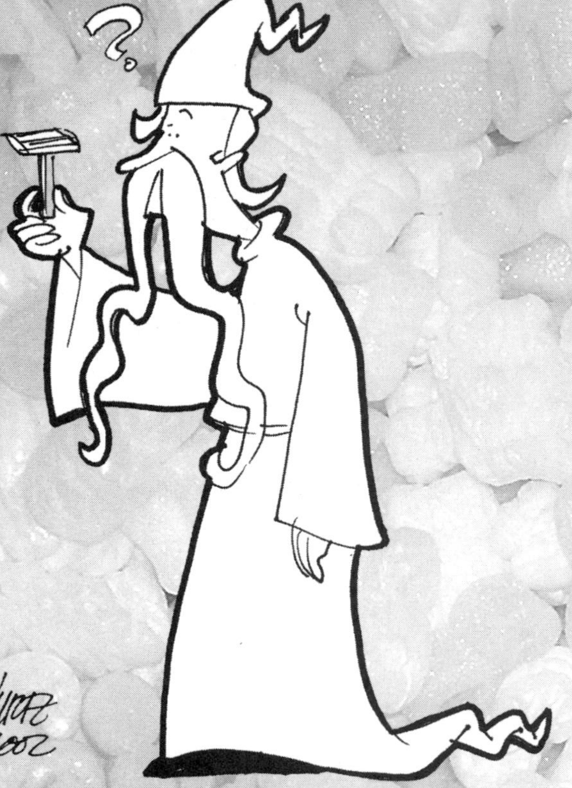
KURTZ
2002

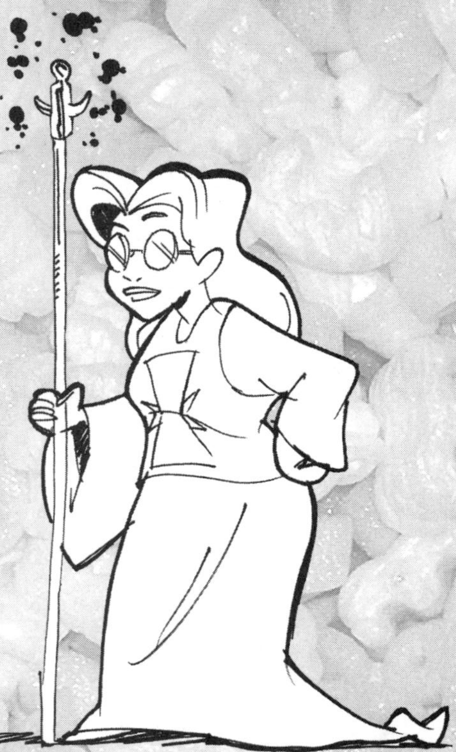
KURTZ
2002

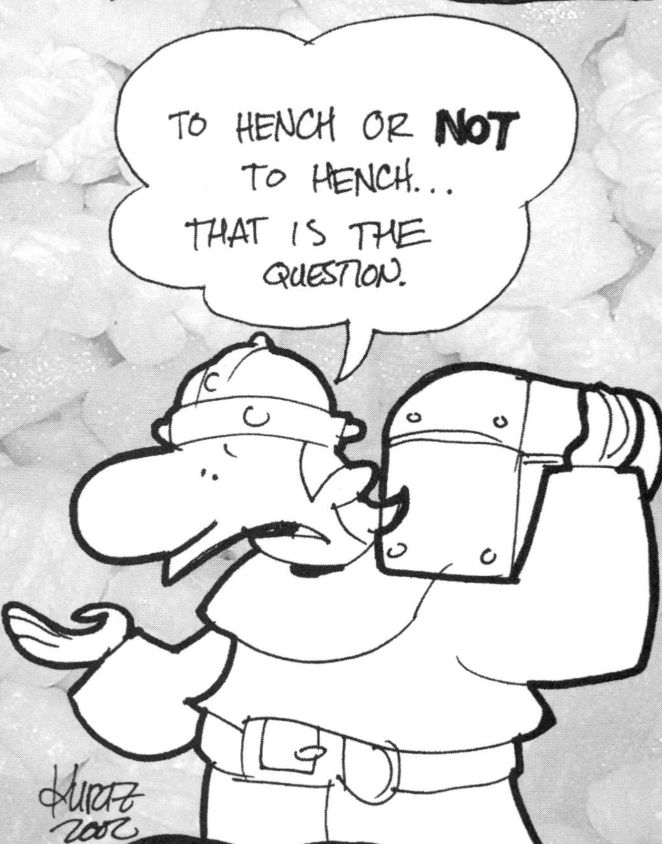
TO HENCH OR **NOT** TO HENCH... THAT IS THE QUESTION.
KURTZ
2002

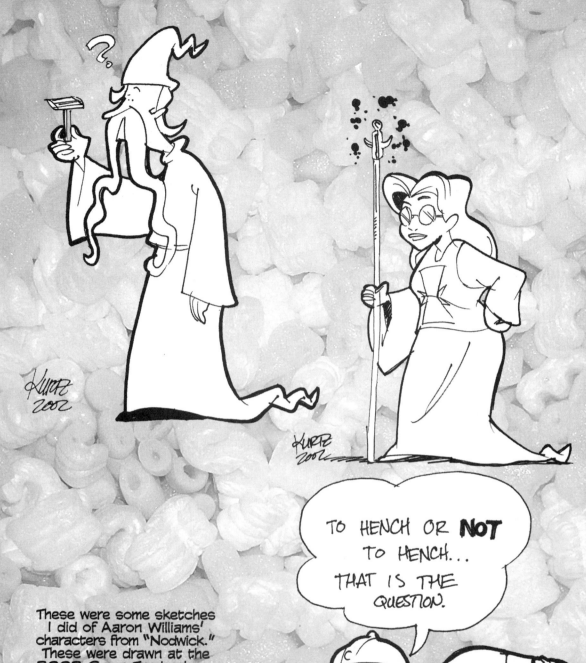

These were some sketches I did of Aaron Williams' characters from "Nodwick." These were drawn at the 2002 Gama Trade show.

This is an unused cover for a collection of five video games that were going to be packaged and sold together. The deal fell through in the end.

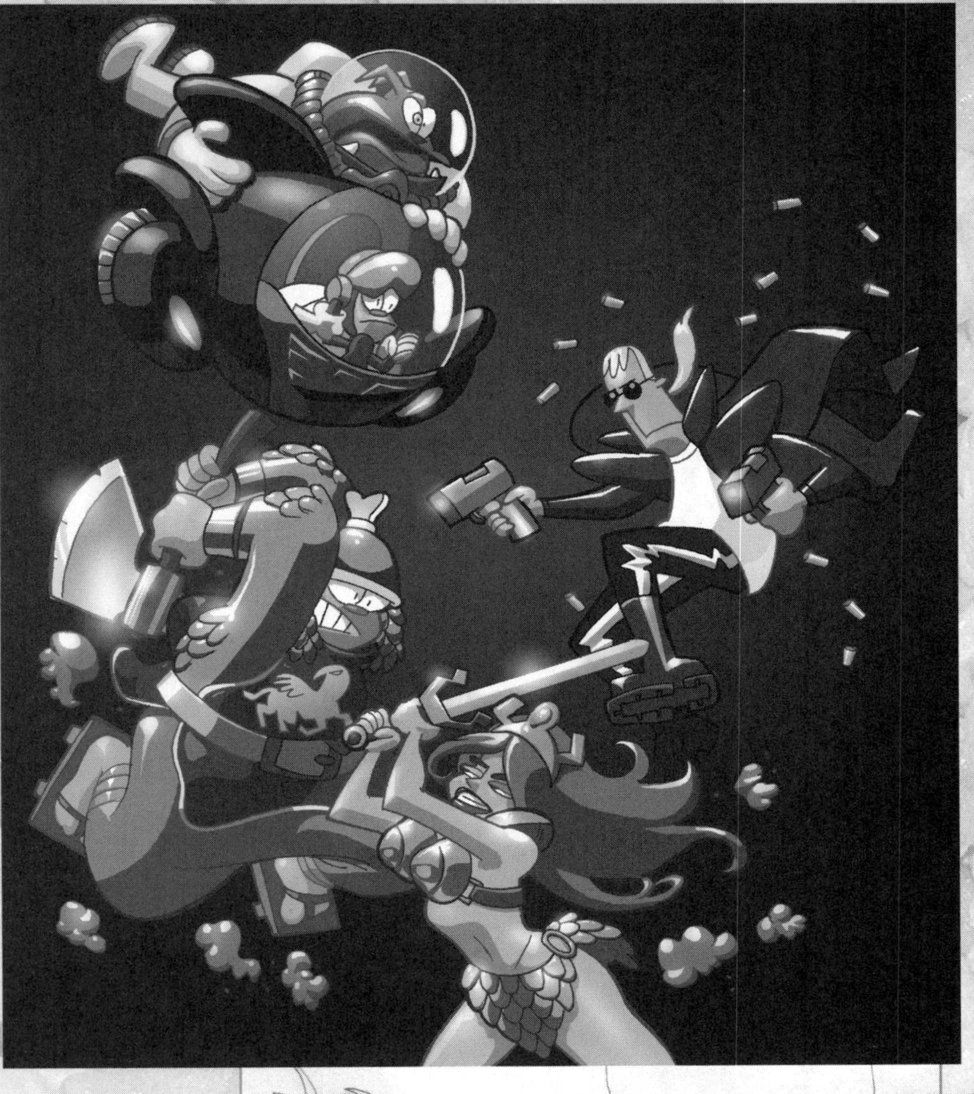

Here are some sketches I did for the piece.

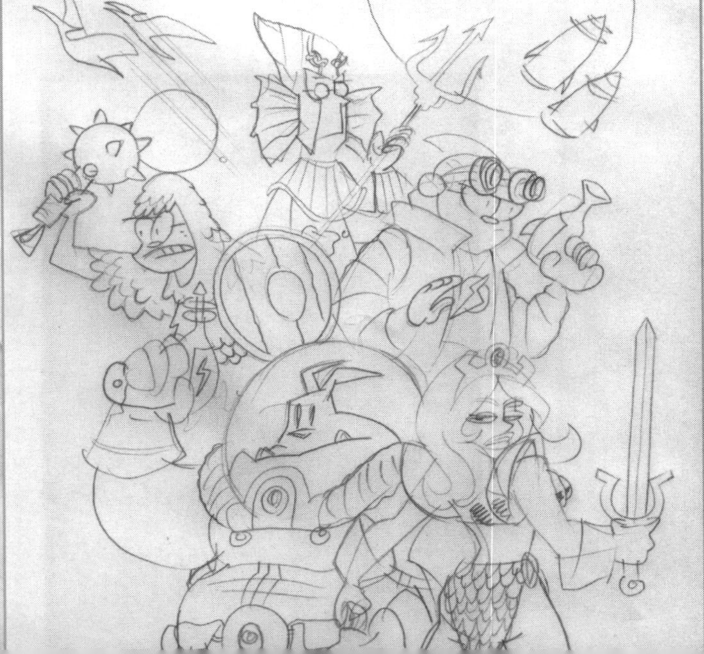

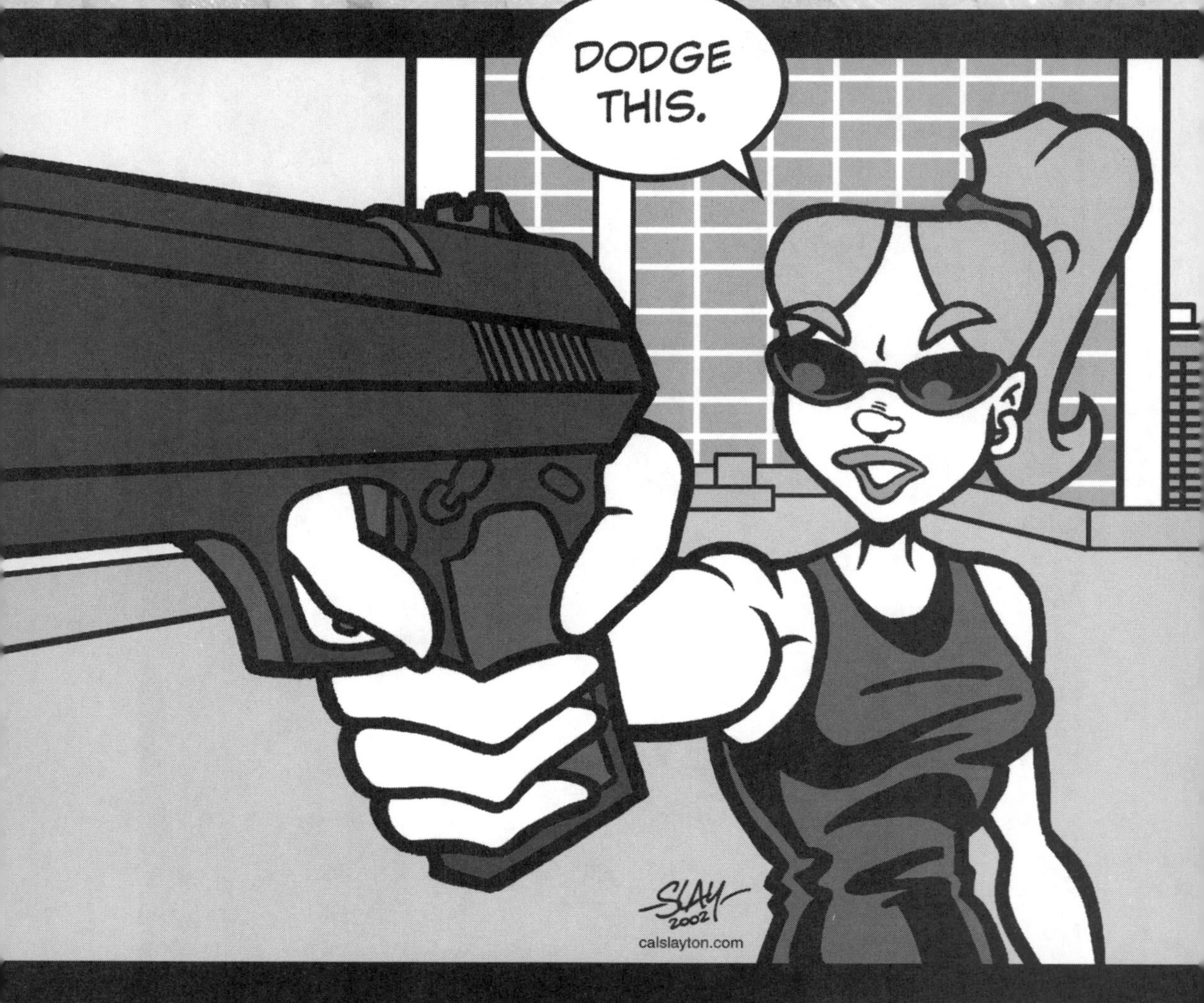
DODGE THIS.
SLAY 2002
calslayton.com

Another piece by Slay, used for the cover of PvP #5

PIN-UP BY
CAL SLAYTON
ARTIST OF

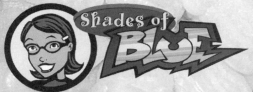

Shades of BLUE

CHECK IT OUT AT
WWW.AMPCOMICS.COM

Cal Slayton drew this great pin up of the entire PvP crew admiring Jade's beauty. I love how Skull is oblivious to her.

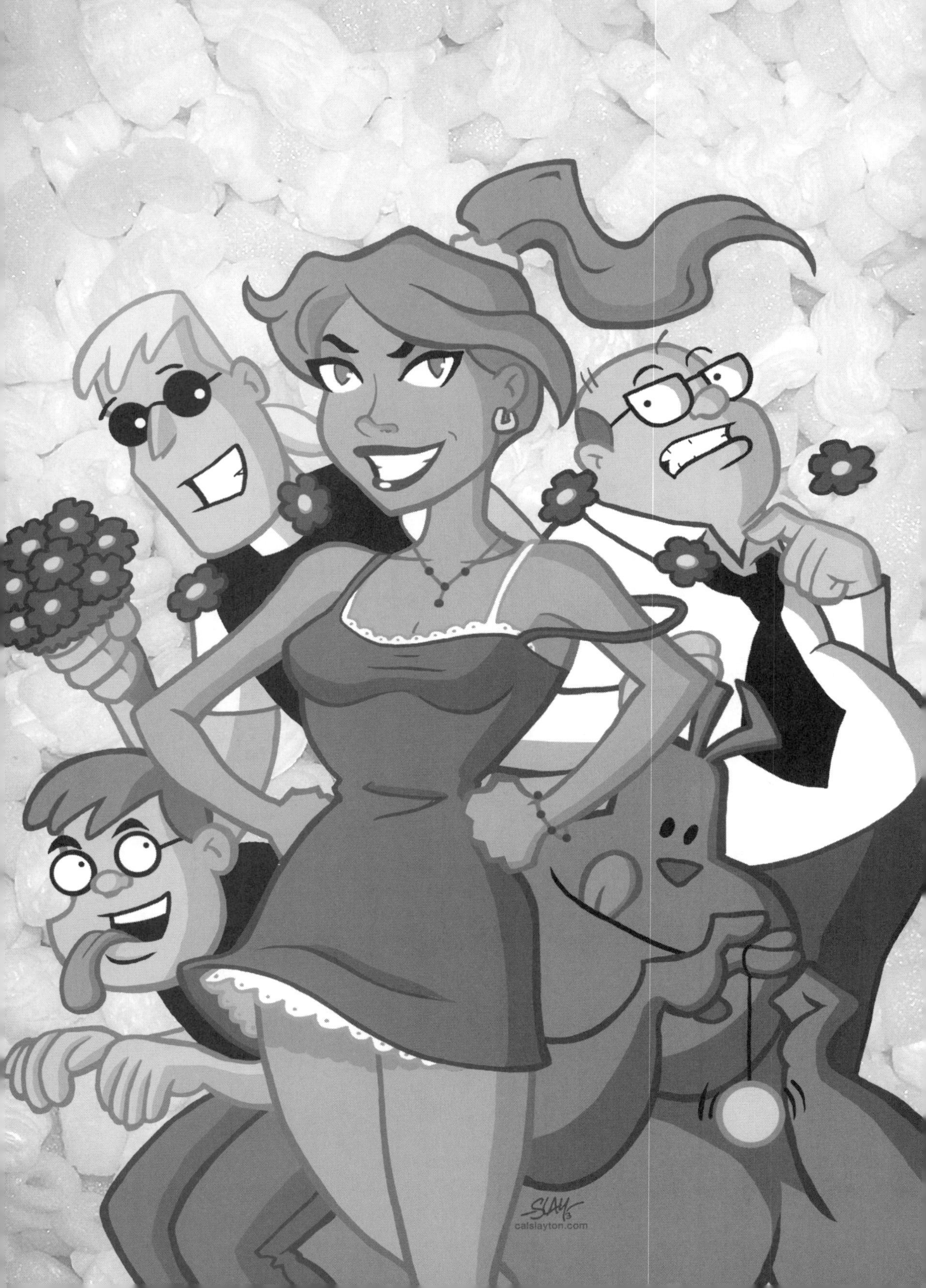
calslayton.com

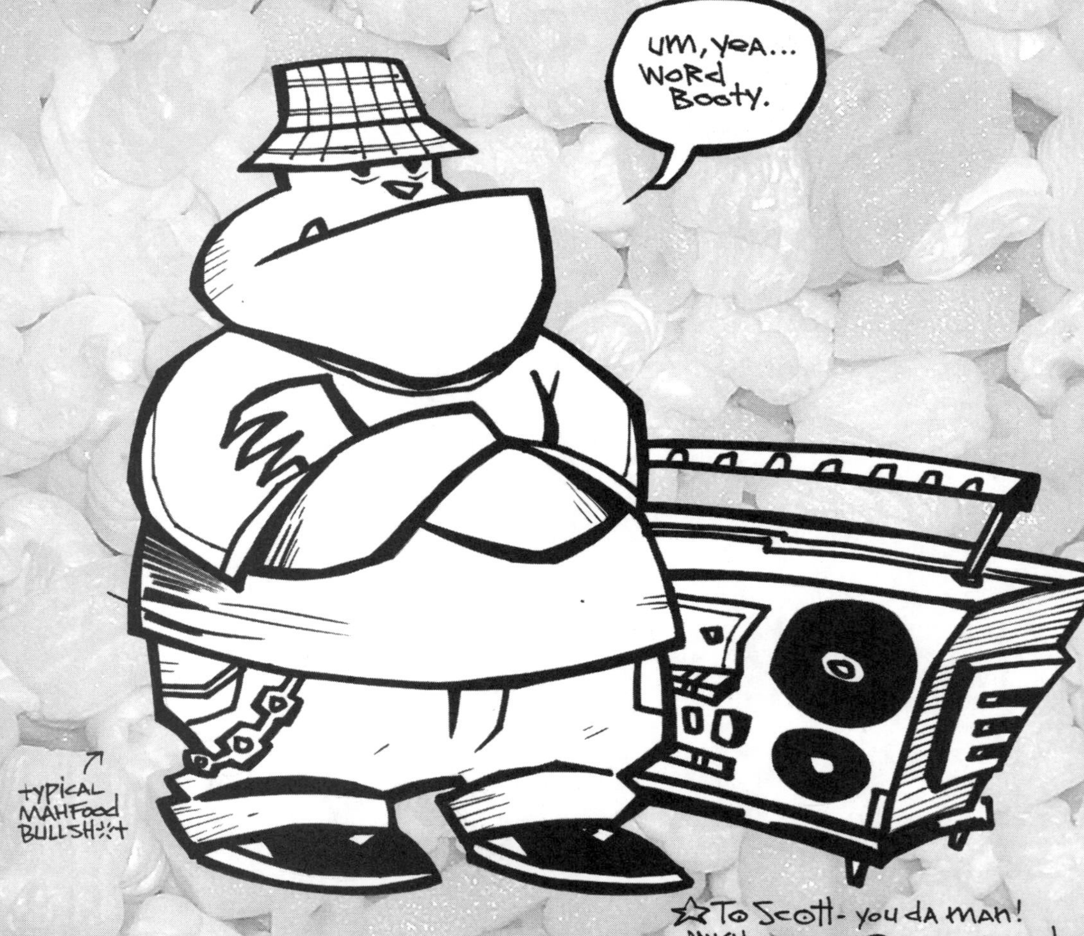
UM, YEA... WORD BOOTY.
TYPICAL MAHFOOD BULLSH*T
To Scott- you da man!
MUCH Respect! JIMMAHFOOD
2002

Pinup by Jim Mahfood

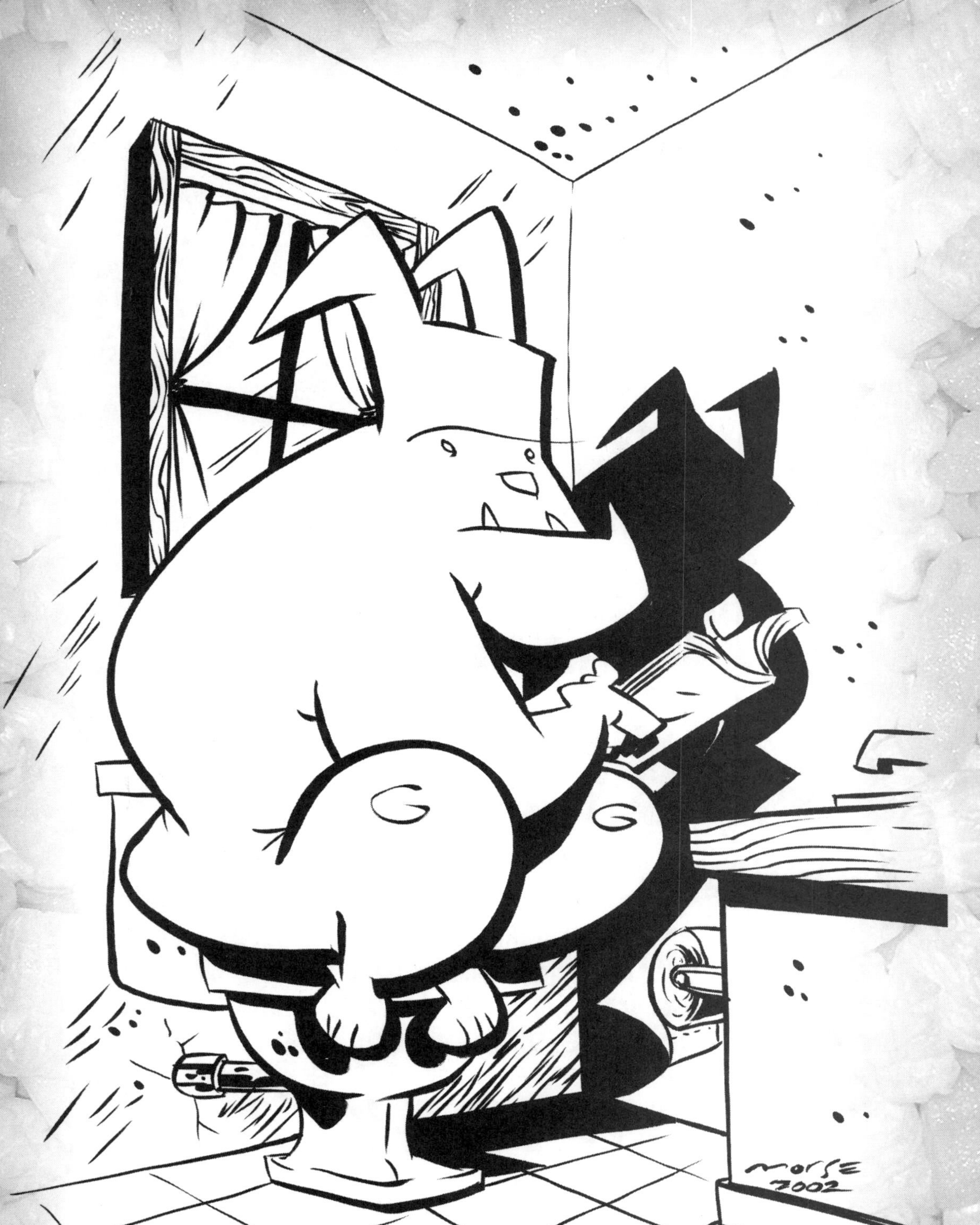
MORSE
2002

Pinup by Scott Morse.

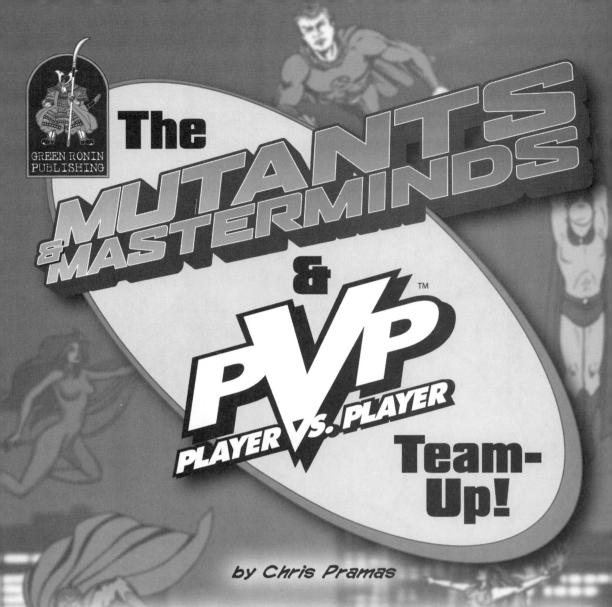

The MUTANTS & MASTERMINDS & PVP PLAYER VS. PLAYER™ Team-Up!

GREEN RONIN PUBLISHING

by Chris Pramas

Now that you've thrilled to the adventures of the Justice 8 and their new nemesis, the Blue Skull, you can bring these iconic characters into your own superhero game! This article provides game stats for these PVP characters, using Green Ronin's hit Mutants & Masterminds roleplaying game. You can now take on the role of Brunhilde, Chessmaster, or Silly Putty, or match wits with the Blue Skull. For more information on Mutants & Masterminds, speed your way down the information superhighway to www.mutantsandmasterminds.com. There you can download previews and bonus material, see what's available for the game, and engage in discussion on the lively forums. Mutants & Masterminds is available in fine hobby, book, and comic stores the world over.

CHESSMASTER

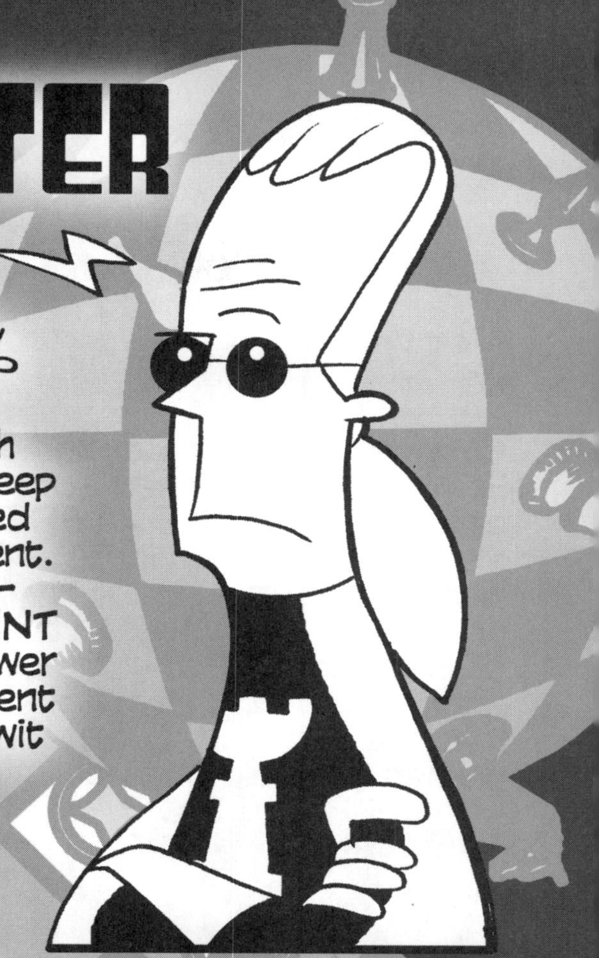

Quote: Are you SURE you want to move THAT piece?

Origin: During a chess match between Gary Kasparov and Deep Blue, a water bottle was spilled causing a freak electrical accident. Kasparov, Deep Blue and mild-mannered IBM technician BRENT SIENNA were caught in a shower of sparks. The accident left Brent with a mind unequalled and a wit unbearable.

Power Level: 10

STR	DEX	CON	INT	WIS	CHA	INITIATIVE	DEFENSE	SPEED
12	14	12	18	16	14	+2	19	30ft

DAMAGE SAVE	FORTITUDE SAVE	REFLEX SAVE	WILL SAVE	MELEE	RANGED	MENTAL BLAST RANGED
+5	+1	+2	+7	+7	+8	+9

Skills: Computers +15, Disable Device +15, Knowledge (games) +17, Knowledge (history) +15, Science (Chemistry) +15, Science (Genetics) +15, Science (Mathematics) +15, Search +16, Sense Motive +7, Taunt +5.

Powers: Force Field +4 [*Extras:* Invisible, Mental Shield; Source: Psionic; Cost: 3 pp; Total: 12 pp], Gadgets +8 [*Source:* Super-Science; Cost: 1 pp; Total: 8 pp], Mental Blast +4 [*Source:* Psionic; Cost: 3 pp; Total: 12 pp], Super-Intelligence +10 [*Source:* Psionic; Cost: 2 pp; Total: 40 pp], Telepathy +4 [*Source:* Psionic; Cost: 2 pp; Total: 8 pp].

Feats: Assessment, Photographic Memory.

Weakness: Quirk (Smart Mouth).

BRUNHILDE

Quote: Mine eyes are up here, knave!

Origin: Museum curator JADE FONTAINE happened across an enchanted IRON BRASSIERE inscribed with the words "Whoever wears this brassiere, if her bosom be worthy, shall possess the power of Brunhilde!" Transformed by her enchanted support, Jade has become the next in a noble line of women to wield the power of the LIVING BATTLEAXE!

Power Level: 10

STR	DEX	CON	INT	WIS	CHA		INITIATIVE	DEFENSE	SPEED/FLY
20	14	16	10	13	14		+2	20	30ft

DAMAGE SAVE	FORTITUDE SAVE	REFLEX SAVE	WILL SAVE			*LIGHTNING BLAST*
					MELEE	RANGED
+7	+3	+4	+1		+15	+12

Skills: Intimidate +5, Listen +3, Spot +3.

Powers: Amazing Save (Damage) +4 [*Source:* Mystical; Cost: 1 pp; Total: 4 pp], Energy Blast (Lightning) +10 [*Flaw:* Full Power; Source: Mystical; Cost: 1 pp; Total: 10 pp], Flight +6 [*Source:* Mystical; Cost: 2 pp; Total: 12 pp], Super-Strength +8 [*Extra:* Protection; Power Stunt: Lethal; Source: Mystical; Cost: 5 pp; Total: 42 pp].

Feats: Immunity (Aging), Indomitable Will, Lightning Reflexes, Move-by Attack, Power Attack, Rapid Strike.

Weakness: Quirk (Strikes Very Dramatic Poses!)

Silly Putty

Quote: I'm rubber and you're glue. Anything you say bounces off me and sticks to you.

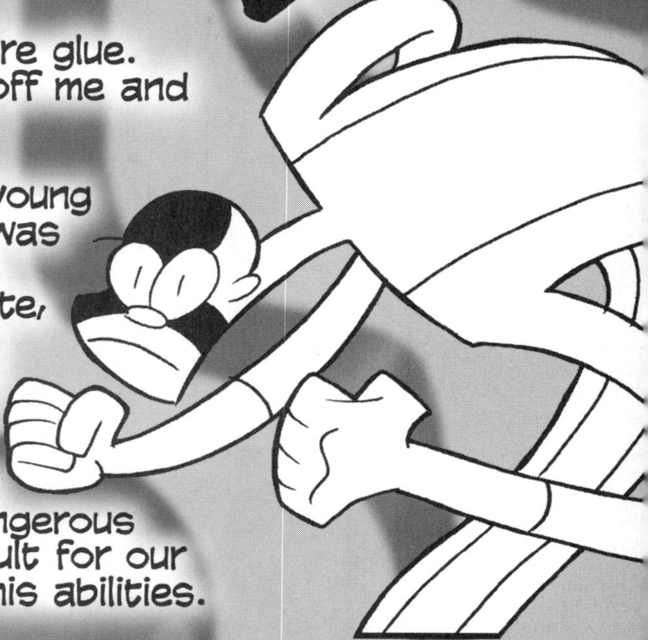

Origin: As a pre-schooler, young FRANCIS RAY OTTOMAN was prone to eating anything. A steady diet of non-toxic paste, rubber cement and modeling clay was enough to alter the cells of his body, granting him the ability to mold his body into any shape. Puberty and super-powers are a dangerous combination making it difficult for our spunky strecher to master his abilities.

Power Level: 10

STR	DEX	CON	INT	WIS	CHA	INITIATIVE	DEFENSE	SPEED
16	18	14	10	12	14	+4	26	30ft

DAMAGE SAVE	FORTITUDE SAVE	REFLEX SAVE	WILL SAVE	MELEE
+2	+2	+4	+1	+12

Skills: Acrobatics +8, Escape Artist +16, Hide +8, Intimidate +5, Move Silently+8, Spot +2.

Powers: Elasticity +8 [*Extra:* Protection; Power Stunts: Bouncing, Gliding; Source: Mutation; Cost: 5 pp; Total: 44 pp], Super-Dexterity +3 [*Flaw:* Limited (no Reflex Save bonus); Source: Mutation; Cost: 3 pp; Total: 9 pp], Super-Strength +4 [*Source:* Mutation; Cost: 4 pp; Total: 16 pp].

Feats: Chokehold, Rapid Strike.

THE BLUE SKULL

Quote: Unleash the villain within.

Origin: Not much is known about the enigma known as THE BLUE SKULL. With a tongue both silver and forked, the blue skull uses his motivational powers to groom the next generation of evil, under the protection of the first amendment. Coffee and Bagels are free, just look out for the atom descramblers.

Power Level: 12

STR	DEX	CON	INT	WIS	CHA
18	14	14	14	14	18

INITIATIVE	DEFENSE	SPEED
+2	22	30ft

DAMAGE SAVE	FORTITUDE SAVE	REFLEX SAVE	WILL SAVE
+10	+2	+2	+4

MELEE	ATOM DESCRAMBLER RANGED
+14	+13

Skills: Bluff +17, Diplomacy +15, Forgery +8, Gather Information +15, Innuendo +15, Profession (Motivational Speaker) +6, Science (Sociology) +9, Sense Motive +5, Spot +4.

Powers: Amazing Save (Damage) +8 [*Source:* Alien; Cost: 1 pp; Total: 8 pp], Gadgets +12 [*Source:* Super-Science; Cost: 1 pp; Total: 12 pp], Super-Charisma +10 [*Source:* Alien; Cost: 2 pp; Total: 20 pp], Super-Intelligence +5 [*Source:* Alien; Cost: 2 pp; Total: 10 pp].

Feats: Durability, Fame, Iron Will, Talented (Bluff and Profession [Motivational Speaker]), Weapon Focus (Atom Descrambler).

Weakness: Atom Descrambler [Effect: Disintegration +12; Extra: Disruption; Flaw: Device; Source: Super-Science; Cost: 2 pp; Total: 24 pp].

About the Cartoonist

Born in Watsonville, California, Scott Kurtz has been creating his own original comic strips ever since he was inspired by the first Garfield collection in 1980. He ignored all of his art teachers in high school and college, shunning any and all formal art training (a decision he's come to later regret).

In 1998, his comic strip PvP debuted on the world wide web with 700 daily readers. Over the last five years, PvP has grown into a genuine internet phenomenon, growing in readership to an estimated 75,000 readers per day, a bi-monthly comic book from IMAGE COMICS, and numerous industry accolades as one of the leaders in online comics. Scott quit his day job in 2000, fulfilling a lifelong dream of being a full-time cartoonist.

He could not be more happy or content.

Scott currently resides in North Texas where he's living the dream with his wife Angela, his basset hound Kirby, and Tiffany, the cat that he refuses to admit he likes.